ISBN 978-1-330-91737-4
PIBN 10121187

1 MONTH OF
FREE
READING

at
www.ForgottenBooks.com

By purchasing this book you are eligible for one month membership to ForgottenBooks.com, giving you unlimited access to our entire collection of over 1,000,000 titles via our web site and mobile apps.

To claim your free month visit:

www.forgottenbooks.com/free121187

English
Français
Deutsche
Italiano
Español
Português

www.forgottenbooks.com

Mythology Photography **Fiction**
Fishing Christianity **Art** Cooking
Essays Buddhism Freemasonry
Medicine **Biology** Music **Ancient
Egypt** Evolution Carpentry Physics
Dance Geology **Mathematics** Fitness
Shakespeare **Folklore** Yoga Marketing
Confidence Immortality Biographies
Poetry **Psychology** Witchcraft
Electronics Chemistry History **Law**
Accounting **Philosophy** Anthropology
Alchemy Drama Quantum Mechanics
Atheism Sexual Health **Ancient History**
Entrepreneurship Languages Sport
Paleontology Needlework Islam
Metaphysics Investment Archaeology
Parenting Statistics Criminology
Motivational

ङ्क
२

Books by
JOHN COWPER POWYS

The War And Culture, 1914 .... 60c
Visions And Revisions, 1915 ....2.00
Wood And Stone, A Romance, 1915 ....1.50
Wolf's-bane, Rhymes, 1916 ....1.25
One Hundred Best Books with Commen-
tary 75c
Rodmoor, A Romance, 1916 ....1.50

Published by
G. ARNOLD SHAW,
Grand Central Terminal, New York

ESSAYS ON BOOKS AND SENSATIONS

JOHN COWPER POWYS

ÆRE PERENNIUS

1916
G. ARNOLD SHAW
NEW YORK
D·Y·

Copyright, 1916, by G. Arnold Shaw

Copyright in Great Britain and the Colonies

DEDICATED
TO
MY DEAR FRIEND
BERNARD PRICE O'NEILL

CONTENTS

THE ART OF DISCRIMINATION

THE ART OF DISCRIMINATION

THE world divides itself into people who can discriminate and people who cannot discriminate. This is the ultimate test of sensitiveness; and sensitiveness alone separates us and unites us.

We all create, or have created for us by the fatality of our temperament, a unique and individual universe. It is only by bringing into light the most secret and subtle elements of this self-contained system of things that we can find out where our lonely orbits touch.

Like all primordial aspects of life the situation is double-edged and contradictory. The further we emphasise and drag forth, out of their reluctant twilight, the lurking attractions and antipathies of our destiny, the nearer, at once, and the more obscure, we find ourselves growing, to those about us.

And the wisdom of the difficult game we are called upon to play, lies in just this very antinomy, —in just this very contradiction—that to make ourselves better understood we have to emphasise our differences, and to touch the universe of our friend we have to travel away from him, on a curve of free sky.

The cultivation of what in us is lonely and

unique creates of necessity a perpetual series of shocks and jars. The unruffled nerves of the lower animals become enviable, and we fall into moods of malicious reaction and vindictive recoil.

And yet,—for Nature makes use even of what is named evil to pursue her cherished ends—the very betrayal of our outraged feelings produces no unpleasant effect upon the minds of others. They know us better so, and the sense of power in them is delicately gratified by the spectacle of our weakness; even as ours is by the spectacle of theirs.

The art of discrimination is the art of letting oneself go, more and more wilfully; letting oneself go along the lines of one's unique predilections; letting oneself go with the resolute push of the inquisitive intellect; the intellect whose rôle it is to register—with just all the preciseness it may—every one of the little discoveries we make on the long road.

The difference between interesting and uninteresting critics of life, is just the difference between those who have refused to let themselves be thus carried away, on the stream of their fatality, and those who have not refused. That is why in all the really arresting writers and artists there is something equivocal and disturbing when we come to know them.

Genius itself, in the last analysis, is not so much the possession of unusual vision—some of the most powerful geniuses have a vision quite medi-

ocre and blunt—as the possession of a certain
demonic driving-force, which pushes them on to
be themselves, in all the fatal narrowness and
obstinacy, it may be, of their personal temperament.

The art of discrimination is precisely what
such characters are born with; hence the almost
savage manner in which they resent the beckon-
ings of alien appeals; appeals which would draw
them out of their pre-ordained track.

One can see in the passionate preference dis-
played by men of real power for the society of
simple and even truculent persons over that of
those who are urbanely plastic and versatile, how
true this is.

Between their own creative wilfulness and the
more static obstinacy of these former, there is an
instinctive bond; whereas the tolerant and colourless cleverness of the latter disconcerts and puz-
zles them.

This is why—led by a profound instinct—the
wisest men of genius select for their female companions the most surprising types, and submit to
the most wretched tyranny. Their craving for
the sure ground of unequivocal naturalness helps
them to put up with what else were quite intolerable.

For it is the typical modern person, of normal
culture and playful expansiveness, who is the
mortal enemy of the art of discrimination.

Such a person's shallow cleverness and conventional good-temper is more withering to the soul of the artist than the blindest bigotry which has the recklessness of genuine passion behind it.

Not to like or to dislike people and things, but to tolerate and patronise a thousand passionate universes, is to put yourself out of the pale of all discrimination. To discriminate is to refine upon one's passions by the process of bringing them into intelligent consciousness. The head alone cannot discriminate; no! not with all the technical knowledge in the world; for the head cannot love nor hate, it can only observe and register.

Nor can the nerves alone discriminate; for they can only cry aloud with a blind cry. In the management of this art, what we need is the nerves and the head together, playing up to one another; and, between them, carrying further—always a little further—the silent advance, along the road of experience, of the insatiable soul.

It is indeed only in this way that one comes to recognise what is, surely, of the essence of all criticism; the fact, namely, that the artists we care most for are doing just the thing we are doing ourselves—doing it in their own way and with their own inviolable secret, but limited, just as we are, by the basic limitations of all flesh.

The art of discrimination is, after all, only the art of appreciation, applied negatively as well as positively; applied to the flinging away from us

6

and the reducing to non-existence for us, of all those forms and modes of being, for which, in the original determination of our taste, we were not, so to speak, born.

And this is precisely what, in a yet more rigorous manner, the artists whose original and subtle paths we trace, effected for themselves in their own explorations.

What is remarkable about this cult of criticism is the way in which it lands us back, with quite a new angle of interest, at the very point from which we started; at the point, namely, where Nature in her indiscriminate richness presents herself at our doors.

It is just here that we find how much we have gained, in delicacy of inclusion and rejection, by following these high and lonely tracks. All the materials of art, the littered quarries, so to speak, of its laborious effects have become, in fact, of new and absorbing interest. Forms, colours, words, sounds; nay! the very textures and odours of the visible world, have reduced themselves, even as they lie here, or toss confusedly together on the waves of the life-stream, into something curiously suggestive and engaging.

We bend our attention to one and to another. We let them group themselves casually, as they will, in their random way, writing their own gnomic hieroglyphics, in their own immense and primeval language, as the earth-mothers heave them up from the abyss or draw them down; but we are no more confined to this stunned and be-wildered apprehension.

We can isolate, distinguish, contrast.

We can take up and put down each delicate fragment of potential artistry; and linger at leisure in the work-shop of the immortal gods.

Discrimination of the most personal and vehe-ment kind in its relation to human works of art, may grow largely and indolently receptive when dealing with the scattered materials of such works, spread out through the teeming world.

Just here lies the point of separation between the poetic and the artistic temper. The artist or the art-critic, discriminating still, even among these raw materials of human creation, derives an elaborate and subtle delight from the sugges-tiveness of their colours, their odours, and their fabrics—conscious all the while of wondrous and visionary evocations, wherein they take their place.

The poetical temper, on the other hand, lets it-self go with a more passive receptivity; and per-mits the formless, wordless brooding of the vast earthpower to work its magic upon it, in its own place and season. Not, however, in any destruc-tion of the defining and registering functions of the intellect does this take place.

Even in the vaguest obsessions of the poetical mind the intellect is present, watching, noting, weighing, and, if you will, discriminating.

For, after all, poetry, though completely different in its methods, its aims, and its effects from the other arts, is itself the greatest of all the arts and must be profoundly aware, just as they are aware, of the actual sense-impressions which produce its inspiration.

The difference, perhaps, is that, whereas the materials for the other arts become most suggestive when isolated and disentangled from the mass, the materials of poetry, though bringing with them, in this case or in the other, their particular sense-accompaniment, must be left free to flow organically together, and to produce their effect in that primeval wanton carelessness, wherein the gods themselves may be supposed to walk about the world.

One thing at least is clear. The more we acquire a genuine art of discrimination amid the subtler processes of the mind the less we come to deal in formulated or rationalistic theory.

The chief rôle of the intellect in criticism is to protect us from the intellect; to protect us from those tiresome and unprofitable "principles of art" which in everything that gives us thrilling pleasure are found to be magnificently contradicted!

Criticism, whether of literature or art, is but a dead hand laid upon a living thing, unless it is genuine response, to the object criticised, of something reciprocal in us. Criticism in fact, to be of any value, must be a stretching out of our whole organic nature, a sort of sacramental partaking,

9

with both senses and soul, of the bread and wine of the "new ritual."

The actual written or spoken word in explanation of what we have come to feel about the thing offered, is after all a mere subordinate issue.

The essential matter is that what we experience in regard to the new touch, the new style, should be a personal and absorbing plunge into an element which we feel at once to have been, as it were, "waiting" to receive us with a predestined harmony.

The point I am seeking to make is that what is called the "critical attitude" towards new experiments in art is the extreme opposite of the mood required in genuine criticism.

That negation of interest in any given new thing which is not only allowable but commendable, if we are to preserve the outlines of our identity from the violence of alien intrusion, becomes a sheer waste of energy when it is transmuted into ponderous principles of rejection.

Give us, ye gods, full liberty to pass on our way indifferent. Give us even the illuminating insight of unbounded hate. But deliver us—that at least we pray—from the hypocrisy of judicial condemnation!

More and more does it become necessary, as the fashion of new things presses insolently upon us, to clear up once for all and in a largely generous manner, the difficult question of the relation of experiment to tradition.

THE ART OF DISCRIMINATION

The number of shallow and insensitive spirits who make use of the existence of these new forms, to display—as if it were a proof of æsthetic superiority—their contempt for all that is old, should alone lead us to pause and consider.

Such persons are as a rule quite as dull to real subtleties of thought and feeling as any absolute Philistine; and yet they are the ones who with their fuss about what they call "creative art" do so much to make reasonable and natural the ordinary person's prejudices against the whole business.

They actually have the audacity to claim as a mark of higher æsthetic taste their inability to appreciate traditional beauty. They make their ignorance their virtue; and because they are dull to the delicate things that have charmed the centuries, they clamorously acclaim the latest sensational novelty, as though it had altered the very nature of our human senses.

One feels instinctive suspicion of this wholesale way of going to work, this root and branch elimination of what has come down to us from the past. It is right and proper—heaven knows—for each individual to have his preferences and his exclusions. He has not, one may be quite sure, found himself if he lacks these. But to have as one's basic preference a relinquishing in the lump of all that is old, and a swallowing in the lump of all that is new, is carrying things suspiciously far.

One begins to surmise that a person of this brand is not a rebel or a revolutionary, but quite simply a thick-skin; a thick-skin endowed with that insolence of cleverness which is the enemy of genius and all its works.

True discrimination does not ride rough-shod over the past like this. It has felt the past too deeply. It has too much of the past in its own blood. What it does, allowing for a thousand differences of temperament, is to move slowly and warily forward, appropriating the new and assimilating, in an organic manner, the material it offers; but never turning round upon the old with savage and ignorant spleen.

But it is hard, even in these most extreme cases, to draw rigorous conclusions.

Life is full of surprises, of particular and exceptional instances. The abnormal is the normal; and the most thrilling moments some of us know are the moments when we snatch an inspiration from a quarter outside our allotted circle.

There are certain strangely constituted ones in our midst whose natural world, it might seem, existed hundreds or even thousands of years ago. Bewildered and harassed they move through our modern streets; puzzled and sad they gaze out from our modern windows. They seem, in their wistful way, hardly conscious of the movements about them, and all our stirring appeals leave them wearily cold.

It is with the very wantonness of ironic insult

that our novelty-mongers come to these, bringing fantastic inventions. What is it to them, children of a nobler past, that this or the other newly botched-up caprice should catch for an hour the plaudits of the mob?

On the other hand, one comes now and again, though rarely enough, upon exceptional natures whose proper and predestined habitation seems to be rather with our children's children than with us.

The word has gone forth touching what is called super-man; but the natures I speak of are not precisely that.

Rather are they devoid in some strange manner of the gross weapons, the protective skin, adapted to the shocks and jolts of our rough and tumble civilisation. They seem prepared and designed to exist in a finer, a more elaborate, in a sense a more luxurious world, than the one we live in.

Their passions are not our passions; nor is their scorn our scorn. If the magic of the past leaves them indifferent, the glamour of the present finds them antipathetic and resentful. With glacial coldness they survey both past and present, and the frosty fire of their devotion is for what, as yet, is not.

Dull indeed should we be, if in the search of finer and more delicate discriminations in the region of art, we grew blunt and blind to the subtle-edged pathos of all these delicate differences between man and man.

SUSPENDED JUDGMENTS

It is by making our excursions in the æsthetic world thus entirely personal and idiosyncratic that we are best spared from the bitter remorse implicit in any blunders in this more complex sphere.

We have learned to avoid the banality of the judicial decisions in the matter of what is called beautiful. We come to learn their even greater uselessness in the matter of what is called the good.

To discriminate, to discriminate endlessly, between types we adore and types we suspect, this is well and wise; but in the long result we are driven, whether it is pleasant to our prejudices or not that it should be so, crushingly to recognise that in the world of human character there are really no types at all; only tragic and lonely figures; figures unable to express what they want of the universe, of us, of themselves; figures that can never, in all the æons of time, be repeated again; figures in whose obliquities and ambiguities the mysteries of all the laws and all the prophets are transcended!

MONTAIGNE

MONTAIGNE

W E, who are interested rather in literature than in the history of literature, and rather in the reaction produced upon ourselves by great original geniuses than in any judicial estimate of their actual achievements, can afford to regard with serene indifference the charges of arbitrariness and caprice brought against us by professional students.

Let these professional students prove to us that, in addition to their learning, they have receptive senses and quickly stimulated imagination, and we will accept them willingly as our guides.

We have already accepted Pater, Brandes, de Gourmont, critics who have the secret of combining immense erudition with creative intelligence, and it is under the power and the spell of these authoritative and indisputable names that we claim our right to the most personal and subjective enjoyment, precisely as the occasion and hour calls, of the greatest figures in art and letters.

Most of all we have a right to treat Montaigne as we please, even though that right includes the privilege of *not* reading every word of the famous Essays, and of only reverting—

in our light return to them—to those aspects and qualites which strike an answering chord in ourselves.

This was, after all, what he—the great humanist—was always doing; he the unscrupulous, indiscriminate and *casual* reader; and if we treat him in the same spirit as that in which he treated the classical authors he loved most, we shall at least be acting under the cloak of his approval, however much we annoy the Calvins and Scaligers of our age.

The man must have been a colossal genius. No human writer has done quite what he did, anticipating the methods and spiritual secrets of posterity, and creating for himself, with sublime indifference to contemporary usage and taste, the sort of intellectual atmosphere that suited him.

When one thinks how sensitive we all are to the intellectual environments in which we move —how we submit for instance, at this very moment, without being able to help ourselves, to the ideas set in motion by Nietzsche, say, or Walt Whitman—it seems impossible to overrate as a sheer triumph of personal force, the thing that Montaigne did in disentangling himself from the tendencies of his age, and creating almost "in vacuo," with nothing to help him but his own temperament and the ancient classics, a new emotional attitude toward life, something that might without the least exaggeration be called "a new soul."

18

The magnitude of his spiritual undertaking can best be estimated if we conceive ourselves freeing our minds, at this moment, from the influences of Nietzsche and Dostoievsky and Whitman and Pater and Wilde, and launching out into some completely original attitude toward existence, fortified it may be by the reading of Sophocles or of Lucretius, but with so original a mental vista that we leave every contemporary writer hopelessly behind.

Suppose we looked about us with a view to the undertaking of so huge an intellectual venture, where should we go to discover the original impetus, the first embryonic germ, of the new way?

In ourselves? In our own temperament? Ah! that is the crux of the whole matter. It was in his temperament that he found the force and inexhaustible riches to carry the matter through—but have we got such power at our disposal? It is doubtful. It is hard to even dream that we have. And yet—consider the simplicity of what he did!

He just took himself, Michael de Montaigne, as he was, in the plain unvarnished totality of his vigorous self-conscious temperament, and jotted down, more for his own amusement than for that of posterity, carelessly, frankly, nonchalantly, his tastes, his vices, his apathies, his antipathies, his prejudices and his pleasures.

In doing this—though there is a certain self-revelation in Augustine's confessions and a certain autobiographical frankness in the writings of many of the classical authors—he did what had never been done by any one before his time, and what, not forgetting Rousseau and Heine and Casanova and Charles Lamb, has never been so well done since. But whether, in these latter days, we can achieve this thing as Montaigne achieved it, the fact remains that this is what we are all at the present time trying hard to do.

The "new soul," which he was permitted by the gods to evoke out of the very abyss, has become, in the passionate subjectivity of our age, the very life-blood of our intellect. Not one among our most interesting artists and writers but does his utmost to reveal to the world every phase and aspect of his personal identity. What was but a human necessity, rather concealed and discouraged than revelled in and exploited before Montaigne, has, after Montaigne, become the obsession and preoccupation of us all. We have got the secret, the great idea, the "new soul." It only remains for us to incarnate it in beautiful and convincing form.

Ah! it is just there where we find the thing so hard. It is easy to say—"Find yourself, know yourself, express yourself!" It is extremely difficult to do any of these things.

No one who has not attempted to set down in words the palpable image and body of what he is, or of what he seems to himself, can possibly conceive the difficulty of the task./

More—oh, so much more—is needed than the mere saying, "I like honey and milk better than meat and wine" or "I like girls who are plump and fair better than those who are slim and dark." That is why so much of modern auto-biographical and confessional writing is dull beyond words. Even impertinence will not save our essays upon ourselves from being tedious—nor will shamelessness in the flaunting of our vices. Something else is required than a mere wish to strip ourselves bare; something else than a mere desire to call attention to ourselves. And this "something else" is genius, and genius of a very rare and peculiar kind. It is not enough to say, "I am this or that or the other." The writer who desires to give a convincing picture of what he is must diffuse the essence of his soul not merely into his statements about himself but into the style in which these statements are made.

Two men may start together to write confessions, and one of the two may dissect every nerve and fibre of his inmost soul, while the other may ramble carelessly on about the places he has seen, and the people he has met; yet in the ultimate result it may turn out that it is the latter rather than the former who has revealed his identity.

Human personalities—the strange and subtle differences which separate us from one another

—refuse to give up the secrets of their quality save at the magical summons of what we call "style." Mr. Pepys was a quaint fellow and no Goethean egotist; but he managed to put a peculiar flavour of style—with a rhythm and a colour all its own—into his meticulous gossip.

Montaigne's essays are not by any means of equal value. The more intimately they deal with his own ways and habits, the more *physiological* they become in their shameless candour, the better do they please us. They grow less interesting to my thinking where they debouch into quotations, some of them whole pages in length, from his favourite Roman writers.

He seems to have kept voluminous scrap-books of such quotations, and, like many less famous people, to have savoured a peculiar satisfaction from transcribing them. One can imagine the deliberate and epicurean way he would go about this task, deriving from the mere bodily effort of "copying out" these long and carefully chosen excerpts, an almost sensual pleasure; the sort of pleasure which the self-imposed observance of some mechanical routine in a leisured person's life is able to produce, not unaccompanied by agreeable sensations of physical well-being.

But what, after all, is this "new soul" which Montaigne succeeded in putting into our western civilisation at the very moment when Catholic and Protestant were so furiously striving for the mastery? What is this new tone, this new temper, this new temperamental atmosphere which, in the intervals of his cautious public work and his lazy compiling of scrap-books from the classics, he managed to fling abroad upon the air?

It is a spiritual ingredient, composed, when one comes to analyse it, of two chemical elements; of what might be called æsthetic egoism and of what we know as philosophic scepticism. Let us deal with the former of these two elements first.

Egoism, in the new psychological sense of the word, may be regarded as the deliberate attempt in an individual's life to throw the chief interest and emphasis of his days upon the inward, personal, subjective impressions produced by the world, rather than upon outward action or social progress. Egoism does not necessarily imply the invidious stigma of selfishness. Goethe, the greatest of all egoists, was notoriously free from such a vice. "Who," cried Wieland, when they first met at Weimar, "who can resist the *unselfishness* of this man?"

Egoism does not necessarily imply "egotism," though it must be confessed that in Montaigne's case, though not in Goethe's, there may have been a touch of that less generous attribute.

Egoism is an intellectual gesture, a spiritual attitude, a temperamental atmosphere. It is a thing which implies a certain definite philosophical mood in regard to the riddle of existence; though, of course, between individual egoists there may be wide gulfs of personal divergence.

Between Montaigne and Goethe, for instance, there is an immense difference. Goethe's egoism was creative; Montaigne's receptive. Goethe's was many-sided; driven forward by a tremendous *demonic* urge toward the satisfaction of a curiosity which was cosmic and universal. Montaigne's was in a certain sense narrow, limited, cautious, earth-bound. It had nothing of the large poetic sweep, nothing of the vast mystical horizons and huge imaginative vistas of the great German. But on the other hand, it was closer to the soil, homelier, more humorous, in a certain measure more natural, normal and human.

This "cult of egoism" is obviously not entirely modern. Traces of it, aspects of it, fragments and morsels of it, have existed from all time. It was the latent presence of this quality in his great Romans, much more than their mere "outward triumphs," which led him to brood so incessantly upon their memories.

But Montaigne himself was the first of all writers to give palpable intellectual shape to this diffused spiritual temper.

In recent times, some of the most fascinating of our literary guides have been philosophical egotists. Whitman, Matthew Arnold, Emerson, Pater, Stendhal, Maurice Barrés (in his earlier work), de Gourmont, D'Annunzio, Oscar Wilde

—are all, in their widely different ways, masters of the same cult.

The out-looking activities and the out-looking social interests of Voltaire or Renan, or Anatole France, give to these great writers quite a different psychological tone. The three I have just mentioned are all too inveterately spirits of mockery even to take seriously *their own* "sensations and ideas"; and however ironical and humorous an egoist may be with regard to other people's impressions, with regard to his own he is grave, intent, preoccupied, almost solemn.

When one thinks of it, there is a curious solemnity of preoccupation with themselves and their own sensations about Wilde, Pater, Whitman, Stendhal, D'Annunzio and Barrés. And this "gravity of egoism" is precisely the thing which, for all his humorous humanity, distinguished the great Montaigne and which his early critics found so irritating.

"What do I care—what does any one care," grumbled the learned Scaliger, "whether he prefers white wine to red wine?"

The second element in the compound chemistry of the "modern temper" introduced into the world by Montaigne may be found in his famous scepticism. The formidable levity of that notorious "que sais-je?" "What do I know?" writes itself nowadays across our whole sky. This also—"this film of white light," as some one has called it, floating waveringly beneath each one of our most cherished convictions was, not un-known before his time.

All the great sophists—Protagoras especially, with his "man the measure of all things"—were, in a sense, professional teachers of a refined scepticism.

Plato himself, with his wavering and gracious hesitations, was more than touched by the same spirit.

Scepticism as a natural human philosophy—perhaps as the only natural human philosophy—underlies all the beautiful soft-coloured panorama of pagan poetry and pagan thought. It must have been the habitual temper of mind in any Periclean symposium or Cæsarean salon. It is, pre-eminently and especially, the *civilised* attitude of mind; the attitude of mind most dominant and universal in the great races, the great epochs, the great societies.

It is for this reason that France, among all modern nations, is the most sceptical.

Barbarian peoples are rarely endowed with this quality. The crude animal energy, which makes them successful in business, and even sometimes in war, is an energy which, for all its primitive force, is destructive of civilisation. Civilisation, the rarest work of art of our race's evolution, is essentially a thing created in restraint of such crude energies; as it is created in restraint of the still cruder energies of nature itself.

MONTAIGNE

The Protestant Reformation springing out of the soul of the countries "beyond the Alps" is, of course, the supreme example of this uncivilised force. One frequently encounters sceptical-minded Catholics, full of the very spirit of Montaigne—who died in the Catholic faith—but it is rare to meet a Protestant who is not, in a most barbarous sense, full of dogmatic and argumentative "truth."

So uncivilised and unlovely is this controversial mood that free-thinkers are often tempted to be unfair to the Reformation. This is a fault; for after all it is something, even for ingrained sceptics prepared to offer incense at any official altar, to be saved from the persecuting alliance of church and state.

It is not pleasant to meet argumentative revivalists, and the Puritan influence upon art and letters is no less than deadly; but it is better to be teased with impertinent questions about one's soul than to be led away to the stake for its salvation.

The mention of the situation, in which in spite of Shakespeare and the rest poor modern sceptics still find themselves, is an indication of how hopelessly illusive all talk of "progress" is. Between Calvin on the one hand and the Sorbonne on the other, Montaigne might well shuffle home from his municipal duties and read Horace in his tower. And we, after three hundred odd years, have little better to do.

SUSPENDED JUDGMENTS

Heine, impish descendant of this great doubter, took refuge from human madness at the feet of Venus in the Louvre. Machiavel— for all his crafty wisdom—was driven back to his books and his memories. Goethe built up the "pyramid of his existence" among pictures and fossils and love affairs, leaving the making of history to others, and keeping "religious truth" at a convenient distance.

This scepticism of Montaigne is a much rarer quality among men of genius than the egoism with which it is so closely associated. I am inclined to regard it as the sanest of all human moods. What distinguishes it from other intellectual attitudes is the fact that it is shared by the very loftiest with the very simplest minds. It is the prevailing temper of shepherds and ploughmen, of carters and herdsmen, of all honest gatherers at rustic taverns who discuss the state of the crops, the prospects of the weather, the cattle market and the rise and fall of nations. It is the wisdom of the earth itself; shrewd, friendly, full of unaccountable instincts; obstinate and capricious, given up to irrational and inexplicable superstitions; sluggish, suspicious, cautious, hostile to theory, enamoured of inconsistencies, humorously critical of all ideals, realistic, empirical, wayward, ready to listen to any magical whisper, to any faint pipings of the flutes of Pan, but grumblingly reluctant to follow the voices of the prophets and the high doctrines of the leaders of men.

Its wisdom is the wisdom of lazy noons in spacious corn-fields; of dewy mornings in misty lanes and moss-grown paths; of dreamy shadows in deep grass when the apple boughs hang heavily earthward, and long nights of autumn rain have left amber-coloured pools in the hollow places of the trees and in the mud trodden by the cattle.

Its sanity is the sanity of farm-yards and smoking dung-heaps and Priapian jests beneath wintry hedges, and clear earth-sweet thoughtless laughter under large, liquid, mid-summer stars.

The nonchalant "What do I know?"—"What does any one know?"—of this shrewd pagan spirit has nothing in it of the ache of pessimistic disillusion. It has never had any illusions. It has taken things as they appear, and life as it appears, and it is so close to the kindly earth-mud beneath our feet that it is in no fear of any desperate fall.

What lends the sceptical wisdom of Montaigne such massive and enduring weight is the very fact of its being the natural pagan wisdom of generations of simple souls who live close to the earth. No wonder he was popular with the farmers and peasants of his countryside and with the thrifty burgesses of his town. He must have gathered much wisdom from his wayfaring among the fields, and many scandalous side-lights upon human nature as he loitered among the streets and wharfs of the city.

It is indeed the old joyous, optimistic, pagan spirit, full of courage and gaiety; full too, it must be confessed, of a humorous terror now and then, and yet capable enough sometimes of looking very formidable antagonists squarely in the face and refusing to quit the quiet ways it has marked out and the shrewd middle path it has chosen!

Turning over the pages of Cotton's translation —it is my fancy to prefer this one to the more famous Florio's—there seems to me to arise from these rambling discourses, a singularly whole-some savour. I seem to see Montaigne's mas-sive and benignant countenance as he jogs home, wrapped against the wind in the cloak that was once his father's, along the muddy autumn lanes, upon his strong but not over-impetuous nag. Surely I have seen that particular cast of fea-tures in the weather-beaten face of many a farm labourer, and listened too, from the same lips, to just as relishing a commentary upon the surpris-ing ways of providence with mortal men.

Full of a profound sense of a physical well-being, which the troublesome accidents of chance and time only served to intensify, Montaigne sur-veyed the grotesque panorama of human life with a massive and indelible satisfaction.

His optimism, if you can call it by such a name, is not the optimism of theory; it is not the optimism of faith, far less is it that mystic and transcendental optimism which teases one, in these later days, with its swollen words and windy rhetoric. It is the optimism of simple, shrewd, sane common sense, the optimism of the poor, the optimism of sound nerves, the optimism of cab-men and bus drivers, of fishermen and gardeners, of "tinkers, tailors, soldiers, sailors, apothecaries and thieves."

What Montaigne really does is to bring into the courts of philosophy and to heighten with the classic style of one who was "brought up upon Latin," the sheer, natural, incorrigible love of life, of such persons, rich or poor, as have the earth in their blood and the shrewd wisdom of the earth and the geniality of the earth, and the mischievous wantonness of the earth, and the old, sly chuckling malice of the earth, in their blood and in their soul.

He can record, and does often record, in those queer episodic dips into his scrap-book, the outrageous stories of a thousand freaks of nature. He loves these little impish tricks of the great careless gods. He loves the mad, wicked, astounding, abnormal things that are permitted to happen as the world moves round. He reads Tacitus and Plutarch very much as a Dorsetshire shepherd might read the *Western Gazette,* and makes, in the end, much of the same commentary.

In a certain sense Montaigne is the most human of all great geniuses. The whole turbulent stream of the motley spectacle passes through his consciousness and he can feel equal sympathy with the heroism of a Roman patriot and with the terrors of a persecuted philosopher.

What pleases him best is to note the accidental little things—"life's little ironies"—which so frequently intervene between ideal resolutions and their results in practise and fact. He chuckles over the unfortunate lapses in the careers of great men much as a mischievous gossip in a tavern might chuckle over similar lapses in the careers of local potentates.

Montaigne's scepticism is the result of his looking at the world not through books or through the theories of books, but through his own eyes. He is sceptical because he sees that any one who wishes to live in harmony with the facts of life must be sceptical. Life is made up of such evasive entangled confused elements that any other attitude than this one is a noble madness if it is not knavish hypocrisy. The theories, convictions, moralities, opinions, of every child of Adam are subject to lamentable upheavals, as the incorrigible earth-gods, with their impish malice, seize them and play nine-pins with them.

"All flows away and nothing remains," says the ancient philosopher, and Montaigne shows clearly enough how vain it is to put our trust in any theory or system or principle or idea.

It is a mistake to regard his scepticism as

merely negative. It is far more than that. Like all wise scepticism it is creative and constructive; not out of theories and phrases, nor out of principles and opinions, but out of events and persons and passions and instincts and chances and occasions.

It is realistic—this Montaignesque method—realistic not materialistic. It takes each occasion as it occurs, each person as he presents himself, each passion, each instinct, each lust, each emotion, and out of these he creates a sort of piece-meal philosophy; modest enough and making no claim to finality, but serving us, at a pinch, as a sort of rough-and-ready clue through the confusions of life.

It will always appear presumptuous to the dogmatic type of mind, the mind made up of rationalistic and logical exigencies, to call scepticism like this by the name of "philosophy." It will be still more obscure to such a mind how it is possible for a human being to live happily and joyfully in a complete absence of any synthetic system.

And yet one feels certain enough that amid the jolts and jars and shocks of actual life even the most idealistic of philosophers leave their logic to shift for itself and just drift on as they may in the groove of traditional usages or the track of temperamental bias.

It must not, however, be for a moment supposed that the scepticism of Montaigne is identical with the so-called "pragmatism" of William James or with the "instinct theories" of Bergson.

Both of these modern attitudes make the assumption that a genuine advance in our knowledge of "truth" is really possible; though possible along quite different lines from the old absolute dogmatic metaphysical ones. But the scepticism of Montaigne throws doubt upon every human attempt to get behind the shifting flowing stream of sense impressions. The rough and ready clue which it offers to the confusions of life is not drawn from any individualistic "point d'appui" of pseudo-psychological personal vision, as are these modern clues to the mystery. It is drawn from nothing more recondite than the customary traditions, usages, pieties and customs of the generations of humanity; habits of mind and moods of hope which have behind them, not so much the psychological insight of clever individuals—the William Jameses and Bergsons of past ages—as the primitive and permanent emotions of the masses of average men and women themselves, confronting the eternal silence.

What the scepticism of Montaigne does is to clear out of the path all the individual claims to extraordinary insight of the philosophic great men of the world, by means of showing how, under the pressure of obstinate and malicious reality, such explanations of the universe break down and such great men collapse and become as blind, helpless, groping and uncertain as all the rest of us. Prophets and rationalists alike, logicians and soothsayers together, so collapse and fall away; while in their place the long slow patient wisdom of the centuries, the old shrewd superstitious wisdom of anonymous humanity rises up out of the pagan earth, and offers us our only solution.

Not that what we get in this humble way is really a solution at all. Rather is it a modest working substitute for such solutions, a dim lamp flickering in a great darkness, a faint shadow falling on a long uncertain road; a road of which we can see neither the beginning nor the end, and along which we have nothing better to guide us than such pathetic "omens of the way" as old wives' tales repeat and old traditions hand down from mouth to mouth.

To certain minds the condition of the human race under the burden of such a twilight may well seem intolerable. To Montaigne it was not intolerable. It was his element, his pleasant Arcadia, his natural home. He loved the incongruities and inconsistencies of such a world; its outrageous Rabelaisian jests, its monstrous changes and chances, its huge irrelevancy. He loved its roguish and goblinish refusal to give up its secret to grave and solemn intellects, taking upon themselves the rôle of prophets. He loved a world that hides its treasures from the "wise and prudent" and reveals them—or at any rate all that will ever be revealed of them—to "babes and sucklings."

Those who read Montaigne with a natural affinity for his peculiar turn of mind, will find themselves in a position to regard very humorously and lightly the portentous claims of modern philosophers whether they be rationalists or intuitivists. "There are more things in Heaven and earth," they will retort to these scholarly Horatios in the very vein of that Prince of Denmark who—according to reliable critical opinion—was actually modelled on Montaigne himself.

They will be encouraged to go on, as before, making the best of what the traditional wisdom of the centuries brings them, but not taking even this with more seriousness than its pathetic weight of human experience demands, and not dreaming that, with even this to help them, they are very closely initiated into the ultimate mystery.

They will be encouraged to go on as before, enjoying the books of the writers with a pinch of pleasant salt, but enjoying them with infinite zest and profit, and, at least, with full *aesthetic* appreciation.

They will be encouraged to fall back upon the kindly possibilities and broad hopeful vistas to which the unsophisticated heart of man naturally and spontaneously turns.

They will be encouraged to go to the "highways

and hedges" for their omens, to the felicitous encounters of the common road for their auguries
and inspirations. They will listen reverently to
the chatter of very simple people, and catch the
shadow of the wings of fate falling upon very
homely heads. The rough earth-wisdom of
ploughed fields, heavy with brown sun-lit mud,
will be redolent for them with whispers and hints
and intimations of things that no philosophy can
include and no psychology explain.

Out of the coarse rankness of rude primitive
natures strange sweet mysteries will come to light,
and upon the sensual lusts of satyrs, gambolling
grossly in rain-soaked leafy midnights, the moon
of tender purity will shed down her virginal benediction.

For them the grotesque roots of trees will leer
magically from the wayside to meet the uncouth
gestures of the labourer and his trull; while in the
smoke-thick air of mellow tavern-corners the
shameless mirth of honest revellers philosophis-
ing upon the world will have a smack of true
divinity.

They will be encouraged—the people who read
Montaigne—to sink once more into their own
souls and enjoy the rare sensations permitted to
their own physical and psychological susceptibil-
ity, as the great world sweeps by them.

I sometimes think that the wisdom of Montaigne, with its essential roots in physiological
well-being, is best realised and understood when

on some misty autumn morning, full of the smell of leaves, one lies, just newly awakened out of pleasant dreams, and watches the sunshine on wall and window and floor, and listens to the traffic of the town or the noises of the village. It is then, with the sweet languor of awakening, that one seems conscious of some ineffable spiritual secret to be drawn from the material sensations of the nerves of one's body.

Montaigne, with all his gravity, is quite shameless in the assumption that the details of his bodily habits form an important part, not by any means to be neglected, of the picture he sets out to give of himself.

And those who read Montaigne with sympathetic affinity will find themselves growing into the habit of making much of the sensations of their bodies. They will not rush foolishly and stupidly, like dull economic machines, from bedroom to "lunch counter" and from "lunch counter" to office. They will savour every moment which can be called *their own* and they will endeavour to enlarge such moments by any sort of economic or domestic change.

They will make much of the sensations of waking and bathing and eating and drinking and going to sleep; just as they make much of the sensations of reading admirable books. They will cross the road to the sunny side of the street; they will pause by the toy-shops and the flower-shops. They will go out into the fields, before breakfast, to look for mushrooms.

They will miss nothing of the caprices and humours and comedies of every day of human life; for they will know that in the final issue none of us are wiser than the day and what the day brings; none of us wiser than the wisdom of street and field and market-place; the wisdom of the common people, the wisdom of our mother, the earth.

In the enjoyment of life spent thus fastidiously in the cultivation of our own sensations, and thus largely and generously in a broad sympathy with the emotions of the masses of men, there is room for many kinds of love. But of all the love passions which destiny offers us, none lends itself better to the peculiar path we have chosen than the passion of friendship. It is the love of an "alter ego," a second self, a twin soul, which more than anything else is able to heighten and deepen our consciousness of life.

The "love of women" has always about it something tragic and catastrophic. It means the plunging of one's hands into frozen snow or burning fire. It means the crossing of perilous glades in tropic jungles. It means the "sowing of the whirlwind" on the edge of the avalanche and the hunting of the mirage in the desert. The ecstasy brought by it is too blinding to serve as an illumination for our days; and for all the tremulous sweetness of its approach it leaves behind it the poison of disillusion and the scars of rancour and remorse.

But the passion of friendship for one of one's own sex burns with a calm clear flame. A thousand little subtleties of observation, that would mean nothing were we alone, take to themselves a significant and symbolic value and lead us down pleasant and flower-strewn vistas of airy fancy. In the absence of our friend the colour of his imagination falls like a magical light upon the saddest and dullest scenes; while with him at our side, all the little jerks and jars and jolts and ironical tricks of the hour and the occasion lose their brutish emphasis and sink into humorous perspective. The sense of having some one for whom one's weakest and least effective moments are of interest and for whom one's weariness and unreason are only an additional bond, makes what were otherwise intolerable in our life easy and light to bear.

And what a delicious sense, in the midst of the open or hidden hostilities of our struggle against the world, to feel one has some one near at hand with whom, crouched in any "corner of the hubbub," we may "make game of *that*" which makes as much of us!

Love, in the sexual sense, fails us in the bitterest crisis of our days because love, or the person loved, is the chief cause of the misery. Scourged and lacerated by Aphrodite it is of little avail to flee to Eros. But friendship—of the noble, rare, *absolute* kind such as existed between Montaigne and his sweet Etienne—is the only antidote, the only healing ointment, the only ano-dyne, which can make it possible for us to endure without complete disintegration "the pangs of despised love" and love's bitter and withering reaction.

Love too—in the ordinary sense—implies jealousy, exclusiveness, insatiable exactions; whereas friendship, sure of its inviolable roots in spiritual equality, is ready to look generously and sympathetically upon every wandering obses-sion or passing madness in the friend of its choice.

With the exception of the love of a parent for a child this is the only human love which is out-ward-looking and centrifugal in its gaze; and even in the case of the love of a mother there is often something possessive and indrawing.

How beautifully, how finally, Montaigne, in his description of this high passion, sweeps aside at one stroke all that selfish emphasis upon "advan-tage" of which Bacon makes so much, and all that idealistic anxiety to retain one's "separate identity" in which Emerson indulges!

"I love him because he is he and he loves me because I am I." This is worthy to be compared with the beautiful and terrible "I *am* Heathcliff" of the heroine in the Brontë novel.

Emerson speaks as though, having sounded the depths of one's friend's soul, one moved off, with a wave of the hand, upon one's lonely quest, having none but God as one's eternal companion.

This translunar preference for the "Oversoul" over every human feeling is not Montaigne's notion of the passion of friendship. He is more earth-bound in his proclivities.

"He is he and I am I," and as long as we are what we are, in our flesh, in our blood, in our bones, nothing, while we live, can sever the bond between us. And in death? Ah! how much nearer to the pagan heart of this great mystery is the cry of the son of Jesse over the body of his beloved than all the Ciceronian rhetoric in the world—and how much nearer to what that loss means!

Montaigne does not really, as Pater so charmingly hints, break the flexible consistency of his philosophic method when he loves his friends in this unbounded manner. He is too great a sceptic to let his scepticism stand in the way of high adventures of this sort.

The essence of his unsystematic system is that one should give oneself freely up to what the gods throw in one's way. And if the gods—in their inescapable predestination—have made him "for me" and me "for him," to cling fast with cold cautious hands to the anchor of moderation were to be false to the philosophy of the "Eternal Now."

The whole of life is an enormous accident—a dice-throw of eternity in the vapours of time and space. Why not then, with him we love by our side, make richer and sweeter the nonchalant gaiety of our amusement, in the great mad purposeless preposterous show, by the "quips and cranks" of a companionable scepticism; canvassing all things in earth and heaven, reverencing God and Cæsar on *this side* of idolatry, relishing the foolish, fooling the wise, and letting the world drift on as it will?

"What do I know?" There may be more in life than the moralists guess, and more in death than the atheists imagine.

PASCAL

PASCAL

THERE are certain figures in the history of human thought who in the deepest sense of the word must be regarded as *tragic;* and this not because of any accidental sufferings they have endured, or because of any persecution, but because of something inherently *desperate* in their own wrestling with truth.

Thus Swift, while an eminently tragic figure in regard to his personal character and the events of his life, is not tragic in regard to his thought.

It is not a question of pessimism. Schopenhauer is generally, and with reason, regarded as a pessimist; but no one who has read his "World as Will and Idea" can visualise Schopenhauer, even in the sphere of pure thought, as a tragic personality.

The pre-eminent example in our modern world of the sort of desperate thinking which I have in mind as worthy of this title is, of course, Nietzsche; and it is a significant thing that over and over again in Nietzsche's writings one comes upon passionate and indignant references to Pascal.

The great iconoclast seemed indeed, as he groped about like a blind Samson in the temple of human faith, to come inevitably upon the figure of Pascal, as if this latter were one of the main pillars of the formidable edifice. It is interesting to watch this passionate attraction of steel for steel.

Nietzsche was constantly searching among apologists for Christianity for one who in intellect and imagination was worthy of his weapons; and it must be confessed that his search was generally vain. But in Pascal he did find what he sought.

His own high mystical spirit with its savage psychological insight was answered here by something of the same metal. His own "desperate thinking" met in this instance a temper equally "desperate," and the beauty and cruelty of his merciless imagination met here a "will to power" not less abnormal.

It is seldom that a critic of a great writer has, by the lucky throwing of life's wanton dice, an opportunity of watching the very temper he is describing, close at hand. But it does sometimes happen, even when the subject of one's criticism has been dead two hundred years, that one comes across a modern mind so penetrated with its master's moods; so coloured, so dyed, so ingrained with that particular spirit, that intercourse with it implies actual contact with its archetype.

Such an encounter with the subtlest of Christian apologists has been my own good fortune in my association with Mr. W. J. Williams, the friend of Loisy and Tyrrel, and the interpreter, for modern piety, of Pascal's deepest thoughts.

The superiority of Pascal over all other defenders of the faith is to be looked for in the peculiar angle of his approach to the terrific controversy—an angle which Newman himself, for all his serpentine sagacity, found it difficult to retain.

Newman worked in a mental atmosphere singularly unpropitious to formidable intellectual ventures, and one never feels that his essentially ecclesiastical mind ever really grasped the human plausibility of natural paganism. But Pascal went straight back to Montaigne, and, like Pater's Marius under the influence of Aristippus, begins his search after truth with a clean acceptance of absolute scepticism.

Newman was sceptical too, but his peculiar kind of intellectual piety lacked the imagination of Pascal. He could play, cleverly enough, with hypothetical infidelity, and refute it, so to say, "in his study" with his eye on the little chapel door; but there was a sort of refined shrinking from the jagged edges of reality in his somewhat Byzantine temperament which throws a certain suspicion of special pleading over his crafty logic.

Newman argues like a subtle theologian who has been clever enough to add to his "repertoire" a certain evasive mist of pragmatic modernism, under the filmy and wavering vapours of which the inveterate sacerdotalism of his temperament

49

covers its tracks. But with Pascal we get clean away from the poison-trail of the obscurantist.

Pascal was essentially a layman. There was nothing priestly in his mood; nothing scholastic in his reasoning; nothing sacerdotal in his conclusions. We breathe with him the clear sharp air of mathematics; and his imagination, shaking itself free from all controversial pettifogging, sweeps off into the stark and naked spaces of the true planetary situation.

One feels that Newman under all conceivable circumstances was bound to be a priest. There was priestliness writ large upon his countenance. His manner, his tone, his beautiful style, with something at once pleading and threatening, and a kind of feminine attenuation in its vibrant periods, bears witness to this.

Stripped of his cassock and tossed into the world's "hurly-burly," Newman would have drawn back into himself in Puritan dismay, and with Puritan narrowness and sourness would have sneered at the feet of the dancers. There was, at bottom, absolutely nothing in Newman of the clear-eyed human sweetness of the Christ of the Gospels; that noble, benignant, tolerant God, full of poetic imagination, whose divine countenance still looks forth from the canvasses of Titian.

Newman's piety, at best, was provincial, local, distorted. His Christ is the Christ of morbid Seminarists and ascetic undergraduates; not the

Christ that Leonardo da Vinci saw breaking bread with his disciples; not the Christ that Paolo Veronese saw moving among the crowds of the street like a royal uncrowned king.

It is a mistake to regard Pascal as a Protestant. It is equally a mistake to press hard upon his Catholicity. He was indeed too tragically preoccupied with the far deeper question as to whether faith in Christ is possible at all, to be limited to these lesser disputes.

His quarrel with the Jesuits was not essentially a theological quarrel. It was the eternal quarrel between the wisdom and caution and casuistry of the world and the uncompromising vision of the poet and prophet.

Nietzsche would never have singled out Pascal as his most formidable enemy if the author of "The Thoughts" had been nothing but a theological controversialist. What gives an eternal value to Pascal's genius, is that it definitely cleared the air. It swept aside all blurring and confusing mental litter, and left the lamentable stage of the great dilemma free for the fatal duel.

Out of the immense darkness of the human situation, that forlorn stage rises. The fearful spaces of the godless night are its roof, and row above row, tier above tier in its shadowy enclosure, the troubled crowds of the tribes of men wait the wavering issue of the contest. Full on the high stage in this tragic theatre of the universe Pascal throws the merciless searchlight of his imaginative logic, and the rhythm of the duality of man's fate is the rhythm of the music of his impassioned utterances.

The more one dreams over the unique position which Pascal has come to occupy, the more one realises how few writers there are whose imagination is large enough to grapple with the sublime horror of being born of the human race into this planetary system.

They take for granted so many things, these others. They have no power in them to lift eagle wings and fly over the cold grey boundless expanse of the shadowy waters.

They take for granted—materialists and mystics alike—so much; so much, that there is no longer any tragic dilemma left, any sublime "parting of the ways," any splendid or terrible decision.

Pascal's essential grandeur consists in the fact that he tore himself clear of all those peddling and pitiful compromises, those half humorous concessions, those lazy conventionalisms, with which most people cover their brains as if with wool, and ballast their imagination as if with heavy sand.

He tore himself clear of everything; of his own temperamental proclivities, of his pride, of his scientific vanity, of his human affections, of his lusts, of his innocent enjoyments. He tore himself clear of everything; so as to envisage the universe in its unmitigated horror, so as to look the emptiness of space straight between its ghastly lidless eyes.

One sees him there, at the edge of the world, silhouetted against the white terror of infinity, wrestling desperately in the dawn with the angel of the withheld secret.

His pride—his pride of sheer intellect—ah! that, as Nietzsche well knew, was the offering that had the most blood in it, the sacrifice that cried the loudest, as he bound it to the horns of the altar. The almost insane howl of suppressed misery which lurks in the scoriating irony of that terrible passage about sprinkling oneself with "holy water" and rendering oneself "stupid," is an indication of what I mean. Truly, as his modern representative does not hesitate to hint, the hand of Pascal held Christianity by the hair.

To certain placid cattle-like minds, the life we have been born into is a thing simple and natural enough. To Pascal it was monstrously and insolently unnatural. He had that species of grand and terrible imagination which is capable of piercing the world through and through; of rising high up above it, and of pulverising it with impassioned logic.

The basic incongruities of life yawned for him like bleeding eye-sockets, and never for one moment could he get out of his mind the appalling nothingness of the stellar spaces.

Once, after thinking about Pascal, I dreamed I saw him standing, a tall dark figure, above a chaotic sea. In his hand he held a gigantic whip, whose long quivering lash seemed, as he cracked it above the moaning waters, to summon the hidden monsters of the depths to rise to the surface. I could not see in my dream the face of this figure, for dark clouds kept sweeping across his head; but the sense of his ferocious loneliness took possession of me, and since then I have found it increasingly difficult to confine his image to mild Jansenistic heresies, ironic girdings at Jesuitical opponents, philosophic strolls with evangelical friends.

What Pascal does is a thing that, curiously enough, is very rarely done, even by great metaphysical writers; I mean the bringing home to the mind, without any comfortable illusive softenings of the stark reality, of what life really implies in its trenchant outlines. To do this with the more complete efficacy, he goes back to Montaigne and uses the scepticism of Montaigne as his starting point.

The Christian faith, in order to be a thing of beauty and dignity, must necessarily have something *desperate* about it, something of the terrible sweat and tears of one who wrestles with the ultimate angel. Easy-going Christianity, the Christianity of plump prelates and argumentative presbyters, is not Christianity at all. It is simply the "custom of the country" greased with the unction of professional interests.

PASCAL

One remembers how both Schopenhauer and Heine sweep away the Hegelian Protestantism of their age and look for the spirit of Christ in other quarters.

That so tremendous a hope, that so sublime a chance should have appeared at all in the history of the human race is a thing to wonder at; and Pascal, coming upon this chance, this hope, this supreme venture, from the depths of a corrosive all-devouring scepticism, realised it at its true value.

Hung between the infinitely great and the infinitely little, frozen by the mockery of two eternities, this "quintessence of dust" which is ourselves, cries aloud to be delivered from the body of its living death.

A reed that thinks! Could there anywhere be found a better description of what we are? Reed-like we bow ourselves to the winds of the four horizons—reed-like we murmur repetitions of the music of forest and sea—reed-like we lift our heads among the dying stalks of those who came before us—reed-like we wither and droop when our own hour comes—but with it all, we *think!*

Pascal looking at the face of the world sees evidence on all sides of the presence of something blighting and poisonous, something diabolic and malign in the way things are now organised. He traces the cause of this to the wilful evil in the heart of man, and he finds the only cure for it in the acceptance of God's grace.

There may be something irritating to the pagan mind about this arbitrary introduction of the idea of "sin" as the cause of the lamentable misery of the world. Among modern writers the idea of "sin" is ridiculed, and the notion of its supernaturalism scouted. But is this true psychology?

Whatever its extraordinary origin, this thing which we call "conscience" has emerged as a definite and inalienable phenomenon among us. To be exempt from the power of *remorse* is still, even in these modern days, to be something below or above the level of ordinary humanity. If the thing is everywhere present with us, then, as an actual undeniable experience; if we feel it, if we suffer from it, where is the philosophical or human advantage of slurring over its existence and refusing to take account of it?

The great artists are wiser in these matters than the philosophers. Are we to suppose that the depths of malignity in an Iago, or the "dark backward and abysm" of remorse in a Macbeth, are things purely relative and illusive?

"Hell is murky," whispers the sleep-walker, and the words touch the nerves of our imagination more closely than all the arguments of the evolutionists.

We will not follow Pascal through the doctrinal symbols of his escape from the burden of this consciousness. Where we must still feel the grandeur of his imagination is in his recognition of the presence of "evil" in the world as an objective and palpable thing which no easy explanations can get rid of and only a stronger spiritual force can overcome.

The imagination of Pascal once more makes life terrible, beautiful and dramatic. It pushes back the marble walls of mechanical cause and effect, and opens up the deep places. It makes the universe porous again. It restores to life its strange and mysterious possibilities. It throws the human *will* once more into the foreground, and gives the drama of our days its rightful spaciousness and breadth.

The kind of religious faith which lends itself to our sense of the noble and the tragic is necessarily of this nature. Like the tight-rope dancer in Zarathrustra, it balances itself between the upper and the nether gulfs. It makes its choice between eternal issues; it throws the dice upon the cosmic gaming-table; it wagers the safety of the soul against the sanity of the intellect.

And it is pre-eminently the mark of a great religion that it should be founded upon a great scepticism. Anything short of this lacks the true tragic note; anything short of this is mere temperamental cheerfulness, mere conventional assent to custom and tradition.

The great religion must carve its daring protest against the whole natural order of the universe upon the flaming ramparts of the world's uttermost boundary. The great religion must engrave its challenge to eternity upon the forehead of the Great Sphinx.

And after all, even supposing that Pascal is wrong; even supposing that making his grand wager he put his money upon the *wrong horse,* does that diminish the tragedy of his position? Does that lessen the sublimity of his imagination?

Obviously it is the practical certainty that he is wrong, and that he did put his money on the wrong horse, which creates the grandeur of the whole desperate business. If he were right, if the universe were really and truly composed in the manner he conceived it—why then, so far from his figure being a tragic one, he would present himself as a shrewd magician, who has found the "wonderful lamp" of the world's Aladdin's cave, and has entered upon inestimable treasures while disappearing into the darkness.

The sublimity of Pascal's vision depends upon its being illusive. The grandeur of his world-logic depends upon its being false. The beauty of his heroic character depends upon his philosophy being a lie.

If all that is left of this desperate dicer with eternity is a little dust and a strangely shaped skull, how magnificently dramatic, in the high classic sense, was his offering up of his intellect upon the altar of his faith!

In the wise psychology of the future—interesting itself in the historic aberrations of the human mind—it is likely that many chapters will be devoted to this strange "disease of desperation" full of such wild and fatal beauty.

The Spectacle of the world will lack much contrasting shadow when this thing passes away. A *certain deep crimson upon black* will be missing from the tapestry of human consciousness. There will be more sun-light but less Rembrantian chiaroscuro in the pigments of the great Picture. At any rate this is certain; by his tragic gambling in the darkness of the abyss between the unfathomed spaces, Pascal has drawn the perilous stuff of the great disease to a dramatic head. The thing can no longer diffuse itself like an attenuated evil humour through every vein of the world-body.

Customary piety, conventional religion, the thin security of self-satisfied morality, can now no more tease us with their sleek impertinence. In the presence of a venture of this high distinction, of a faith of this tragic intensity, such shabby counterfeits of the race's hope dwindle and pale and fade.

We now perceive what the alternative is, what the voice of "deep calling unto deep" really utters, as the constellation of Hercules draws the solar world toward it through the abysmal night. No more ethical foolery; no more pragmatic insolence; no more mystical rhetoric.

The prophets of optimism "lie in hell like

sheep." The world yawns and quivers to its foundations. Jotunheim rushes upon Asgard. From the pleasant fields of sun-lit pagan doubt comes to our ears the piping of the undying Pan —older than all the "twi-lights" of all the "gods."

But for the rest the issue is now plain, the great dilemma clear. No more fooling with shadows when faith has lost its substance; no more walking on the road to Emmaus when the Master is transformed to a stream of tendency; no more liberal theology when Socrates is as divine as Jesus.

The "Thinking Reed" bows before the wind of the infinite spaces. It bows. It bends. It is broken.

Aut Christus aut Nihil!

VOLTAIRE

VOLTAIRE

THE immense bulk of Voltaire's writings is profoundly uninteresting to me. I once saw—I think it must have been in Liverpool—a wonderful edition of his complete works published during the Revolution and with a duplicate copy of every illustrative print. I couldn't afford the price of the thing just then, amazingly low though it was, but in my devotion to that great name, I swore that, when I made my library, that noble edition should be in it.

I have never made any library and never intend to. The sight of classical authors in row upon row depresses me beyond words. Public Libraries are still worse. I have no wish to be helped "to get on in the world" by Mr. Carnegie. I resent the association between literature and "public benefactions." Does he propose to dole out the exquisite taste necessary to appreciate these rare things, on condition that our "home town" pay half the cost? Thank Heaven, a feeling for what is noble and distinguished in human thought is beyond the reach of any philanthropist. I mean beyond his power of giving or taking away, and I do not believe that those among the poor who really have this feeling are often found in libraries. They probably have their "Oxford Book of English Verse"—a gift from their gentlest acquaintance—just as I have; and, for the rest, they can sell their school prizes to buy Hardy and Henry James.

Except for "Candide" and a few excerpts from the "Philosophical Dictionary," I must confess I have no wish to turn over another page of Voltaire. It is simply incredible to me that human beings possessed of the same senses as ours could find satisfaction for their imagination in the sterile moralising, stilted sentiment, superficial wit, and tiresome persiflage of that queer generation. I suppose they didn't really. I suppose they used to go off on the sly, and read Rabelais and Villon. I suppose it was only the preposterous "social world" of those days who enjoyed nothing in literature except pseudo-classic attitudes and gestures; just as it is only the preposterous "social world" with us who enjoy nothing but Gaelic mythology and Oriental Mysticism.

Those pseudo-classic writers of the eighteenth century, in England and France, have their admirers still. I confess such admiration excites in me as much wonder as the works themselves excite distaste. What can they find in them that is thrilling or exciting or large or luminous or magical? I would pile up the whole lot of them along with those books that are no books —biblia a-biblia—of which Charles Lamb speaks

so plaintively. Backgammon boards with let-
tering behind them should be their companions.

What a relief to turn from contemplation of
the works of Voltaire to that bust of him by
Houdon!

Ah! there we have him, there we apprehend
him, there we catch his undying spirit! And
what a man he was! As one looks at that face
wherein a mockery more trenchant than the
world is able to endure leers and wags the tongue,
one feels certain that the soul of the eighteenth
century was not really contented with its heroic
sentimental mask. The look upon that face, with
its aristocratic refinement, its deadly intellect, its
beautiful cynicism, is worth all the sessions of
the Academy and all the seasons of the Salons.
It makes one think somehow of the gardens of
Versailles. One seems to see it as a mocking
fragment of heathen marble—some Priapian
deity of shameless irreverence, peering forth in
the moonlight from among the yew hedges and
the fountains; watching the Pierrot of the Min-
ute make love to Columbine, and the generations
of men drift by like falling leaves.

Voltaire!— He was well advised to choose
that name for himself; a name which sounds
even now like the call of a trumpet. And a call
it is; a call to the clear intelligences and the un-
clouded brains; a call to the generous hearts and
the unperverted instincts; a call to sanity and
sweetness and clarity and noble commonsense;

65

to all that is free and brave and gay and friendly, to rally to the standard of true civilisation against the forces of stupidity, brutality and obscurantism!

Voltaire was one of those great men whose thoughts are armies and whose words are victories in the cause of the liberation of humanity. If we do not read his books, we look at his image and we read his life. We name his name and we seal ourselves of his tribe; the name and tribe of such as refuse to bow their knees to Baal, and if they worship in the house of Rimmon, worship with a large reservation!

Voltaire is much more than a man of letters. He is a prophet of the age to come, when the execrable superstitions of narrow minds shall no longer darken the sunlight, and the infamous compulsion of human manners, human intellects, human tastes, into the petty mould of oppressive public opinion shall be ended forever.

That bust in the Louvre and the sublime story of his life will outlast all but one of those half a hundred volumes of his which Mr. Carnegie's liberality has put at the disposal of our "home town."

We too, like the populace of Paris, on the day when he came back to his own, flock out to see the "saviour of the Calas." We too, like the passionate actresses who crowned his image in the great comedy-house while—as they say—he bowed his head so low that his forehead touched the front of his box, acclaim him still as the Messiah of the Liberty of the human intellect.

How admirable it is to come back to the spirit and temper of Voltaire from the fussy self-love and neurotic introspections of our modern egoists. The new fashionable doctrine among the "intellectuals" is that one is to live in one's ivory tower and let the world go; live in one's ivory tower while brutal and detestable people tyrannise over the gentle and sensitive; live in one's ivory tower while the heavy hand of popular ignorance lies like a dead weight upon all that is fine and rare; live in one's ivory tower while complacent well-paid optimism whispers acquiescence in the "best of all possible worlds."

The great Voltaire was made in another mould. Few enjoyed the pleasures of life more than he; but the idea of the stupid brutality and ignorant tyranny from which in this world so many harmless people suffer filled him with fury. The Calas were only one—only the best known—of a long list of victims on whose behalf he entered the arena. In these campaigns of justice, he was tireless, inexhaustible, insatiable. He flooded Europe with pamphlets on behalf of his protegés. He defied Church and State in his crusades to defend them. His house at Ferney became a sort of universal refuge and sanctuary for the persecuted persons of the civilised world.

A great and good man! I sometimes think that of all the heroic champions of sensitiveness against insensitiveness, of weakness against strength, of the individual against public opinion, I would soonest call up the noble shade of Voltaire and kiss his pontifical hand!

The Pantheistic Carlyle grumbles at his levity and rails against his persiflage. One hopes there will always be a "persiflage" like that of Voltaire to clear the human stage of stupid tyranny and drive the mud-monsters of obscurantism back into their mid-night caverns. He was a queer kind of Apollo—this little great man with his old-fashioned wig and the fur-cloak "given him by Catherine of Russia"—but the flame which inspired him was the authentic fire, and the arrows with which he fought were dipped in the golden light of the sun.

I said there was one book of Voltaire's to which the souls of honest people who love literature must constantly return. This, of course, is "Candide"; a work worthy to be bound up in royal vellum and stained in Tyrian dyes. If it were not for "Candide"—so stiff and stilted was the fashionable spirit of that age—there would be little in Voltaire's huge shelf of volumes, little except stray flashes of his irrepressible gaiety, to arrest and to hold us. But into the pages of "Candide" he poured the full bright torrent of his immortal wit, and with this book in our hands we can feel him and savour him as he was.

One has only to glance over the face of Europe at this present hour to get the sting and Pythian poison of this planetary irony. It is like a Circean philtre of sweet sunbrewed wine, sparkling with rainbow bubbles and gleaming with the mockery of the deathless gods. Once for all in this scandalous and beautiful book, the lying optimism of the preachers receives its crushing blow. "Candide" is the final retort of all sane and generous spirits, full of magnanimity and laughter, to that morbid and shameful propitiation of the destinies which cries "peace when there is no peace."

One feels when one reads it as if it were written by some wanton and gracious youth, in the marble courts of some happy palace of Utopia, commenting upon the mad delusions and diseased hypocrisies of the men of the old time when superstition still reigned. No book in the world has more spontaneous gaiety, more of the triumphant spirit of human boyishness in its blood. Certainly the great Voltaire was to the end of his life—and you can see that very thing in the old-young face of the famous bust—inspired by the immortal flame of youth. He never grew old. To the last his attitude toward life was the attitude of that exuberant and unbounded energy which takes nothing seriously and loves the contest with darkness and stupidity for the sake of the divine "sport" of the struggle. There is a certain sun-born sanity of *commonsense* about such natural youthfulness, which contradicts all popular fallacies.

It is the Mercutio spirit, striking up the swords of both Montagus and Capulets and fooling them all on their grey-haired obsessions. It comes into this solemn custom-ridden world, as if from some younger and gayer star, and makes wanton sport of its pious hypocrisies. ,It opens its astonished laughing eyes upon the meanness of men and the cruelties of men and the insane superstitions and illusions of men, and it mocks them all with mischievous delight. It refuses to bow its head before hoary idols. It refuses to go weeping and penitent and stricken with a sense of "sin" in the presence of natural fleshly instincts. It is absolutely irresponsible—what, in a world like this, should one be responsible for? —and it is shamelessly frivolous. Why not? Where the highest sanctities are so lamentably human, and where the phylacteries of the moralists are embroidered with such earth-spun threads, why go on tip-toe and with forlorn visage? It is outrageously indecent. Why not? Who made this portentous "decency" to be the rule of free-born life? Who put fig-leaves upon the sweet flesh of the immortals? Decency after all is a mere modern barbarism; the evocation of morbid vulgarity and a perverted heart.

The great classic civilisations included a poetic obscenity with easy nonchalance. They had a god to protect its interests, and its sun-burnt youthful wantonness penetrates all their art. This modern cult of "decency"—thrust down the throat of human joy by a set of Calvins and John Knoxes—is only one of the indications in our wretched commercialised age of how far we have sunk from the laughter of the gods and the dancing of the morning stars.

To sit listening in the forlorn streets of a Puritan city—when for one day the cheating tradesmen leave their barbarous shops—to the wailing of unlovely hymns, empty of everything except a degraded sentimentality that would make an Athenian or a Roman slave blush with shame, is enough to cause one to regard the most scandalous levity of Voltaire as something positively sacred and holy.

One wonders that scholars are any longer allowed even to read Aristophanes—far less translate him. And cannot they see—these perverts of a purity that insults the sunshine—that *humour*, decent or indecent, is precisely the thing that puts sex properly in its place? Cannot they see that by substituting morbid sentiment for honest Rabelaisianism they are obsessing the minds of every one with a matter which after all is only one aspect of life?

The great terrible Aphrodite—ruler of gods and men—is not to be banished by conventicle or council. She will find her way back, though she has to tread strange paths, and the punishment for the elimination of natural wantonness is the appearance of hideous hypocrisy. Driven from the haunts of the Muses, expelled from the symposia of the wise and witty, the spirit of sexual irreverence takes refuge in the streets; and the scurrilous vulgarities of the tavern balance the mincing proprieties of the book-shop.

After all sex *is* a laughable thing. The tragedies connected with it, the high and thrilling pleasures connected with it, do not obliterate its original absurdity. And Voltaire—this sane sun-born child of the shameless intellect—never permits us for a moment to forget how ridiculous in the last resort all this fuss about the matter is.

Puritanical suppression and neurotic obsession are found invariably together. It is precisely in this way that the great goddess revenges herself upon those who disobey her laws. Voltaire, the least Puritanical of men, is also the least neurotic. The Satyrish laughter of his eternally youthful energy clears the air of the world.

Humour of all human things is the most transitory and changing in its moods. As a perambulating interpreter of literature, ancient as well as modern, this has especially been borne in upon me. I have been guilty, in that sickening academic way which makes one howl with shame in one's self-respecting moments, of "trying out" upon people the old stock humours of the standard authors.

I have dragged poor Bottom back to life and made the arms of the Cervantian wind-mill turn and the frogs of Aristophanes croak. But oh, shade of Yorick! how the sap, the ichor, the sharp authentic tang, that really tickles our sensibilities, has thinned out and fallen flat during the centuries. My hearers have smiled and tittered perhaps—with a pathetic wish to be kind, or a desire to show themselves not quite dull to these classic amenities—and between us we have, in a kind of chuckling pedantry, shuffled through the occasion; but it is not pleasant to recall such moments.

Of course a sly comedian could make anything amusing; but one cannot help feeling that if the humour of these famous scenes were really permanent it would force its way even through the frosty air of academic culture into our human nerves.

"We are not wood; we are not stones, but men" —and being men the essential spirit of outrageous humour ought surely to hit us, however poorly interpreted. And it does; only the proprieties and the decencies sheer us off from what is permanently appealing!

I recollect on one occasion, how, after making my hearers cry over the natural and permanent tragedy of Shylock, I asked the fatuous question, addressing it, as one does, to the vague air—

"What are we to say about Launcelot Gobbo?"

Now obviously any one but a professional interpreter of literature would know that there's *nothing* to say about this harmless fool. Shakespeare threw him in as "a comic relief" and probably felt his strongest appeal to the native genius of the actor who impersonated him. But I can recall now, with that sense of humiliation which wrings one's withers, the sweetly murmured tones of some tactful woman who answered— and the last thing one wants is an answer to these inanities—

"Oh, we must say that Launcelot Gobbo is charming!"

But Gobbo or no Gobbo, the fact remains that humour is one of the most delicate, the most evasive, and the most unstable of human qualities. I am myself inclined to hold that sheer outrageous ribaldry, especially if graced with an undertone of philosophic irony, is the only kind of humour which is really permanent. To give permanence to any human quality in literature, there must be an appeal to something which is beyond the power of time and change and fashion and custom and circumstance. And, as a matter of fact, nothing in the world except sex itself answers this requirement.

The absurdities of men are infinite, but they alter with every generation. What never alters or can alter, is the absurdity of being a man at all.

Where Shakespeare's humour still touches us most nearly is precisely in those scenes which the superficial custom of our age finds least endurable. It is not in his Gobbos or in his frolicsome boy-girls, that his essential spirit must be looked for; but in his Falstaffs and Mercutios.

But Shakespeare's humour is largely, after all, a lovely, dreamy, poetical thing. I doubt if it has the weight or the massive solidity of the humour of Rabelais. I think the humour of Charles Lamb wears well; but that is probably because it has a most indisputable flavour of Rabelaisian roguery underlying its whimsical grace. Anatole France has the true classic spirit. His humour will remain fresh forever, because it is the humour of the eternal absurdity of sexual desire. Heine can never lose the sharpness of his bite, for his irreverence is the eternal irreverence of the soul that neither man nor God can scourge into solemn submission.

Humour to be really permanent and to outlast the changes of fashion must go plummet-like to the basic root of things. It is nothing less than extraordinary that Voltaire, living in the age of all ages the most obsessed with the modishness of the hour, should have written "Candide," a book full of the old unalterable laughter. For "Candide" is not only a clever book, a witty book, a wise book. It is a book preposterously and outrageously funny. It tickles one's liver and one's gall; it relaxes one's nerves; it vents the suppressed spleen of years in a shout of irrepressible amusement. Certain passages in it—and, as one would have suspected they are precisely the passages that cannot be quoted in a modern book—compel one to laugh aloud as one thinks of them.

Personally I hold the opinion that "Candide"

is the most humorous piece of human writing in the world. And yet its ribaldry, its irreverence, is unbounded. It sticks at nothing. It says everything. It wags the philosophic tongue at every conceivable embodiment of popular superstition.

If the best books are the books which the authors of them have most enjoyed writing, the books that have the thrill of excellent pleasure on every page, then "Candide" certainly bears away the palm. One would like to have watched Voltaire's countenance as he wrote it. The man's superb audacity, his courage, his aplomb, his god-like shamelessness, appear in every sentence.

What an indictment of the human race! What an arraignment of the "insolence of office"! What a tract for the philanthropists! What a slap in the face for the philosophers! And all done with such imperturbable good temper, such magnanimity of fine malice.

Poor Candide! how loyally he struggled on, with Pangloss as his master and his ideal; and what shocks he experienced! I would sooner go down to posterity as the author of "Candide" than of any volume in the world except Goethe's "Faust."

There is something extraordinarily reassuring about the book. It reconciles one to life even at the moment it is piling up life's extravagant miseries. Its buoyant and resilient energy, full of the unconquerable irreverence and glorious shamelessness of youth, takes life fairly by the throat and mocks it and defies it to its face. It indicates courageous gaiety as the only victory, and ironical submission to what even gaiety cannot alter as the only wisdom.

There are few among us, I suppose, who in going to and fro in the world, have not come upon some much-persecuted, much-battered Candide, "cultivating his garden" after a thousand disillusions; and holding fast, in spite of all, to the doctrines of some amazing Pangloss. Such encounters with such invincible derelicts must put us most wholesomely to shame. Our neurotic peevishness, our imaginary grievances, our vanity and our pride, are shown up at such moments in their true light.

If complacent optimism appears an insolent falsifying of life's facts, a helpless pessimism appears a cowardly surrender to life's impertinence. Neither to gloss over the outrageous reality nor to lose our resistant obstinacy, whatever such reality may do to us, is the last word of noble commonsense. And it is a noble commonsense which, after all, is Voltaire's pre-eminent gift.

The Voltairian spirit refuses to be fooled by man or god. The universe may batter it and bruise it, but it cannot break it. The brutality of authority, the brutality of public opinion, may crush it to the earth; but from the earth it mocks still, mocks and mocks and mocks, with the eternal youthfulness of its wicked tongue! Voltaire took the world as he found it. With the weapons of the world he fought the world; with the weapons of the world he overcame the world. The neurotic modern vulgarity which, misinterpreting the doctrines of Nietzsche, worships force and bows down in the dust before the great unscrupulous man, finds no support in Voltaire. Honest people, cultivating their gardens and keeping the prophets away from their back-yards, find in the Voltairian spirit their perpetual refuge.

The old Horatian wisdom, clear-eyed, cynical and friendly, leaps up once again from the dust of the centuries, a clean bright flame, and brings joyousness and sanity back to the earth.

Voltaire could be kind and generous without calling to his aid the "immensities" and the "eternities." He could strike fiercely on behalf of the weak and the oppressed without darkening the sunshine by any worship of "sorrow." He could be thoroughly and most entirely "good," while spitting forth his ribald irreverences against every pious dogma. He could be long-suffering and considerate and patient, to a degree hardly ever known among men of genius, while ruling Europe with his indomitable pen.

The name of Voltaire is more than a trumpet call of liberty for the oppressed artists and thinkers of the world; it is a challenge to the individual Candides of our harassed generation to rise above their own weaknesses and introspections and come forth into the sunshine.

The name of Voltaire is a living indictment of the madness of politicians and the insanity of parties and sects. It brings us back to the commonsense of honest men, who "care for none of these things."

He was a queer Apollo of light and reason—this lean bewigged figure with cane and snuffbox and laced sleeves—but the powers of darkness fled from before his wit as they have not fled from before the wit of any other; for the wit of Voltaire is in harmony with the spirit of the human race, as it shakes itself free from superstition "and all uncharitableness."

He was a materialist if you will, for his "deism" meant no more to him than a distant blue sky giving the world space and perspective and free air; but a materialism that renders men kind and courteous, urbane and sweet-tempered, honest and clear-headed, is better than a spirituality that leads to intolerance and madness.

He was a ribald and a scoffer in the presence of much that the world holds sacred; but the most sacred thing of all—the *sanity of human reason*—has never been more splendidly defended.

He mocked at the traditions of men; but he remains a champion of man's highest prerogative. He turned the churches into indecent ridicule; but wherever an honest man strikes at tyrannous superstition, or a solitary "cultivator of his garden" strikes at stupid mob-rule, one stone the more is added to that great "ecclesia" of civilisation, which "Deo erexit Voltaire"; which Voltaire built—and builds—to God.

ROUSSEAU

ROUSSEAU

NOTHING is more clear than that the enjoyment of art and letters is forbidden, in any rich or subtle degree, to the apprehension of the moralist. It is also forbidden, for quite other reasons, to the apprehension of the extravagantly vicious.

The moralist is debarred from any free and passionate love of literature by the simple fact that all literature is created out of the vices of men of letters. The extravagantly vicious man is debarred from such a love by the still simpler fact that his own dominant obsession narrows down his interest to the particular writers who share his own vice.

When I encounter a catholic and impassioned lover of books—of many books and many authors—I know two things about him—I know that he is the opposite of a moralist, and I know that he is free from any maniacal vice. I might go further and say that I know he has a rooted hatred of moralists and a tolerant curiosity about every other form of human aberration.

When I say that literature is created out of the vices of men of letters, I use the word in a large and liberal sense. A vice is a pleasant sensation condemned by Puritans.. It is an over-emphasis laid upon some normal reaction; or it is a perverse and morbid deviation from the normal path.

It would not require any fantastic stretch of psychological interpretation to show how all the great men of letters are driven forward along their various paths by some demoniac urge, some dynamic impulse, that has its sensual as well as its intellectual origin. The "psychology of genius" is still in its infancy. It seems a pity that so much of the critical interpretation of the great writers of the world should be in the hands of persons who—by the reason of their academic profession—are naturally more interested in the effect of such work upon youthful minds than in its intrinsic quality.

The barbaric vulgarity of our commercial age is largely responsible for the invidious slur cast upon any genuine critical psychology; upon any psychology which frankly recognises the enormous influence in literature exercised by normal or abnormal sexual impulses.

Criticism of literature which has nothing to say about the particular sexual impulse—natural or vicious, as it may happen—which drives a writer forward, becomes as dull and unenlightening as theology without the Real Presence.

Among the influences that obstruct such free criticism among us at present may be noted Puritan fanaticism, academic professionalism (with its cult of the "young person"), popular vulgarity, **and** that curious Anglo-Saxon uneasiness and reticence in these things which while in no sense a sign of purity of mind invokes an invincible prejudice against any sort of **straightforward** discussion.

It is for these reasons that the art of criticism in England and America is so childish and pedantic when compared with that of France. In France even the most reactionary of critics—persons like Léon Bloy, for instance—habitually use the boldest sexual psychology in elucidating the mysterious caprices of human genius; and one can only wish that the conventional **inhibition** that renders such freedom impossible with us could come to be seen in its true light, that is to say as itself one of the most curious examples of sexual morbidity ever produced by unnatural conditions.

Rousseau is perhaps of all great original geniuses the one most impossible to deal with without some sort of recognition of the sexual peculiarities which penetrated his passionate and restless spirit. No writer who **has** ever lived had so sensitive, so nervous, **so** vibrant a physiological constitution. Nothing that he achieved in literature or in the creation of a new atmosphere of feeling in Europe, can be understood without at least a passing reference to the impulses which pushed him forward on his wayward road.

As we watch him in his pleasures, his passions,

his pilgrimages, his savage reactions, it is difficult to avoid the impression that certain kinds of genius are eminently and organically anti-social.

It is perhaps for this reason at bottom that the political-minded Anglo-Saxon race, with its sturdy "good citizen" ideals, feels so hostile and suspicious toward these great anarchists of the soul.

Rousseau is indeed, temperamentally considered, one of the most passionately anarchical minds in the history of the race. The citizen of Geneva, the lover of humanity, the advocate of liberty and equality, was so scandalous an individualist that there has come to breathe from the passage of his personality across the world an intoxicating savour of irresponsible independence.

The most ingrained pursuer of his own path, the most intransigeant "enemy of the people," would be able to derive encouragement in his obstinate loneliness from reading the works of this philanthropist who detested humanity; this reformer who fled from society; this advocate of domesticity who deserted his children; this pietist who worshipped the god of nature.

The man's intellect was so dominated by his sensualism that, even at the moment he is eloquently protesting in favour of a regenerated humanity living under enlightened laws, there emanates from the mere physical rhythm of his sentences an anti-social passion, a misanthropic self-worship, a panic terror of the crowd, which remains in the mind when all his social theories are forgotten.

He is the grand example of a writer whose sub-conscious intimate self contradicts his overt dogmas and creates a spiritual atmosphere in which his own reforming schemes wither and vanish.

Rousseau is, from any moral or social or national point of view, a force of much more disintegrating power than Nietzsche can ever be. And he is this for the very reason that his sensual and sentimental nature dominates him so completely.

From the austere Nietzschean watch-tower, this man's incorrigible weakness presents itself as intrinsically more dangerous to the race than any unscrupulous strength. The voluptuous femininty of his insidious eloquence lends itself, as Nietzsche saw, to every sort of crafty hypocrisy.

Rousseau's rich, subtle, melodious style—soft as a voice of a choir of women celebrating some Euripidean Dionysus—flows round the revolutionary figure of Liberty with an orgiastic passion worthy of the backward flung heads, bared breasts and streaming hair of a dance of Bassarids.

Other symbolic figures besides that of Liberty emerge above the stream of this impassioned

"Return to Nature." The figure of justice is there and the figure of fraternity; while above them all the shadowy lineaments of some female personification of the Future of Humanity, crowned with the happy stars of the Age of Gold, looks down upon the rushing tide.

"Oh, Liberty!" one can hear the voice of many heroic souls protesting, "Oh, Liberty—what things are done in thy name!"

For it is of the essential nature of Rousseau's eloquence, as it is of the essential nature of his temperament, that any kind of sensual abandonment, slurred over by rich orchestral litanies of human freedom, should be more than tolerated.

This Religion of Liberty lends itself to strange hypocrisies when the torrent of his imaginative passion breaks upon the jagged rocks of reality. That is why—from Robespierre down to very modern persons—the eloquent use of such vague generalisations as Justice, Virtue, Simplicity, Nature, Humanity, Reason, excites profound suspicion in the psychological mind.

From the antinomian torrent of this voluptuous anarchy the spirits of Epicurus, of Spinoza, of Goethe, of Nietzsche, turn away in horror. This is indeed an insurrection from the depths; this is indeed a breaking loose of chaos; this is indeed a "return to Nature." For there is a perilous intoxication in all this, and, like chemical ingredients in some obsessing drug these great vague names work magically and wantonly upon us, giving scope to all our weaknesses and perversities.

If I were asked—taking all the great influences which have moulded human history together—what figure, what personality, I would set up as the antipodal antagonist of the influence of Nietzsche, I would retort with the name of Rousseau.

Here is an "immoralism" deeper and far more anti-social than any "beyond good and evil." Nietzsche hammered furiously at Christian ethics; but he did so with the sublime intention of substituting for what he destroyed a new ethical construction of his own.

Rousseau, using with stirring and caressing unction symbol after symbol, catch-word after catch-word, from the moral atmosphere of Christendom, draws us furiously after him, in a mad hysterical abandonment of all that every human symbol covers, toward a cataract of limitless and almost inhuman subjectivity.

To certain types of mind Rousseau appears as a noble prophet of what is permanent in evangelic "truth" and of what is desirable and lovely in the future of humanity. To other types—to the pronounced classical or Goethean type, for instance—he must appear as the most pernicious, the most disintegrating, the most poisonous, the most unhealthy influence that has ever been brought to bear upon the world. Such minds—

confronting him with a genuine and logical anarchist, such as Max Stirner—would find him
far more dangerous. For Rousseau's anarchy is
of an emotional, psychological, feminine kind; a
kind that carries along upon the surface of its
eloquence every sort of high-sounding abstrac-
tion; while, all the time, the sinuous waters of its
world-sapping current filter through all the flood-
gates of human institution.

One cannot but be certain that Rousseau
would have been one of those irresistible but most
injurious persons whom, honorably crowned with
fillets of well-spun wool and fresh-grown myrtle,
Plato would have dismissed from the gates of the
great Republic.

One asks oneself the question—and it is a
question less often asked than one would expect
—whether it is really possible that a man of immense genius and magnetic influence can actually, as the phrase runs, "do more harm than
good" to the happiness of the human race. We
are so absurdly sheep-like and conventional in
these things that we permit our old-fashioned belief in a benignant providence turning all things
to good, to transform itself into a vague optimistic trust in evolutionary progress; a progress
which can never for one moment fail to make
everything work out to the advantage of humanity.

We have such pathetic trust too in the inherent friendliness of the universe that it seems

inconceivable to us that a great genius, inspired from hidden cosmic depths, should be actually a power of evil, dangerous to humanity. And yet, why not? Why should there not appear sometimes from the secret reservoirs of Being, powerful and fatal influences that, in the long result, are definitely baleful and malign in their effect upon the fortunes of the human race?

This was the underlying belief in the Middle Ages, and it led to the abominable persecution of persons who were obviously increasing the sum of human happiness. But may not there have been behind such unpardonable persecution, a legitimate instinct of self-protection—an instinct for which in these latter days of popular worship of "great names" there is no outlet of expression?

The uneasiness of the modern English-speaking world in the presence of free discussion of sex is, of course, quite a different matter. This objection is a mere childish prejudice reinforced by outworn superstitions. The religious terror excited by certain formidable free-thinkers and anti-social philosophers in earlier days went much deeper than this, and was quite free from that mere prurient itch of perverted sensuality which inspires the Puritans of our time.

This religious terror, barbarous and hideous as it was in many of its manifestations, may have been a legitimate expression of subconscious panic in the presence of something that, at least now and then, was really antagonistic to the general welfare.

Why should there not arise sometimes great demonic forces, incarnated in formidable personalities, who are really and truly "humani generis hostes," enemies of the human race? The weird mediæval dream of the antiChrist, drawn from Apocalyptic literature, symbolises this occult possibility.

Because a writer has immense genius there is no earthly reason why his influence upon the world should be good. There is no reason why it should be for the happiness of the world, putting the moral question aside.

In the classic ages the State regulated literature. In the Middle Ages, the Church regulated it. In our own age it is not regulated at all; it is neglected by ignorance and expurgated by stupidity. The mob in our days cringes before great names, the journalist exploits great names, and the school-master dishes them up for the young. No one seriously criticises them; no one seriously considers their influence upon the world.

The business man has a shrewd suspicion that they have no influence at all; or certainly none comparable with that of well placed advertisements. Meanwhile under the surface, from sensitive minds to sensitive minds, there run the electric currents of new intellectual ideas, setting in motion those psychic and spiritual forces which still, in spite of all our economic philosophers, up-heave the world.

Was Rousseau, more than any one, more than Voltaire, more than Diderot, responsible for the French Revolution? I am inclined to hold that he was, and if so, according to the revolutionary instincts of all enemies of oppression, we are bound to regard his influence as "good"; unless by chance we are among those who consider the tyranny of the middle-class no less outrageous than the tyranny of the aristocracy. But Rous-seau's influence—so far stretching is the power of personal genius—does not stop with the French Revolution. It does not stop with the Commune or with any other outburst of popular indignation. It works subterraneanly in a thou-sand devious ways until the present hour. Wherever, under the impassioned enthusiasm of such words as Justice, Liberty, Equality, Reason, Nature, Love, self-idealising, self-worshipping, self-deceiving prophets of magnetic genius give way to their weaknesses, their perversities, their anti-social reactions, the vibrant nerves of the great citizen of Geneva may still be felt, quiv-ering melodiously; touching us with the trem-ulousness of their anarchical revolt against every-thing hard and stern and strong.

Suppose for a moment that Rousseau were the equivocal pernicious influence, half-priest, half-pandar, half-charlatan, half-prophet of a world-disintegrating orgy of sentiment, should I for one, I am tempted to ask, close the gates of our platonic republic against him?

Not so! Let the world look to itself. Let the sheep-like crowd take the risks of its docility. Let the new bourgeois tyrants cuddle and cosset the serpent that shall bite them, as did the salon ladies of the old régime.

No! Let the world look to itself and let progress look to itself.

There seems something exhilarating about this possible appearance upon the earth of genuinely dangerous writers, of writers who exploit their vices, lay bare their weaknesses, brew intoxicating philtres of sweet poison out of their obsessions and lead humanity to the edge of the precipice! And there is something peculiarly stimulating to one's psychological intelligence when all this is done under the anæsthesia of humanitarian rhetoric and the lulling incantations of pastoral sentiment.

Rousseau is, in one very important sense, the pioneer of that art of delicate egoism in which the wisest epicureans of our day love to indulge. I refer to his mania for solitude, his self-conscious passion for nature. This feeling for nature was absolutely genuine in him and associates itself with all his amours and all his boldest speculations.

The interesting thing about it is that it takes the form of that vague, intimate magical rapport between our human souls and whatever mysterious soul lurks in the world around us, which has become in these recent days the predominant secret of imaginative poetry.

Not that Rousseau carries things as far as Wordsworth or Shelley. He is a born prose writer, not a poet. But for the very reason that he is writing prose, and writing it with a sentimental rather than a mystical bias, there are aspects of his work which have a simple natural *personal* appeal that the sublime imagination of the great spiritual poets must necessarily lack.

There is indeed about Rousseau's allusions to places and spots which had become dear to him from emotional association a lingering regretful tenderness, full of wistful memories and a vague tremulous yearning, which leaves upon the mind a feeling unlike that produced by any other writer. The subconscious music of his days seems at those times to rise from some hidden wells of emotion in him and overflow the world.

When he speaks of such places the mere admixture in his tone of the material sensuousness of the eighteenth century with something new and thrilling and different has itself an appealing charm. The blending of a self-conscious artificial, pastoral sentiment, redolent of the sophisticated Arcadias of Poussin and Watteau, and suggestive of the dairy-maid masquerades of Marie Antoinette in the gardens of Versailles, with a direct passionate simplicity almost worthy

95

of some modern Russian, produces a unique and memorable effect upon a sympathetic spirit.

The mere fact that that incorrigible egoist and introspective epicurean, William Hazlitt, whose essays are themselves full of an ingratiating and engaging sensuousness, should have taken Rousseau as his special master and idealised him into a symbolic figure, is a proof of the presence in him of something subtle, arresting and unusual.

I always like to bring these recondite odours and intimations of delicate spiritual qualities down to the test of actual experience, and I am able to say that, through the help of Hazlitt's intuitive commentaries, the idea of Rousseau has twined itself around some of the pleasantest recollections of my life.

I can see at this moment as I pen these lines, a certain ditch-bordered path leading to a narrow foot-bridge across a river in Norfolk. I can recall the indescribable sensations which the purple spikes of loosestrife and the tall willow-herb, growing with green rushes, produced in my mind on a certain misty morning when the veiled future bowed toward me like a vision of promise and the dead past flew away over the fens like a flight of wild swans.

The image of Rousseau cherishing so tenderly every rose-tinged memory and every leafy oasis in his passionate pilgrimage, came to me then, as it comes to me now, a thing that no harsh blows of the world, no unkind turns of fate, no "coining of my soul for drachmas" can ever quite destroy.

There is, after all, a sort of spiritual second self, a sort of astral residuum left behind by a personality of this kind, which to certain natures becomes more sacred and suggestive than any of those tedious speculations or literary theories about which the historians may argue.

Most human beings—especially in these "centres of civilisation," which are more hideous than anything the sun has looked upon since it watched the mammoths tusking the frozen earth or the ichtheosauruses wallowing in the primeval mud —go through this life blindly, mechanically, unconsciously, fulfilling their duties, snatching at their pleasures, and shuddering at the thought of the end.

Few men and women seem really conscious of what it is to be alive, to be alive and endowed with imagination and memory, upon this time-battered planet.   It needs perhaps the anti-social instincts of a true "philosophic anarchist" to detach oneself from the absorbing present and to win the larger perspective.

Rousseau was of so fluid, so irrresponsible a temperament that he never could be brought to take seriously, to take as anything but as suggestive subjects for eloquent diatribes, the practical and domestic relations between human beings in organised society.

He played lightly with these relations, he laughed over them and wept over them, he wrote impassioned and dithyrambic orations upon them. But they were not his real life. His real life was the life he lived with his music and his botany and his love affairs, the life of his dreamy wanderings from refuge to refuge among the woods and châteaux of France; the life of his delicate memories and wistful regrets; the life of his thrilling indescribable thoughts, half sensual and half spiritual, as he drifted along the lonely roads and under the silent stars, or sat staring at the fire-light in his Paris attic while the city roared about him.

No lonely introspective spirit, withdrawn from the crowd and hating the voices of the world, can afford to lose touch with the secret of Rousseau; with what his self-centred and impassioned existence really meant.

We need not tease ourselves with his pious speculations, with his philanthropic oratory or his educational proposals. These can be left to those who are interested in such things. What we find arresting and suggestive in him, after this lapse of years, is a certain quality of personal passion, a certain vein of individual feeling, the touch of which still has a living power.

How interesting, for example, is that voluptuous desire of his to lay bare all his basest and meanest lusts, all his little tricks and devices and vanities and envies and jealousies. This mania for self-exposure, this frantic passion for self-laceration and self-humiliation is all of a piece with the manner in which he seemed to enjoy being ill-used and tyrannised over in his singular love-affairs.

More interesting still, and still more morbid, is that persecution mania which seized him in his later days—the mania that all the world loathed him and laughed at him and plotted to make a fool of him. Though betrayed into using the popular phrase, "persecution mania," I am myself inclined to resent, on Rousseau's behalf and on behalf of those who temperamentally resemble him, this cool assumption by the normal world that those whom it instinctively detests are "mad" when they grow aware of such detestation.

There seems no doubt that certain human beings appear at intervals on the world stage, whose sentient organisation, attuned to an abnormal receptivity, renders them alien and antagonistic to the masses of mankind.

They seem like creatures dropped upon the earth from some other planet, and, do what they may, they cannot grow "native and endued unto the element" of our terrestrial system. This difference in them is not only irritating to the normal herd; it is also provocative of bitter hostility in those among their contemporaries who are themselves possessed of genius.

These other wooers of posterity feel outraged

and piqued to the limit of their endurance at having to contend in the same arena with an antagonist who seems to obey no human rules. "A conspiracy of silence" or of scandalous aspersions is almost instinctively set on foot.

Rousseau's so-called mania of persecution can easily be explained. There was morbidity; there was neurotic unwisdom, in the manner in which he dealt with all these people. But he was probably perfectly right in assuming that they came to hate him.

In his Confessions he does his best to make posterity hate him; and in private life he must have been constantly, like one of those strange self-lacerating persons in Dostoievsky, bringing to the front, with shameless indecency, his vanities and jealousies, his weakness and his manias. When he couldn't enjoy the society of some friendly lady—and his friends were nearly always uneasy under the infliction—he poured forth his childish petulances and his rare imaginations on the bosom, so to speak, of society in general; and society in general flung him back in wondering contempt.

His clever contemporaries would naturally, under the pressure of the moment, concentrate their critical attention upon the weakest part of his genius—that is to say upon his reforming theories and large world-shaking speculations—while the portion of him that interests us now would merely strike them as tiresome and irrelevant.

He grew more and more lonely as he neared his end. It might be said that he deserved this fate; he who refused to accept even the responsibility of paternity. But one cannot resist a certain satisfaction in noting how the high-placed society people who came to visit him as he sat in his attic, copying music for a livelihood, were driven from his door.

The great Sentimentalist must have had his exquisite memories, even then, as he sat brooding over his dull mechanical work, he whose burning eloquence about Liberty and Justice and Simplicity and Nature was already sowing the seed of the earthquake.

Queer memories he must have had of his early tramp life through the roads and villages of France; of his conversations with the sceptical Hume among the hills of Derbyshire; of his sweet romantic sojournings in old historic houses, and his strange passions and fatal loves. But the rarest of his memories must have been of those hours and days when, in the pastoral seclusion of some cherished hiding-place, he let the world go by and sank, among patient leaves and flowers that could not mock him, into his own soul and the soul of nature.

He has been hugely vituperated by evolutionary philosophers for his mania for the "age of gold" and his disbelief in progress.

One of his favourite themes that civilisation is a curse and not a blessing excited the derision of his best friends. Others said that he stole the idea. But we may be sure that as he copied his daily portion of music with the civilisation of the Salons clamouring unheeded around him, his mind reverted rather to those exquisite moments when he had been happy alone, than to all the triumphs of his genius.

He was just the type that the world would naturally persecute. Devoid of any sparkling wit, devoid of any charm of manner, singularly devoid of the least sense of proportion, he lent himself to every sort of social rancour. He was one of those persons who take themselves seriously, and that, in his world as in the world of our own time, was an unpardonable fault.

He loved humanity better than men and women. He loved nature better than humanity.

He was a man with little sense of humour and with little interest in other men. He lived for his memories and his dreams, his glimpses and his visions.

Turning away from all dogmatic creeds, he yet sought God and prayed to him for his mercy.

Born into a world whose cleverness he dreaded, whose institutions he loathed, whose angers he provoked, whose authorities he scandalised, whose crowds he hated, he went aside "botanizing" and "copying music"; every now and then hurling forth from his interludes of sentimental journeying a rhythmical torrent of eloquent prophecy in which he himself only half believed and of which, quite often, "the idea was stolen."

In his abnormal receptivity, he was used as a reed for the invisible powers to blow their wild tunes through and to trouble the earth. He produced one great Revolution, and he may, through the medium of souls like his own, produce another; but all the time his real happiness was in his wanderings by field and hedge and road and lane, by canal side and by river bank, thinking the vague delicious thoughts of sensuous solitude and dreaming over the dumb quiescence of that mute inanimate background of our days into which, with his exasperated human nerves, he longed to sink and be at rest.

BALZAC

BALZAC

THE real value of the creations of men of genius is to make richer and more complicated what might be called the imaginative margin of our normal life. We all, as Goethe says, have to bear the burden of humanity—we have to plunge into the bitter waters of reality, so full of sharp rocks and blinding spray. We have to fight for our own hand. We have to forget that we so much as possess a soul as we tug and strain at the resistant elements out of which we live and help others to live.

It is nonsense to pretend that the insight of philosophers and the energy of artists help us very greatly in this bleak wrestling. They are there, these men of genius, securely lodged in the Elysian fields of large and free thoughts—and we are here, sweating and toiling in the dust of brutal facts.

The hollow idealism that pretends that the achievements of literature and thought enter profoundly into the diurnal necessity which prods us forward is a plausible and specious lie. We do not learn how to deal craftily and prosperously with the world from the Machiavels and Talleyrands. We do not learn how to love the world and savour it with exquisite joy from the Whitmans and Emersons. What we do is to struggle on, as best we may; living by custom, by prejudice, by hope, by fear, by envy and jealousy, by ambition, by vanity, by love.

They call it our "environment," this patched up and piecemeal panorama of mad chaotic blunderings, which pushes us hither and thither; and they call it our "heredity," this confused and twisted amalgam of greeds and lusts and conscience-stricken reactions, which drives us backward and forward from within. But there is more in the lives of the most wretched of us than this blind struggle.

There are those invaluable, unutterable moments, which we have *to ourselves,* free of the weight of the world. There are the moments—the door of our bedroom, of our attic, of our ship's cabin, of our monastic cell, of our tenement-flat, shut against the intruder—when we can enter the company of the great shadows and largely and freely converse with them to the forgetting of all vexation.

At such times, it is to the novelists, to the inventors of stories, that we most willingly turn for the poppied draught that we crave. The poets hurt us with the pang of too dear beauty. They remind us too pitifully of what we have missed. There is too much Rosemary which is "for remembrance" about their songs; too many dead violets between their leaves!

But on the large full tide of a great human romance, we can forget all our troubles. We can live in the lives of people who resemble ourselves and yet are not ourselves. We can put our own misguided life into the sweet distance, and see it —it also—as an invented story; a story that may yet have a fortunate ending!

The philosophers and even the poets are too anxious to convert us to their visions and their fancies. There is the fatal odour of the prophet in their perilous rhetoric, and they would fain lay their most noble fingers upon our personal matters. They want to make us moral or immoral. They want to thrust their mysticism, their materialism, their free love, or their imprisoned thoughts, down our reluctant throats.

But the great novelists are up to no such mischief; they are dreaming of no such outrage. They are telling their stories of the old eternal dilemmas; stories of love and hate and fear and wonder and madness; stories of life and death and strength and weakness and perversion; stories of loyalty and treachery, of angels and devils, of things seen and things unseen. The greatest novelists are not the ones that deal in sociological or ethical problems. They are the ones that make us forget sociological and ethical problems. They are the ones that deal with the beautiful, mad, capricious, reckless, tyrannous passions, which will outlast all social systems and are beyond the categories of all ethical theorising.

First of all the arts of the world was, they say, the art of dancing. The aboriginal cave-men, we are to believe, footed it in their long twilights to tunes played on the bones of mammoths. But I like to fancy, I who have no great love for this throwing abroad of legs and arms, that there were a few quiet souls, even in those days, who preferred to sit on their haunches and listen to some hoary greybeard tell stories, stories I suppose of what it was like in still earlier days, when those lumbering Diplodocuses were still snorting in the remoter marshes.

It was not, as a matter of fact, in any attic or ship's cabin that I read the larger number of Balzac's novels. I am not at all disinclined to explain exactly and precisely where it was, because I cannot help feeling that the way we poor slaves of work manage to snatch an hour's pleasure, and the little happy accidents of place and circumstance accompanying such pleasure, are a noteworthy part of the interest of our experience. It was, as it happens, in a cheerful bow-window in the Oxford High Street that I read most of Balzac; read him in the dreamy half-light of late summer afternoons while the coming on of evening seemed delayed by something golden in the drowsy air which was more than the mere sinking of the sun behind the historic roofs.

Oxford is not my Alma Mater. The less courtly atmosphere which rises above the willows and poplars of the Cam nourished my youthful dreams; and I shall probably to my dying day never quite attain the high nonchalant aloofness from the common herd proper to a true scholar.

It was in the humbler capacity of a summer visitor that I found myself in those exclusive purlieus, and it amuses me now to recall how I associated, as one does in reading a great romance, the personages of the Human Comedy with what surrounded me then.

It is a far cry from the city of Matthew Arnold and Walter Pater to the city of Vautrin and Rastignac and Lucien de Rubempré and Gobsec and Père Goriot and Diane de Maufrigneuse; and the great Balzacian world has the power of making every other milieu seem a little faded and pallid. But one got a delicious sense of contrast reading him just there in those golden evenings, and across the margin of one's mind floated rich and thrilling suggestions of the vast vistas of human life. One had the dreamy pleasure that some sequestered seminarist might have, who, on a sunny bench, under high monastic walls, reads of the gallantries and adventures of the great ungodly world outside.

Certainly the heavy avalanches of scoriac passion which rend their way through the pages of the Human Comedy make even the graceful blasphemies of the Oscar Wilde group, in those fastidious enclosures, seem a babyish pretence of naughtiness.

I remember how I used to return after long rambles through those fields and village lanes which one reads about in "Thyrsis," and linger in one of the cavernous book-shops which lie—like little Bodleians of liberal welcome—anywhere between New College and Balliol, hunting for Balzac in the original French. Since then I have not been able to endure to read him in any edition except in that very cheapest one, in dusty green paper, with the pages always so resistently uncut and tinted with a peculiar brownish tint such as I have not seemed to find in any other volumes. What an enormous number of that particular issue there must be in Paris, if one can find so many of them still, sun-bleached and weather-stained, in the old book-shops of Oxford!

Translations of Balzac, especially in those "editions de luxe" with dreadful interpretative prefaces by English professors, are odious to me. They seem the sort of thing one expects to find under glass-cases in the houses of cultured financiers. They are admirably adapted for wedding presents. And they have illustrations! That is really too much. A person who can endure to read Balzac, or any other great imaginative writer, in an edition with illustrations, is a person utterly outside the pale. It must be for barbarians of this sort that the custom has arisen of having handsome young women, representing feminine prettiness in general, put upon the covers of books in the way they put them upon chocolate

boxes. I have seen even "Tess of the d'Urber-
villes" prostituted in this manner. It is all on a
par with every other aspect of modern life. Indeed it may be said that what chiefly distinguishes
our age from previous ages is its habit of leaving
nothing to the imagination.

On the whole, Balzac must still be regarded as
the greatest novelist that ever lived. Not to love
Balzac is not to love the art of fiction, not to love
the huge restorative pleasure of wandering at
large through a vast region of imaginary characters set in localities and scenes which may be
verified and authenticated by contact with original
places.

I would flatly refuse to two classes of persons,
at any rate, any claim to be regarded as genuine
lovers of fiction. The first class are those who
want nothing but moral support and encouragement. These are still under the illusion that Balzac is a wicked writer. The second class are
those who want nothing but neurotic excitement
and tingling sensual thrills. These are under the
illusion that Balzac is a dull writer.

There is yet a third class to whom I refuse the
name of lovers of fiction. These are the intellectual and psychological maniacs who want nothing but elaborate social and personal problems,
the elucidation of which may throw scientific light
upon anthropological evolution. Well! We
have George Eliot to supply the need of the first;
the author of "Homo Sapiens" to supply the need

of the second; and Paul Bourget to deal with the last.

It is difficult not to extend our refusal of the noble title of real Fiction-Lovers to the whole modern generation. The frivolous craze for short books and short stories is a proof of this. *The unfortunate illusion which has gone abroad of late that a thing to be "artistic" must be concise and condensed and to the point, encourages this heresy. I would add these "artistic" persons with their pedantry of condensation and the "exact phrase" to all the others who don't really love this large and liberal art. To a genuine fiction-lover a book cannot be too long. What causes such true amorists of imaginative creation real suffering is when a book comes to an end. It can never be enjoyed again with quite the same relish, with quite the same glow and thrill and ecstasy. /

To listen to certain fanatics of the principle of unity is to get the impression that these mysterious "artistic qualities" are things that may be thrust into a work from outside, after a careful perusal of, shall we say, Flaubert's Letters to Madame Something-or-other, or a course of studies of the Short Story at Columbia University. Chop the thing quite clear of all "surplusage and irrelevancy"; chop it clear of all "unnecessary detail"; chop the descriptions and chop the incidents; chop the characters; "chop it and pat it and mark it with T," as the nursery rhyme says, "and put it in the oven for Baby and me!" It is an impertinence, this theory, and an insult to natural human instincts.

⌐ Art is not a "hole and corner" thing, an affair of professional preciosities and discriminations, a set of tiresome rules to be learned by rote.

Art is the free play of generous and creative imaginations with the life-blood of the demiurgic forces of the universe in their veins. There is a large and noble joy in it, a magnanimous nonchalanee and aplomb, a sap, an ichor, a surge of resilient suggestion, a rich ineffable magic, a royal liberality

Devoid of the energy of a large and free imagination, art dwindles into an epicene odalisque, a faded minion of pleasure in a perfumed garden. It becomes the initiatory word of an exclusive Rosicrucian order. It becomes the amulet of an affected superiority, the signet ring of a masquerading conspiracy. ⌐

The habitation of the spirit of true art is the natural soul of man, as it has been from the beginning and as it will be to the end. The soul of man has depths which can only be fathomed by an art which breaks every rule of the formalists and transgresses every technical law.

The mere fact that the kind of scrupulous artistry advocated by these pedants of "style" is a kind that can be defined in words at all writes its own condemnation upon it. For the magical evocations of true genius are beyond definition.

As Goethe says the important thing in all great art is just what cannot be put in words. Those who would seek so to confine it are the bunglers who have missed the mark themselves, and "they like"—the great critic adds malignantly—"they like to be together."

The so-called rules of technique are nothing when you come to analyse them but a purely empirical and pragmatic deduction from the actual practise of the masters. And every new master creates new laws and a new taste capable of appreciating these new laws. There is no science of art. These modern critics, with their cult of "the unique phrase" and the "sharply defined image," are just as intolerant as the old judicial authorities whose prestige they scout; just as intolerant and just as unilluminating.

It is to the *imagination* we must go for a living appreciation of genius, and many quite simple persons possess this, to whom the jargon of the studios is empty chatter.

No human person has a right to say "Balzac ought to have put more delicacy, more subtlety into his style," or to say, "Balzac ought to have eliminated those long descriptions." Balzac is Balzac; and that ends it. If you prefer the manner of Henry James, by all means read him and let the other alone.

There is such a thing as the mere absence of what the "little masters" call style being itself a quite definite style.

BALZAC

A certain large and colourless fluidity of manner is often the only medium through which a vision of the world can be expressed at all; a vision, that is to say, of a particular kind, with the passion of it carried to a particular intensity.

In America, at this present time, the work of Mr. Theodore Dreiser is an admirable example of this sort of thing. Mr. Dreiser, it must be admitted, goes even beyond Balzac in his contempt for the rules; but just as none of the literary goldsmiths of France convey to us the flavour of Paris as Balzac does, so none of the clever writers of America convey to us the flavour of America as Mr. Dreiser does.

Indeed I am ready to confess that I have derived much light in regard to my feeling for the demonic energy of the great Frenchman from watching the methods of this formidable American. I discern in Mr. Dreiser the same obstinate tenacity of purpose, the same occult perception of subterranean forces, the same upheaving, plough-like "drive" through the materials of life and character.

Balzac is undoubtedly the greatest purely creative genius that has ever dealt with the art of fiction. It is astonishing to realise how entirely the immense teeming world through which he leads us is the product of unalloyed imagination.

Experience has its place in the art of literature; it would be foolish to deny it; but the more one contemplates the career of Balzac the more evident does it become that his art is the extreme opposite of the art of the document-hunters and the chroniclers.

The life which he habitually and continually led was the life of the imagination. He lived in Paris. He knew its streets, its tradesmen, its artists, its adventurers, its aristocratic and its proletarian demi-monde.

He came from the country and he knew the country; its peasants, its farmers, its provincial magnates, its village tyrants, its priests, its doctors, its gentlemen of leisure.

But when one comes to calculate the enormous number of hours he spent over his desk, night after night, and day after day, one comes to see that there was really very scant margin left for the conscious collecting of material. The truth is he lived an abnormally sedentary life. Had he gone about a little more he would probably have lived much longer. The flame of his genius devoured him, powerful and titanic though his bodily appearance was, and unbounded though his physical energy. He *lived by the imagination* as hardly another writer has ever done and his reward is that, as long as human imagination interests itself in the panorama of human affairs, his stories will remain thrilling. How little it really matters whether this story or the other rounds itself off in the properly approved way!

Personally I love to regard all the stories of Balzac as one immense novel—of some forty volumes—dealing with the torrential life of the human race itself as it roars and eddies in its huge turbulency with France and Paris for a background. I am largely justified in this view of Balzac's work by his own catholic and comprehensive title—The Human Comedy—suggestive certainly of a sort of uniting thread running through the whole mass of his productions. I am also justified by his trick of introducing again and again the same personages; a device which I daresay is profoundly irritating to the modern artistic mind, but which is certainly most pleasing to the natural human instinct.

This alone, this habit of introducing the same people in book after book, is indicative of how Balzac belongs to the company of the great natural story-tellers. A real lover of a story wants it to go on forever; wants nobody in it ever to die; nobody in it ever to disappear; nobody in it ever to round things off or complete his life's apprenticeship, with a bow to the ethical authorities, in that annoying way of so many modern writers.

No wonder Oscar Wilde wept whenever he thought of the death of Lucien de Rubempré. Lucien should have been allowed at least one more "avatar." That is one of the things that pleases me so much in that old ten-penny paper edition published by the great Paris house. We have a list of the characters in the index, with all their other appearances on the stage; just exactly as if it were real life! It was all real enough at any

rate to Balzac himself, according to that beautiful tale of how he turned away from some trouble-some piece of personal gossip with the cry:
"Come back to actualities! Come back to my books!"

And in the old ideal platonic sense it *is* the true reality, this reproduction of life through the creative energy of the imagination.

The whole business of novel writing lies in two things; in the creating of exciting situations and imaginatively suggestive characters—and in making these situations and characters *seem real*.

They need not be dragged directly forth from personal experiences. One grows to resent the modern tendency to reduce everything to auto-biographical reminiscence. These histories of free-thinking young men breaking loose from their father's authority and running amuck among Paris studios and Leicester Square act-resses become tedious and banal after a time. Such sordid piling up of meticulous detail, drawn so obviously from the writer's own adventures, throws a kind of grey dust over one's interest in the narrative.

One's feeling simply is that it is all right and all true; that just in this casual chaotic sort of way the impact of life has struck oneself as one drifted along. But there is no more in it than a clever sort of intellectual photography, no more in it than a more or less moralised version of the ordinary facts of an average person's life-story.

BALZAC

One is tempted to feel that, after all, there is a certain underlying justification for the man in the street's objection to this kind of so-called "realism." ⁄ We have a right after all to demand of art something more than a clever reproduction of the experiences we have undergone. We have a right to demand something creative, something exceptional, something imaginative, something that lifts us out of ourselves and our ordinary environments, something that has *deep holes* in it that go down into unfathomable mystery, something that has vistas, horizons, large and noble perspectives, breadth, sweep, and scope.

The truth is that these grey psychological histories of typical young persons, drearily revolting against dreary conventions, are, in a deep and inherent sense, false to the mystery of life. ⁄

One feels certain that even the clever people who write them have moods and impulses far more vivid and thrilling, far more abnormal and bizarre, than they have the audacity to put into their work. A sort of perverted Puritanism restrains them. They have the diseased conscience of modern art, and they think that nothing can be true which is not draggle-tailed and nothing can be real which is not petty and unstimulating. And all the while the maddest, beautifulest fantasticalest things are occurring every day, and every day the great drunken gods are tossing the crazy orb of our fate from hand to hand and making it shine with a thousand iridescent hues!

The natural man takes refuge from these people's drab perversions of the outrageous reality, in the sham wonders of meretricious romances which are not real at all.

What we cry out for is something that shall have about it the liberating power of the imagination and yet be able to convince us of its reality. We need an imaginative realism. We need a romanticism which has its roots in the solid earth. We need, in fact, precisely what Balzac brings.

So far from finding anything tedious or irksome in the heavy massing up of animate and inanimate back-grounds which goes on all the while in Balzac's novels, I find these things most germane to the matter. What I ask from a book is precisely this huge weight of formidable verisimilitude which shall surround me on all sides and give firm ground for my feet to walk on. I love it when a novel is thick with the solid mass of earth-life, and when its passions spring up volcano-like from flaming pits and bleeding craters of torn and convulsed materials. I demand and must have in a book a four-square sense of life-illusion, a rich field for my imagination to wander in at large, a certain quantity of blank space, so to speak, filled with a huge litter of things that are not tiresomely pointing to the projected issue.

I hold the view that in the larger aspects of the creative imagination there is room for many free margins and for many materials that are not slavishly symbolic. I protest from my heart against this tyrannous "artistic conscience" which insists that every word "should tell" and every object and person referred to be of "vital importance" in the evolution of the "main theme." I maintain that in the broad canvas of a nobler, freer art there is ample space for every kind of digression and by-issue. I maintain that the mere absence of this self-conscious vibrating pressure upon one string gives to a book that amplitude, that nonchalance, that huge friendly discursiveness, which enables us to breathe and loiter and move around and see the characters from all sides—from behind as well as from in front! The constant playing upon that one string of a symbolic purpose or a philosophical formula seems to me to lead invariably to a certain attenuation and strain. The imagination grows weary under repeated blows upon the same spot. We long to debouch into some path that leads nowhere. We long to meet some one who is interesting in himself and does nothing to carry anything along.

Art of this tiresomely technical kind can be taught to any one. If this were all—if this were the one thing needful—we might well rush off en masse to the lecture-rooms and acquire the complete rules of the Short Story. Luckily for our pleasant hours there is still, in spite of everything, a certain place left for what we call genius in the manufacture of books; a place left for that sudden thrilling lift of the whole thing to a level where the point of the interest is not in the mere accidents of one particular plot but in the vast stream of the mystery of life itself.

Among the individual volumes of the Human Comedy, I am inclined to regard "Lost Illusions" —of which there are two volumes in that ten-penny edition—as the finest of all, and no one who has read that book can forget the portentous weight of realistic background with which it begins.

After "Lost Illusions" I would put "Cousin Bette" as Balzac's master-piece, and, after that, "A Bachelor's Establishment." But I lay no particular stress upon these preferences. With the exception of such books as "The Wild Ass's Skin" and the "Alkahest" and "Seraphita," the bulk of his work has a sort of continuous interest which one would expect in a single tremendous prose epic dealing with the France of his age.

Balzac's most remarkable characteristic is a sort of exultant revelling in every kind of human passion, in every species of desire or greed or ambition or obsession which gives a dignity and a tragic grandeur to otherwise prosaic lives. There is a kind of subterranean torrent of blind primeval energy running through his books which focusses itself in a thick smouldering fuliginous eruption when the moment or the occasion arises. The "will to power," or whatever else you may call it, has never been more terrifically exposed. I cannot but feel that as a portrayer of such a "will to power" among the obstinate, narrow, savage personages of small provincial towns, no one has approached Balzac.

Here, in his country scenes, he is a supreme master; and the tough, resistant fibre of his slow-moving, massively egotistic provincials, with their backgrounds of old houses full of wicked secrets and hoarded wealth, lends itself especially well to his brooding materialistic imagination, ready to kindle under provocation into crackling and licking flames.

His imagination has transformed, for me at least, the face of more than one country-side. Coming in on a windy November evening, through muddy lanes and sombre avenues of the outskirts of any country town, how richly, how magically, the lights in the scattered high walled houses and the faces seen at the windows, suggest the infinite possibilities of human life! The sound of wheels upon cobblestones, as the street begins and as the spire of the church rises over the moaning branches of its leafless elm-trees has a meaning for me now, since I have read Balzac, different from what it had before. Is that muffled figure in the rumbling cart which passes me so swiftly the country doctor or the village priest, summoned to the death-bed of some notorious atheist? Is the slender white hand which closes those heavy shutters in that gloomy house the hand of some heart-broken Eugénie, desolately locking herself up once more, for another lonely night, with her sick hopes and her sacred memories?

I feel as though no one but Balzac has expressed the peculiar brutality, thick, impervious, knotted and fibrous like the roots of the tree-trunks at his gate, of the small provincial farmer in England as well as in France.

I am certain no one but Balzac—except it be some of the rougher, homelier Dutch painters—has caught the spirit of those mellow, sensual "interiors" of typical country houses, with their mixture of grossness and avarice and inveterate conservatism; where an odour of centuries of egotism emanates from every piece of furniture against the wall and from every gesture of every person seated over the fire! One is plunged indeed into the dim, sweet, brutal heart of reality here, and the imagination finds starting places for its wanderings from the mere gammons of dried bacon hanging from the smoky rafters and the least gross repartee and lewd satyrish jest of the rustic Grangousier and Gargamelle who quaff their amber-coloured cider under the flickering of candles.

If he did not pile up his descriptions of old furniture, old warehouses, old barns, old cellars, old shops, old orchards and old gardens, this thick human atmosphere—overlaid, generation after generation, by the sensual proclivities of the children of the earth—would never possess the unction of verisimilitude which it has.

If he were all the while fussing about his style in the exhausting Flaubert manner, the rich dim reek of all this time-mellowed humanity would never strike our senses as it does. Thus much one can see quite clearly from reading de Maupassant, Flaubert's pupil, whose stark and savage strokes of clean-cut visualisation never attain the imaginative atmosphere or Rabelaisian aplomb of Balzac's rural scenes.

But supreme as he is in his provincial towns and villages, one cannot help associating him even more intimately with the streets and squares and river banks of Paris.

I suppose Balzac has possessed himself of Paris and has ransacked and ravished its rare mysteries more completely than any other writer.

I once stayed in a hotel called the Louis le Grand in the Rue Louis le Grand, and I shall never forget the look of a certain old Parisian Banking-House, now altered into some other building, which was visible through the narrow window of my high-placed room. That very house is definitely mentioned somewhere in the Human Comedy; but mentioned or not, its peculiar Balzacian air, crowded round by sloping roofs and tall white houses, brought all the great desperate passionate scenes into my mind.

I saw old Goriot crying aloud upon his "unkind daughters." I saw Baron Hulot dragged away from the beseeching eyes and clinging arms of his last little inamorata to the bedside of his much wronged wife. I saw the Duchesse de Langeais, issuing forth from the chamber of her victim-victor, pale and tragic, and with love and despair in her heart.

It is the thing that pleases me most in the stories of Paul Bourget that he has continued the admirable Balzacian tradition of mentioning the Paris streets and localities by their historic names, and of giving circumstantial colour and body to his inventions by thus placing them in a milieu which one can traverse any hour of the day, recalling the imaginary scenes as if they were not imaginary, and reviving the dramatic issues as if they were those of real people.

A favourite objection to Balzac among æsthetic critics is that his aristocratic scenes are lacking in true refinement, lacking in the genuine air and grace of such fastidious circles. I do not give a fig for that criticism. To try and limit a great imaginative spirit, full of passionate fantasy and bizarre inventions, to the precise and petty reproduction of the tricks of any particular class seems to me a piece of impertinent pedantry. It might just as well be said that Shakespeare's lords and ladies were not euphuistic enough. I protest against this attempt to turn a Napoleonic superman of literature, with a head like that head which Rodin has so admirably recalled for us,

into a bourgeois chronicler of bourgeois mediocri-
ties.

Balzac's characters, to whatever class they belong, bear the royal and passionate stamp of their
demiurgic creator. They all have a certain mag-
nificence of gesture, a certain intensity of tone, a
certain concentrated fury of movement.

There is something tremendous and awe-inspiring about the task Balzac set himself and the
task he achieved.

⁄One sees him drinking his black coffee in those
early hours of the morning, wrapped in his dress-
ing-gown, and with a sort of clouded Vulcanian
grandeur about him, hammering at his population
of colossal figures amid the smouldering images
of his cavernous brain. He was wise to work in
those hours when the cities of men sleep and the
tides of life run low; at those hours when the sick
find it easiest to die and the pulses of the world's
heart are scarcely audible. There was little at
such times to obstruct his imagination. He could
work "in the void," and the spirit of his genius
could brood over untroubled waters.⁄

There was something formidable and noble in
the way he drove all light and casual loves, the
usual recreations of men of literary talent, away
from his threshold. Like some primordial
Prometheus, making men out of mud and fire, he
kept the perilous worshippers of Aphrodite far-
distant from the smoke of his smithy, and re-

fused to interrupt his cosmic labour for the sake of dalliance.

That high imaginative love of his—itself like one of the great passions he depicts—which ended, in its unworthy fulfilment, by dragging him down to the earth, was only one other proof of how profoundly cerebral and psychic that demonic force was which drove the immense engine of his energy.

It is unlikely that, as the world progresses and the generations of the artists follow one another and go their way, there will be another like him.

Such primal force, capable of evoking a whole world of passionate living figures, comes only once or twice in the history of a race. There will be thousands of cleverer psychologists, thousands of more felicitous stylists, thousands of more exact copiers of reality.

There will never be another Balzac.

VICTOR HUGO

VICTOR HUGO

M Y first notions of Victor Hugo were associated with the sea. It was from the old Weymouth harbour that as a child I used to watch those Channel-Island steamers with red funnels setting forth on what seemed to me in those days a wondrous voyage of mystery and peril. I read "The Toilers of the Sea" at my inland school at Mr. Hardy's Sherton Abbas; whither, it may be remembered, poor Giles Winterbourne set off with such trembling anxiety to fetch home his Grace.

I read it in what was probably a very quaint sort of translation. The book was bound in that old-fashioned "yellow back" style which at that time was considered in clergymen's families as a symbol of all that was dissipated and dangerous; and on the outside of the yellow cover was a positively terrifying picture of the monstrous devilfish with which Gellert wrestled in that terrible sea-cavern.

Certain scenes in that romance lodged themselves in my brain with diabolic intensity. That scene, for instance, when the successful scoundrel, swimming in the water, "feels himself seized by one foot," that scene where the man buys the revolver in the little gunsmith's shop; that appalling scene at the end where Gellert drowns himself, watching the ship that bears his love away to happiness in the arms of another—all these held my imagination then, as indeed they hold it still, with the vividness of personal experience.

It was long after this, not more than five or six years ago in fact, that I read "Notre Dame de Paris." This book I secured from the ship's library of some transatlantic liner and the fantastic horrors it contains, carried to a point of almost intolerable melodrama, harmonised well enough with the nightly thud of the engines and the day-long staring at the heaving water.

"Notre Dame" is certainly an amazing book. If it were not for the presence of genius in it, that ineffable all-redeeming quality, it would be one of the most outrageous inventions of flagrant sensationalism ever indulged in by the morbidity of man. But genius pervades it from beginning to end; pervades even its most impossible scenes; and on the whole I think it is a much more arresting tale than, say, "The Count of Monte Cristo," or any of Dumas' works except "The Three Musketeers."

I have never, even as a child, cared greatly for Dumas, and I discern in the attitude of the persons who persist in preferring him to Victor Hugo the presence of a temperamental cult so alien to my own that I am tempted to regard it as no better than an affected pose.

Nowhere is Victor Hugo's genius more evident

than in his invention of names. Esmeralda, Quasimodo, Gellert, Cosette, Fantine—they all have that indescribable ring of genuine romance about them which more than anything else restores to us the "long, long thoughts" of youth.

I think that Fantine is the most beautiful and imaginative name ever given to any woman. It is far more suggestive of wild and delicate mysteries than Fragoletta or Dolores or Charmian or Ianthe.

I am inclined to maintain that it is in the sphere of pure poetic imagination that Victor Hugo is greatest; though, like so many other foreigners, I find it difficult to read his formal poetry. It is, I fancy, this poetic imagination of his which makes it possible for him to throw his isolated scenes into such terrific relief that they lodge themselves in one's brain with such crushing force. In all his books it is the separate individual scenes of which one finds oneself thinking as one recalls the progress of this narrative or the other. And when he has struck out with a few vivid lightning-like flashes the original lineaments of one of his superb creations, it is rather in separate and detached scenes that he makes such a person's indelible characteristics gleam forth from the surrounding darkness, than in any continuous psychological process of development.

His psychology is the psychology of a child; but none the worse perhaps for that; for it is remarkable how often the most exhaustive psychological analysis misses the real mystery of human character. Victor Hugo goes to work by illuminating flashes. He carries a flaring torch in his hand; and every now and then he plunges it into the caverns of the human heart, and one is conscious of vast stupendous Shadows, moving from midnight to midnight.

His method is gnomic, laconic, oracular; never persuasive or plausible. It is "Lo—here" and then again "Lo—there!" and we are either with him or not with him. There are no half measures, no slow evolutionary disclosures.

One of his most interesting literary devices, and it is an essentially poetic one, is the diffusion through the story of some particular background, a background which gathers to itself a sort of brooding personality as the tale proceeds, and often becomes before the book is finished far more arresting and important than any of the human characters whose drama it dominates.

Such is the sea itself, for instance, in "The Toilers." Such is the historic cathedral in "Notre Dame." Such is the great Revolution—certainly a kind of natural cataclysm—in "Ninety-three." Such are the great sewers of Paris in "Les Misérables." Such—though it is rather a symbol than a background—is the terrible fixed smile of the unfortunate hero in "L'Homme qui Rit."

It is one of the most curious and interesting phenomena in the history of literature, this turning of a poet into a writer of romances, romances which have at least as much if not more of the poetic quality in them than the orthodox poetry of the same hand.

One is led to wonder what kind of stories Swinburne would have written had he debouched into this territory, or what would have been the novels conceived by Tennyson. Thomas Hardy began with poetry and has returned to poetry; and one cannot help feeling that it is more than anything else the absence of this quality in the autobiographical studies of sex and character which the younger writers of our day spin out that makes them after a time seem so sour and flat.

It is the extravagance of the poetic temper and its lack of proportion which leads to some of the most glaring of Victor Hugo's faults; and it is the oracular, prophetic, gnomic tone of his genius which causes those queer gaps and rents in his work and that fantastic arbitrariness which makes it difficult for him to evoke any rational or organic continuity.

It is an aspect of the poetic temper too, the queer tricks which the humour of Victor Hugo will condescend to play. I suppose he is by nature the least endowed with a sense of humour of all the men of genius who have ever lived. The poet Wordsworth had more. But like so many poetic natures, whose vivid imagination lends itself to every sort of human reaction, even to those not really indigenous, Victor Hugo cannot resist in indulging in freakish sallies of jocularity which sometimes become extraordinarily strained and forced, and even remind one now and then of the horrible mechanical smile on the countenance of the mutilated man in his own story.

Poet-like too is the portentous pedantry of his archæological vein; the stupendous air of authority with which he raps out his classical quotations and his historic allusions. He is capable sometimes of producing upon the mind the effect of a hilarious school-master cracking his learned jokes to an audience only too willing to encourage him. At other times, so bizarre and out of all human proportion are his fantasies, one receives an impression as if one of the great granite effigies representing Liberty or Equality or the Rights of Man, from the portico of some solemn Palais de Justice, had suddenly yielded to the temptation of drink and was uttering the most amazing levities. Victor Hugo in his lighter vein is really, we must honestly confess, a somewhat disconcerting companion. One has such respect for the sublime imaginations which one knows are lurking behind "that cliff-like brow" that one struggles to find some sort of congruity in these strange gestures. It is as though when walking by the side of some revered prophet, one were suddenly conscious that the man was skipping or putting out his tongue. It is as though we caught Ajax masquerading as a mummer, or Æschylus dressed up in cap and bells.

There are persons who interest themselves still in Victor Hugo's political attitudes, in his orations on the balcony of the Hotel de Ville; in his theatrical visits to the barricades where "he could be shot, but could not shoot"; in his diatribes against Napoleon the Third; in his defence of the Commune from the safe remoteness of Brussels. There are persons who suffer real disillusion when they discover how much of a conservative and a courtier he was in his youth. There are persons who are thrilled to recall how he carried his solemn vengeance against his imperial enemy so far as to rebuke in stern language Queen Victoria for her friendliness towards the Empress.

I must confess I find it difficult to share these emotions. I seem to smell the foot-lights of the opera in these heroic declamations, and indeed poor Napoleon the Little was himself so much of an operatic hero that to exalt him into a classic tyrant seems little short of ridiculous.

We derive a much truer picture of Victor Hugo's antagonist from Disraeli's "Endymion" than we do from the poet's torrential invectives. I have a shrewd idea that the Emperor was a good deal more amiable, if not more philosophical, than his eloquent judge.

Victor Hugo was an impassioned lover of children. Who can forget those scenes in "Les Misérables" about little Cosette and the great wonderful doll which Valjean gave her? He loved children and—for all his lack of humour;

sometimes I think because of it—he thoroughly understood them. He loved children and he was a child himself.

No one but a child would have behaved as he did on certain occasions. The grave naïveté of his attitude to the whole spectacle of life was like the solemnity of a child who takes very seriously every movement of the game which he is playing. A child is solemn when it is pretending to be an engine-driver or a pilot, and Victor Hugo was solemn when he pretended to be a saviour of society. No one but a person endowed with the perfect genius of childishness could have acted toward his mistress and his wife in the way he did, or have been so serenely blind to the irony of the world.

There is as little of the sensual in Victor Hugo's temperament as there is in the temperament of a pure-minded child; but like a child he finds a shuddering pleasure in approaching the edge of the precipice; like a child he loves to loiter in melancholy fields where the white moon-daisies are queerly stained with the old dark blood of weird and abnormal memories.

Irony of any kind, worldly or otherwise, never crossed so much as the margin of his consciousness. He is shamelessly, indecently, monstrously lacking in the ironic sense.

"What are we going to do?" he dramatically asked his sons when they had established themselves in their island home; and after they had each replied according to their respective tastes, "I," he added, "am going to contemplate the ocean!"

I am ready to confess that I feel a certain shame in thus joining the company of the godless and making sport of my childhood's hero. "He was a man, take him for all in all," and *we* at any rate shall not live to see his like again.

There was something genuinely large and innocent and elemental in Victor Hugo. The austere simplicity of his life may have been perhaps too self-consciously flung at the world's face; but it was a natural instinct in him. I hesitate to call him a charlatan. Was it Goethe who said "There is something of charlatanism in all genius"? Victor Hugo hardly deserves to have Goethe quoted in his favour, so ignorantly did he disparage, in his childish prejudice, the great German's work; but what perhaps the world calls charlatanism in him is really only the reaction of genius when it comes into conflict with the brutal obstinacy of real life.

What is charlatanism? I am almost scared to look up the word in the dictionary for fear of discovering that I am myself no better than that opprobrious thing. But still, if Victor Hugo was really a charlatan, one can safely say one would sooner be damned with the author of "L'Homme qui Rit" than saved with many who have no charlatanism in them.

But what is charlatanism? Does it imply false

and extravagant claims to qualities we do not possess? Or is there the spirit of the Mountebank in it? If one were a deliberate Machiavel of dissimulation, if one fooled the people thoroughly and consciously, would one be a charlatan? Or are charlatans simply harmless fools who are too embarrassed to confess their ignorance and too childish to stop pretending?

There is something nobly patriarchal about the idea of Victor Hugo in his old age. The man's countenance has certainly extraordinary genius "writ large" there for all men to see. His head is like something that has been carved by Michelangelo. Looking at his face one realises where the secret of his peculiar genius lay. It lay in a certain tragic abandonment to a sublime struggle with the elements. When in his imagination he wrestled with the elements he forgot his politics, his prejudices, his moral bravado.

Whatever this mysterious weakness may have been which we call his "charlatanism," it certainly dropped away from him like a mask when he confronted the wind or sea or such primitive forms of human tragedy as are elemental in their simple outlines. Probably for all his rhetoric Victor Hugo would have made an obstinate invincible sailor on the high seas. I discern in the shape of his head something of the look of weather-beaten mariners. I can fancy him holding fast the rudder of a ship flying before the fury of an Atlantic storm.

The sea-scenes in his books are unequalled in all prose literature. To match them you would have to go to the poets—to Shakespeare—to Swinburne. A single line of Hugo has more of the spirit of the sea, more of its savagery, its bitter strength, its tigerish leap and bite, than pages of Pierre Loti. Whether I am prejudiced by my childish associations I do not know, but no other writer makes me smell the sea-weed, catch the sharp salt tang, feel the buffeting of the waves, as Victor Hugo does. Yes, for all his panoramic evocations of sea-effects, Pierre Loti does not touch the old eternal mystery of the deep, with its answer of terror and strange yearning in the heart of man, in the way this other touches it. The great rhetorician found a rhetoric here that put his eloquence to silence and he responded to it with sentences as sharp, as brief, as broken, as abrupt, as stinging and wind-driven, as the rushing waves themselves pouring over a half drowned wreck.

And just as he deals with the sea, so he deals with the wind and rain and snow and vapour and fire. Those who love Victor Hugo will think of a hundred examples of what I mean, from the burning castle in "Ninety-three," to the wind-rocked gibbet on the Isle of Portland, when the child hero of the "Man who Laughs" escapes from the storm.

When one tries to cast one's critical plummet into the secret motive forces of Hugo's genius, one is continually being baffled by the presence there of conflicting elements. For instance no one who has read "Notre Dame" can deny the presence of a certain savage delight in scenes of grotesque and exaggerated terror. No one who has read "Les Misérables" can deny the existence in him of a vein of lovely tenderness that, with a little tiny push over the edge, would degenerate into maudlin sentiment of the most lamentable kind.

The performances of the diabolical "archdeacon" in "Notre Dame" to the moment when Quasimodo watches him fall from the parapet, are just what one might expect to enjoy in some old-fashioned melodramatic theatre designed for such among the pure in heart as have a penchant for ghastliness. But one forgets all this in a moment when some extraordinary touch of illuminating imagination gets hold of one by the throat.

I do not think that Victor Hugo will go down to posterity honoured and applauded because of his love for the human race. I suspect those critics who hold him up as a grand example of democratic principles and libertarian ideals of not being great lovers of his stories. He is a name for them to conjure with and that is all.

Victor Hugo loved children and he loved the mothers of children, but he was too great a soul to spoil his colossal romance with any blatant humanitarianism. I do not say he was the high, sad, lonely, social exile he would have liked the world to believe him; for he was indeed of kind, simple, honest domestic habits and a man who got much happiness from quite little things. But when we come to consider what will be left of him in the future I feel sure that it will be rather by his imagination than by his social eloquence that he will touch our descendants. It is indeed not in the remotest degree as a rhetorician that he arrests us in these unique tales. It is by means of something quite different from eloquence.

His best effects are achieved in sudden striking images which seem to have in them a depth of fantastic diablerie worthy of the wreck-strewn "humming waters" whose secrets he loved to penetrate.

It is not sufficiently realised how much there was of the "macabre" about Victor Hugo. Like the prophet Ezekiel, he had strange visions from the power he served, and in the primordial valleys of his imagination there lie, strewn to the bleaching winds, the bones of men and of demons and of gods; and the breath that blows upon them and makes them live—live their weird phantasmal life of mediæval goblins in some wild procession of madness—is the breath of the spirit of childhood's fancies.

GUY DE MAUPASSANT

GUY DE MAUPASSANT

TO read for the first time, one of the short stories of Guy de Maupassant is to receive a staggering enlargement of one's ideas as to what mere literature can do. They hardly seem like literature at all, these blocks from the quarry of life, flung into one's face with so unerring an aim.

"If you prick them, they bleed. If you tickle them, they laugh." The rough rain-smelling earth still clings to them; when you take them in your hands, the mud of the highway comes off upon your fingers. Is it really, one wonders, mere literary craft, mere cunning artfulness, which gives these sentences the weight of a guillotine-blade crashing down upon the prostrate neck of bound helpless reality?

Is it simply the art of a pupil of the euphonious Flaubert, this power of making written sentences march full-armed like living men, and fall, when their work is done, with a metallic ring of absolute finality—"as a dead body falls"?

As one reads Guy de Maupassant one breathes heavily as if it were oneself and not another upon whom the tension and the sweat of the crisis has come. One touches with one's naked hand every object he describes. One feels the gasping breath of every person he brings forward. His images slap one's cheeks till they tingle, and his situations wrestle with one to the ground.

Not for nothing was he a descendant of that race which, of all races except the Turks, has loved love better than literature and war better than love. Words are resounding blows and smacking kisses to Guy de Maupassant. He writes literature as a Norman baron, and when he rounds off a sentence it is as if he dug a spur into the flanks of a restless filly. There is nothing like his style in the world.

They never taught me Tacitus when I was at school. My Latinity stops short at Cæsar and Cicero. One is, however, led to suppose that the great executioner of imperial reputations was a mighty pruner, in his day, of the "many, too many" words. But I am sure that this other "Great Latin," as Nietzsche calls him, cleans up his litter and chops off his surplusage quite as effectively as Tacitus, and I suspect that neither Tacitus nor any other classic writer hits the nail on the head with so straight, so steady, so effective a stroke.

I suppose it is the usual habit of destiny to rush into literary paths people who are essentially dreamers and theorists and utopians; people who by instinct and temperament shrink away from contact with brute reality.

GUY DE MAUPASSANT

I suppose even the great imaginative writers, like Balzac, live, on the whole, sedentary and exclusive lives, making a great deal, as far as the materials for their work go, of a very little. Now and then, however, it happens that a man of action, a man of the world, a man of love and war and sport, enters the literary arena; and when that occurs, I have an idea that he hits about him with a more trenchant, more resolute, more crushing force than the others.

The art of literature has become perhaps too completely the monopoly of sedentary people—largely of the bourgeois class—who bring to their work the sedentary sensitiveness, the sedentary refinement, the sedentary lack of living experience, which are the natural characteristics of persons who work all day in studies and studios. That is why the appearance of a Walt Whitman or a Maxim Gorki is so wholesome and airclearing an event.

But not less salutary is the appearance of a ferocious aristocrat from the class which has ridden rough-shod over the fields of submissive actuality for many tyrannous centuries.

In the hard shrewd blows of a Maxim Gorki, the monopolising tribes of sedentary dreamers receive their palpable hit, receive it from the factory and the furrow. In the deadly knocks of a Guy de Maupassant they get their "quietus" from the height, so to speak, of the saddle of a sporting gentleman.

Do what they can to get the sharp bitter tang of reality into their books, the bulk of these people, write they never so cleverly, seem somehow to miss it.

The smell of that crafty old skunk—the genuine truth of things—draws them forward through the reeds and rushes of the great dim forests' edge, but they seldom touch the hide of the evasive animal; no, not so much as with the end of their barge-pole.

But Guy de Maupassant plunges into the thickets, gun in hand, and we soon hear the howl of the hunted.

A love of literature, a reverence and respect for the dignity of words, does not by any means imply a power of making them plastic before the pressure of truth. How often one is conscious of the intervention of "something else," some alien material, marbly and shiny it may be, and with a beauty of its own, but obtruding quite opaquely between the thing said and the thing felt.

In reading Guy de Maupassant, it does not seem to be words at all which touch us. It seems to be things—things living or dead, things in motion or at rest. Words are there indeed; they must be there—but they are so hammered on the anvil of his hard purpose that they have become porous and transparent. Their one rôle now is to get themselves out of the way; or rather to turn themselves into thin air and clean water, through which the reality beyond can come at us with unblurred outlines.

It is a wonderful commentary, when one thinks of it, upon the malleability of human language that it can so take shape and colour from the pressure of a single temperament. The words in the dictionary are all there—all at the disposal of every one of us—but how miraculous a thing to make their choice and their arrangement expressive of nothing on earth but the peculiar turn of one particular mind!

The whole mystery of life is in this; this power of the unique and solitary soul to twist the universe into the shape of its vision.

Without any doubt Guy de Maupassant is the greatest realist that ever lived. All other realists seem idealists in comparison. Many of the situations he describes are situations doubtless in which he himself "had a hand." Others are situations which he came across, in his enterprising debouchings here and there, in curious by-alleys, and which he observed with a morose scowl of amusement, from outside. A few— very few—are situations which he evoked from the more recondite places of his own turbulent soul.

But one cannot read a page of him without feeling that he is a writer who writes from out of his own experiences, from out of the shocks and jolts and rough file-like edges of raw reality.

It is a huge encouragement to all literary ambitions, this immense achievement of his. The scope and sweep of a great creative imagination is given to few among us, and Guy de Maupassant was not one of these. His imagination was rigorously earth-bound, and not only earth-bound but bound to certain obvious and sensual aspects of earth-life. Except when he tore open the bleeding wounds of his own mutilated sensibility and wrote stories of his madness with a pen dipped in the evil humours of his diseased blood, he was a master of a certain brutal and sunburnt objectivity.

But how cheerful and encouraging it is for those among us who are engaged in literature, to see what this astonishing man was able to make of experiences which, in some measure, we must all have shared!

There is never any need to leave one's own town or village or city to get "copy." There is scarcely any need to leave one's own house. The physiological peculiarities of the people who jostle against us in the common routine of things will completely suffice. That is the whole point of de Maupassant's achievement.

The same thing, of course, is true of the great imaginative writers. *They* also are able to derive grist for their mill from the common occurences; they also are free to remain at home. But their sphere is the sphere of the human soul; his was the sphere of the human body.

He was pre-eminently the master of physiology

—the physiological writer. Bodies, not souls, were his "métier"—or souls only in so far as they are directly affected by bodies.

But bodies—bodies of men and women are everywhere; living ones on the earth; dead ones under the earth. One need not go to the antipodes to find the nerves and the tissues, the flesh and the blood, of these planetary evocations, of these microcosms of the universe. The great imaginative writers have the soul of man always under their hand, and Guy de Maupassant has the body of man always under his hand.

It is not the masters who are found journeying to remote regions to get inspiration for their work. Their "America," as Goethe puts it, lies close to their door.

It is singularly encouraging to us men of letters to contemplate what Guy de Maupassant could do with the natural animal instincts and gestures and mutterings and struggles of the bodies of men and women as their desires make them skip.

"Encouraging" did I say? Tantalizing rather, and provocative of helpless rage. For just as the spiritual insensitiveness of our bourgeois tyrants renders them dull and obtuse to the noble imaginations of great souls, so their moral bigotry and stupidity renders them obstinately averse to the freedom of the artist in dealing with the physical eccentricities of the grotesque human animal.

We must not deal at large with the spirit lest we weary the vulgar and the frivolous; we must not deal at large with the body, lest we infuriate the Puritanical and the squeamish.

It is absurd to rail at de Maupassant because of his "brutality." One cannot help suspecting that those who do so have never recognised the absurd comedy of their own bodily activities and desires.

It is idle to protest against the outrageous excursions of his predatory humour. The raw bleeding pieces—each, as one almost feels, with its own peculiar cry—of the living body of the world, clawed as if by tiger claws, are strange morsels for the taste of some among us. But for others, there is an exultant pleasure in this great hunt, with the deep-mouthed hounds of veracity and sincerity, after the authentic truth.

One touches here—in this question of the brutality of Guy de Maupassant—upon a very deep matter; the matter namely of what our pleasure exactly consists, as we watch, in one of his more savage stories, the flesh of the world's truth thus clawed at.

I think it is a pleasure composed of several different elements. The first of these is that deep and curious satisfaction which we derive from the exhibition in art of the essential grossness and unscrupulousness of life. We revenge ourselves in this way upon what makes us suffer. The clear presentation of an outrage, of an insult, of an indecency, is in itself a sort of vengeance upon the power that wrought it, and though it may sound ridiculous enough to speak of being avenged upon Nature, still the basic instinct is there, and we can, if we will, personify the immense malignity of things, and fancy that we are striking back at the gods and causing the gods some degree of perturbation; at least letting them know that we are not deceived by the illusions they dole out to us!

The quiet gods may well be imagined as quite as indifferent to our artistic vengeance as Nature herself, but at any rate, like the man in the Inferno who "makes the fig" at the Almighty, we have found vent for our human feelings. Another element in it is the pleasure we get—not perhaps a very Christian one, but Literature deviates from Christianity in several important ways—from having other people made fully aware, as we may be, of the grossness and unscrupulousness of life.

These other people may easily be assumed to be fidgety, meticulous, self-complacent purists; and as we read the short stories of Guy de Maupassant, we cannot resist calling up an imaginary company of such poor devils and forcing them to listen to a page of the great book of human judgment upon Nature's perversity.

Finally at the bottom of all there is a much more subtle cause for our pleasure; nothing less in fact than that old wild dark Dionysian embracing of fate, of fate however monstrous and bizarre, simply because it is there—an integral part of the universe—and we ourselves with something of that ingredient in our own heathen hearts.

An imaginary symposium of modern writers upon the causes of human pleasure in the grosser elements of art lends itself to very free speculation. Personally I must confess to very serious limitations in my own capacity for such enjoyment. I have a sneaking sympathy with tender nerves. I can relish de Maupassant up to a certain point—and that point is well this side of idolatry—but I fancy I relish him because I discern in him a certain vibrant nerve of revolt against the brutality of things, a certain quivering irony of savage protest. When you get the brutality represented without this revolt and with a certain unction of sympathetic zest, as you do in the great eighteenth century novelists in England, I confess it becomes more than I can endure.

This is a most grievous limitation and I apologise to the reader most humbly for it. It is indeed a lamentable confession of weakness. But since the limitations of critics are, consciously or unconsciously, part of their contribution to the problems at issue, I offer mine without further comment.

It is an odd thing that while I can relish and even hugely enjoy ribaldry in a Latin writer, I cannot so much as tolerate vulgarity in an English or Scotch one. Perhaps it is their own hidden consciousness that, if they once let themselves go, they would go unpleasantly far, which gives this morbid uneasiness to the strictures of the Puritans. Or is it that the English-speaking races are born between the deep sea of undiluted coarseness and the devil of a diseased conscience? Is this the reason why every artist in the world and every critic of art, feels himself essentially an exile everywhere except upon Latin soil?

Guy de Maupassant visualises human life as a thing completely and helplessly in the grip of animal appetites and instincts. He takes what we call lust, and makes of it the main motive force in his vivid and terrible sketches. It is perhaps for this very reason that his stories have such an air of appalling reality.

But it is not only lust or lechery which he exploits. He turns to his artistic purpose every kind of physiological desire, every sort of bodily craving. Many of these are quite innocent and harmless, and the denial of their satisfaction is in the deepest sense tragic. Perhaps it is in regard to what this word *tragic* implies that we find the difference between the brutality of Guy de Maupassant and the coarseness of the earlier English writers.

The very savagery in de Maupassant's humour is an indication of a clear intellectual consciousness of something monstrously, grotesquely, wrong; something mad and blind and devilish

about the whole business, which we miss completely in all English writers except the great
Jonathan Swift.

Guy de Maupassant had the easy magnanimity
of the Latin races in regard to sex matters, but
in regard to the sufferings of men and of animals from the denial of their right to every sort
of natural joy, there smouldered in him a deep
black rage—a *saeva indignatio*—which scorches
his pages like a deadly acid.

In his constant preoccupation with the bodies
of living creatures, it is natural enough that animals as well as men should come into the circle
of his interest. He was a great huntsman and
fisherman. He loved to wander over the frozen
marshes, gun in hand, searching for strange wild-
fowl among the reeds and ditches. But though
he slew these things in the savage passion of the
chase as his ancestors had done for ages, between
his own fierce senses and theirs there was a
singular magnetic sympathy. •

As may be often noticed in other cases, as we
go through the world, there was between the
primitive earth-instincts of this hunter of wild
things and the desperate creatures he pursued, a
far deeper bond of kinship than exists between
sedentary humanitarians and the objects of their
philanthrophy. It is good that there should be
such a writer as this in the world.

In the sophisticated subtleties of our varnished
and velvet-carpeted civilisation, it is well that we

should be brought back to the old essential can-
dours which forever underlie the frills and frip-
pery. It is well that the stark bones of the aboriginal skeleton with its raw "unaccommodated"
flesh should peep out through the embroideries.

It is, after all, the "thing itself" which matters—the thing which "owes the worm no silk,
the cat no perfume." Forked straddling animals
mals are we all, as the mad king says in the play,
and it is mere effeminacy and affectation to cover
up the truth.

Guy de Maupassant is never greater than
when appealing to the primitive link of tragic
affiliation that binds us to all living flesh and
blood. A horse mercilessly starved in the fields;
a wild bird wailing for its murdered mate; a
tramp driven by hunger and primitive desire, and
harried by the "insolence of office"; an old man
denied the little luxuries of his senile greed; an
old maid torn and rent in the flesh that is barren and the breasts that never gave suck; these
are the natural subjects of his genius—the sort
of "copy" that one certainly need not leave one's
"home town" to find.

One is inclined to feel that those who miss the
tragic generosity at the heart of the brutality of
Guy de Maupassant, are not really aware of the
bitter cry of this mad planet. Let them content themselves, these people, with their pretty
little touching stories, their nice blobs of cheerful "local colour" thrown in here and there, and

their sweet impossible endings. Sunday school literature for Sunday school children; but let there be at least one writer who writes for those who know what the world is.

The question of the legitimacy in art of the kind of realism which Guy de Maupassant practised, goes incalculably deep. Consider yourself at this moment, gentle reader, lightly turning over —as doubtless you are doing—the harmless pages of this academic book, as you drink your tea from a well appointed tray in a sunny corner of some friendly cake-shop. You are at this moment— come, confess it—hiding up, perhaps from yourself but certainly from the world, some outrageous annoyance, some grotesque resolution, some fear, some memory, some suspicion, that has— as is natural and proper enough, for your father was a man, your mother a woman—its physiological origin. You turn to this elegant book of mine, with its mild and persuasive thoughts, as if you turned away from reality into some pleasant arbour of innocent recreation. It is a sort of little lullaby for you amid the troubles of this rough world.

But suppose instead of the soothing cadences of this harmless volume, you had just perused a short story of Guy de Maupassant; would not your feelings be different? Would you not have the sensation of being fortified in your courage, in your humour, in your brave embracing of the fantastic truth? Would you not contemplate the most grotesque matters lightly, wisely, sanely and with a magnanimous heart?

The perverted moral training to which we have been all of us subjected, has "sicklied o'er with the pale cast" of a most evil scrupulousness our natural free enjoyment of the absurd contrasts and accidents and chances of life.

French humour may be savage—all the better —we need a humour with some gall in it to deal with the humour of the universe. But our humour, stopping short so timorously of stripping the world to its smock, is content to remain vulgar. That is the only definition of vulgarity that I recognise—a temptation to be coarse without the spiritual courage to be outrageous! Coarseness—our Anglo Saxon peculiarity—is due to temperamental insensitiveness. Outrageous grossness—with its ironical, beautiful blasphemy against the great mother's amazing tricks —is an intellectual and spiritual thing, worthy of all noble souls. The one is the rank breath of a bourgeois democracy, the other is the free laughter of civilised intelligences through all human history.

English and Americans find it difficult to understand each other's humour. One can well understand this difficulty. No one finds any obstacle—except Puritan prejudice—in understanding French humour; because French humour is universal; the humour of the human spirit contemplating the tragic comedy of the human body.

One very interesting thing must be noted here in regard to the method of Guy de Maupassant's writings; I mean the power of the short story to give a sense of the general stream of life which is denied to the long story.

Personally I prefer long stories; but that is only because I have an insatiable love of the story for its own sake, apart from its interpretation of life. I am not in the least ashamed to confess that when I read books, I do so to escape from the pinch of actual facts. I have a right to this little peculiarity as much as to any other as long as I don't let it invade the clarity of my reason. But in the short story—and I have no scruple about admitting it—one seems to get the flavour of the writer's general philosophy of life more completely than in any other literary form.

It is a snatch at the passing procession, a dip into the flowing stream, and one gets from it the sort of sudden illumination that one gets from catching a significant gesture under the street lamp, or meeting a swift tale-telling glance beneath a crowded doorway.

Bitterly inspired as he is by the irony of the physiological tragedy of human life, Guy de Maupassant is at his greatest when he deals with the bizarre accidents that happen to the body; greatest of all when he deals with the last bizarre accident of all, the accident of death.

The appalling grotesqueness of death, its brutal and impious levity, its crushing finality, have never been better written of. The savage ferocity with which he tears off the mask which the sentimental piety of generations has thrown over the features of their dead is no sign of frivolousness in him. The gravity of the undertaker is not an indication of deep emotion; nor is the jesting of Hamlet, as he stands above Ophelia's grave, a sign of an inhuman heart.

The last insult of the scurrilous gods—their flinging us upon oblivion with so indecent, so lewd a disregard for every sort of seemliness—is answered in Guy de Maupassant by a ferocious irony almost equal to their own.

But it would be unfair to let this dark-browed Norman go, without at least a passing allusion to the large and friendly manner in which he rakes up, out of brothel, out of gutter, out of tenement, out of sweat-shop, out of circus-tent, out of wharf shanty, out of barge cabin, every kind and species of human derelict to immortalise their vagrant humanity in the amber of his flawless style.

There is a spacious hospitality about the man's genius which is a rare tonic to weary æsthetes, sick of the thin-spun theories of the schools. The sun-burnt humour of many queer tatterdemalions warms us, as we read him, into a fine indifference to nice points of human distinction. All manner of ragged nondescripts blink at us out of their tragic resignation and hint at a ribald reciprocity of nature, making the whole world kin.

In his ultimate view of life, he was a drastic pessimist, and what we call materialism receives from his hands the clinching fiat of a terrific imprimatur. And this is well; this is as it should be. There are always literary persons to uphold the banners of mysticism and morality, idealism and good hope. There will always be plenty of talent "on the side of the angels" in these days, when it has become a kind of intellectual cant to cry aloud, "I am no materialist! Materialism has been disproved by the latest scientific thinkers!"

To come back to the old, honest, downright, heathen recognition of the midnight, wherein all candles are put out, is quite a salutary experience. It is good that there should be a few great geniuses that are unmitigated materialists, and to whom the visible world is absolutely all there is. One is rendered more tolerant of the boisterousness of the players when one feels the play ends so finally and so soon. One is rendered less exacting towards the poor creatures of the earth when one recognises that their hour is so brief.

There will always be optimists in the countries where "the standards of living are high." There will always be writers—scientific or otherwise—to dispose of materialism. But meanwhile it is well that there should be at least one great modern among us for whom that *pulvis et umbra* is the last word. At least, one, if only for the sake of those whom we mourn most; so that, beholding their lives, like torch-flames against black darkness, we shall not stint them of their remembrance.

ANATOLE FRANCE

ANATOLE FRANCE

ANATOLE FRANCE is probably the most disillusioned human intelligence which has ever appeared on the surface of this planet. All the great civilised races tend to disillusion. Disillusion is the mark of civilised eras as opposed to barbaric ones and if the dream of the poets is ever realised and the Golden Age returns, such an age will be the supreme age of happy, triumphant disillusion.

This was seen long ago by Lucretius, who regarded the fear of the gods as the last illusion of the human race, and looked for its removal as the race's entrance into the earthly paradise.

Nietzsche's noble and austere call to seriousness and spiritual conflict is the sign of a temper quite opposite from this. Zarathustra frees himself from all other illusions, but he does not free himself from the most deadly one of all—the illusion namely, that the freeing oneself from illusion is a high and terrible duty.

The real disillusioned spirit is not the fierce Nietzschean one whose glacial laughter is an iconoclastic battle-cry and whose freedom is a freedom achieved anew every day by a strenuous and desperate struggle. The real disillusioned spirit plays with illusions, puts them on and takes them off, lightly, gaily, indifferently, just as it happens, just as the moment demands.

One feels that in spite of his cosmic persiflage and radiant attempt to Mediterraneanise into "sun-burnt mirth" the souls of the northern nations, Nietzsche was still at heart an ingrained hyperborean, still at heart a splendid and savage Goth.

As in every other instance, we may take it for granted that any popular idea which runs the gamut of the idealistic lecture-halls and pulpits of a modern democracy is false through and through. Among such false ideas is the almost universal one that what is called the decadence of a nation is a sign of something regrettable and deplorable. On the contrary, it is a sign of something admirable and excellent. Such "weakness," in a deeper than a popular sense, is "strength"; such decadence is simply wisdom.

The new cult of the "will to power" which Nietzsche originated is nothing more than the old demiurgic life-illusion breaking loose again, as it broke loose in the grave ecstasies of the early Christians and in the Lutheran reformation. Nietzsche rent and tore at the morality of Christendom, but he did so with the full intention of substituting a morality of his own. One illusion for another illusion. A Roland for an Oliver!

Nietzsche praised with desperate laudation a

classical equanimity which he was never able to reach. He would have us love fate and laugh and dance; but there were drops of scorching tears upon the page of his prophecy and the motif of his challenge was the terrible gravity of his own nature; though the conclusion of his seriousness was that we must renounce all seriousness. It is Nietzsche himself who teaches us that in estimating the value of a philosopher we have to consider the psychology of the motive-force which drove him.

The motive-force that drove Nietzsche was the old savage life-instinct, penetrated with illusion through and through, and praise as he might the classical urbanity, no temper that has ever existed was less urbane than his own.

The history of the human race upon this planet may be regarded—in so far as its spiritual eruptions are concerned—as the pressure upwards, from the abysmal depths, of one scoriac tempest after another, rending and tearing their way from the dark centre fires where demogorgon turns himself over in his sleep, and becoming as soon as they reach the surface and harden into rock, the great monumental systems of human thought, the huge fetters of our imaginations. The central life-fire which thus forces its path at cataclysmic intervals to the devastated surface is certainly no illusion. It is the one terrific cosmic fact.

Where illusion enters is where we, poor slaves

of traditional ratiocination, seek to turn these explosions of eternal lava into eternal systems. The lava of life pours forth forever, but the systems break and crumble; each one overwhelmed in its allotted time by a new outrushing of abysmal energy.

The reiterated eruptions from the fathomless depths make up the shifting material with which human civilisations build themselves their illusive homes; but the wisest civilisations are the ones that erect a hard, clear, bright wall of sceptical "suspension of judgment," from the face of which the raging flood of primordial energy may be flung back before it can petrify into any further mischief.

Such a protective wall from the eruptive madness of primordial barbarism, the scepticism of classical civilisation is forever polishing and fortifying. Through the pearl-like glass of its inviolable security we are able to mock the tempest-driven eagles and the swirling glacial storms. We can amuse ourselves with the illusions from which we are free. We can give the imagination unbounded scope and the fancy unrestricted licence. We have become happy children of our own self-created kingdom of heaven; the kingdom of heaven which is the kingdom of disillusion.

And of this kingdom, Anatole France is surely the reigning king. From the Olympian disenchantment of his tolerant urbanity, all eruptive seriousness foams back spray-tossed and scattered. And yet such a master of the art of "suspended judgment" was he, that he permits himself to dally very pleasantly with the most passionate illusions of the human race. He is too deep a sceptic even to remain at the point of taking seriously his own æsthetic epicureanism.

This is where he differs from Oscar Wilde, from Walter Pater, from Stendhal, from Remy de Gourmont, from Gabriele d'Annunzio. This is where he differs from Montaigne. These great men build up an egoism of grave subjectivity out of their suspicion of other people's cults. They laugh at humanity but they do not laugh at themselves. With the help of metaphysic they destroy metaphysic; only to substitute for the gravity of idealism the gravity of epicureanism.

But Anatole France has no gravity. He respects nothing; least of all himself. That is why there is something singularly winning about him which we miss in these others. There is something which palls upon us and grows heavy and tiresome after a while about this massive gravity in the cult of one's own sensations.

Sensations? Well! We all know how subtle and pleasant they can be; but this perpetual religion of them, this ponderous worship of them, becomes at last something monstrous and inhuman, something which makes us cry aloud for air and space. Not only does it become inhuman and heavy—it becomes comic.

Every religion, even the religion of sensation, becomes comic when the sharp salt breath of intellectual sanity ceases to blow upon it. Its votaries seem to be going to and fro wrapped in sheep's wool. The wool may be stained in Tyrian dyes; but it is wool for all that, and it tends ultimately to impede the steps of the wearer and to dull not a few of his natural perceptions.

If one imagines a symposium in the Elysian fields between Wilde and Pater and d'Annunzio, and the sudden entrance upon them of the great Voltaire, one cannot but believe that after a very short time this religion of æstheticism would prove as tiresome to the old ribald champion of a free humanity as any other ritual.

And in this respect Anatole France is with Voltaire. He has too humorous a soul to endure the solemnity of the cultivated senses. He would desert such a group of pious subjectivists to chat with Horace about the scandals of the imperial court or with Rabelais about the price of sausages.

Sceptical in other matters, egoists of the type I have mentioned are inclined to grow unconscionably grave when questions of sex are brought forward. This illusion at any rate—the illusion of sexual attraction—they would be most loth to destroy.

But Anatole France fools sex without stint.

It affords him, just as it did Voltaire and Rabelais, his finest opportunities. He fools it up hill and down dale. He shakes it, he trundles it, he rattles it, he bangs it, he thumps it, he tumbles it in the mud, in the sand, in the earth—just as Diogenes did with his most noble tub. Fooling sex is the grand game of Anatole France's classic wit. The sport never wearies him. It seems an eternal perennial entertainment. Hardly one of his books but has this sex fooling as its principal theme.

It seems to his detached and speculative mind the most amusing and irresistible jest in the world that men and women should behave as they do; that matters should be arranged in just this manner.

What we arrive at once more in Anatole France is that humorous drawing back from the world, back into some high pitched observation-tower of the mind, from the philosophic seclusion of which the world scene can be easily imagined as different from what it is. Nothing is more salutary in the midst of the mad confusion of the world than these retirements. It is to no mere "ivory tower" of æsthetic superiority that we retreat. It is to a much higher and more spacious eminence. So high indeed do we withdraw that all the ivory towers of the world seem far beneath us; beneath us, and not more or less sacred than other secular erections.

It is from this point of observation that our

humour is suddenly made aware of the startling absurdity of human institution; and not only
of *human* institution; for it is made aware also
of the absurdity of the whole fantastic scheme of
this portentous universe. We regard the world
in these high speculative moods much as children
do when they suddenly enquire of their bewildered parents why it is that human beings
have two legs and why it is that little girls are
different from little boys.

It is one result of these withdrawings to the
translunar empyrean that the life of a man of
action upon this earth does not appear any more
or any less remarkable or important than the
life of a man of letters. All human activities
from that celestial height are equal; and whether
we plunge into politics or into pleasure, into
science or into theology, seems a mere incidental
chance, as indifferent in the great uncaring solar
system as the movements of gnats around a lamp
or midges around a candle.

The great historic revolutions, the great social reformations, ancient or modern, present
themselves from this height as just as important
—as just as unimportant—as the visions of
saintly fanatics or the amours of besotted rakes.

Nothing is important and anything may be
important. It is all a matter of the human point
of view. It is all a matter of taste. Looking at
the whole mad stream of things from this alti-
tude, we see the world as if we were peering

178

through an inverted telescope; or rather, shall we say, through an instrument called an "equiscope"—whose peculiarity it is to make all things upon which it is turned *little and equal.*

The mental temper of Anatole France is essentially one which is interested in historic and contemporary events; interested in the outward actions and movements of men and in the fluctuations of political life. But it is interested in these things with a certain spacious reservation. It is interested in them simply because they are there, simply because they illustrate so ironically the weaknesses and caprices of human nature and the dramatic chances of ineluctable fate. It is not interested in them because they are inherently and absolutely important, but because they are important relatively and humorously as indicative of the absurd lengths to which human folly will go. It is interested in these things, as I have said, with an ample reservation, but it must emphatically be noted that it is a great deal more interested in them than in any works of art or letters or in any achievement of philosophy.

Anatole France seems indeed to take a certain delight in putting human thought into its place as essentially secondary and subordinate to human will. He delights to indicate, just as Montaigne used to do, the pathetic and laughable discrepancies between human thoughts and human actions.

He is more concerned with men and women as they actually live and move in the commerce of the world than in the wayward play of their speculative fancies, and it gives him an ironic satisfaction to show how the most heroic and ideal thoughts are affected by the little wanton tricks of circumstances and character.

This predominant concern with the natural humours and normal animal instincts of the human race, this refusal ever to leave the broad and beaten path of human frailty, gives a tone to his writings, even when he is dealing with art and literature, quite different from other æsthetes'.

He is not really an æsthete at all; he is too Voltairian for that. As a critic he is learned, scholarly, clear-sighted and acute; but his sense of the humorous inconsistencies of normal flesh and blood is too habitually present with him to admit of that complete abandonment to the spirit of his author, which, accompanied by interpretative subtlety, secures the most striking results.

His criticisms are wise and interesting, but they necessarily miss the sinuous clairvoyance of a writer like Remy de Gourmont who is able to give himself up completely and with no ironic reservation to the abnormalities of the temperament he is discussing. Remy de Gourmont's own temperament has something in it more receptive, more psychological, more supple than Anatole France's. He is in himself a far less original genius and for that very reason he can slide more reservedly into the bizarre nooks and crannies of abnormal minds.

Anatole France is one of those great men of genius to whom the gods have permitted an unblurred vision of the eternal normalities of human weakness. This vision he can never forget. He takes his stand upon the ground which it covers, and from that ground he never deviates.

Man for him is always an amorous and fantastic animal, using his reason to justify his passions, and his imagination to justify his illusions. He is always the animal who can laugh, the animal who can cry, the animal who can beget or bear children. He is only in a quite secondary sense the animal who can philosophise.

It is because of his constant preoccupation with the normal eccentricities and pathetic follies of our race that he lays so much stress upon outward action.

The normal man is rather an animal who wills and acts than an animal who dreams and thinks; and it is with willing and acting, rather than with dreaming and thinking, that Anatole France is concerned. One of the main ironic devices of his humour is to show the active animal led astray by his illusions, and the contemplative animal driven into absurdity by his will.

With his outward-looking gaze fixed upon the eternal and pathetic normalities of the human situation, Anatole France has himself, like Voltaire, a constant tendency to gravitate towards politics and public affairs.

In this respect his temperament is most obstinately classical. Like Horace and all the ancient satirists, he feels himself invincibly attracted to "affairs of state," even while they excite his derision. One cannot read a page of his writing without becoming aware that one is in the presence of a mind cast in the true classic mould.

In the manner of the great classical writers of Athens and Rome he holds himself back from any emotional betrayal of his own feelings. He is the type of character most entirely opposite to what might be called the Rousseau-type.

He is un-modern in this and quite alone; for, in one form or another, the Rousseau-type with its enthusiastic neurotic mania for self-revelation dominates the entire literary field. One gets the impression of something massive and self-possessed, something serenely and almost inhumanly sane about him. One feels always that he is the "Grand Gentleman" of literature with whom no liberties may be taken. His tone is quiet, his manner equable, his air smiling, urbane, superior. His reserve is the reserve of the great races of antiquity. With a calm, inscrutable, benevolent malice, he looks out upon the world. There is a sense of much withheld, much unsaid, much that nothing would ever induce him to say.

His point of view is always objective. It

might be maintained, though the thing sounds like a paradox, that his very temperament is objective. Certainly it is a temperament averse to any outbursts of unbalanced enthusiasm.

His attitude toward what we call Nature is more classical than the classics. Virgil shows more vibrant emotion in the presence of the sublimities of the natural elements. His manner when dealing with the inanimate world is the manner of the Eighteenth Century touched with a certain airiness and charm that is perhaps more Hellenic than Latin. As one reads him one almost feels as though the human race detached itself from its surroundings and put between itself and Nature a certain clear and airy space, untroubled by any magnetic currents of spiritual reciprocity. One feels as though Nature were kept decisively and formally in her place and not permitted to obtrude herself upon the consciousness of civilised people except when they require some pleasant lawn or noble trees or smiling garden of roses to serve as a background for their metaphysical discussions or their wanton amorous play. What we have come to call the "magic" of Nature is never for a moment allowed to interrupt these self-possessed epicurean arguments of statesmen, politicians, amorists, theologians, philosophers and proconsuls.

Individual objects in Nature—a tree, a brook, the seashore, a bunch of flowers, a glade in the forest, a terrace in a garden,—are described in that clear, laconic, objective manner, which gives one the impression of being able to touch the thing in question with one's bare hand.

The plastic and tactile value of things is always indicated in Anatole France's writings with brief, clear cut, decisive touches, but "the murmurs and scents" of the great waters, the silences of the shadowy forests are not allowed to cross the threshold of his garden of Epicurus. Each single petal of a rose will have its curves, its colours, its tints; but the mysterious forces of subterranean life which bring the thing to birth are pushed back into the darkness. The marble-cold resistance of Anatole France's classical mind offers a hard polished surface against which the vague elemental energies of the world beat in vain. He walks smilingly and pensively among the olive-trees of the Academia, plucking a rose here and an oleander there; but for the rest, the solemn wizardries of Nature are regarded with an urbane contempt.

His style is a thing over which the fastidious lovers of human language may ponder long and deep. The art of it is so restrained, so aristocratic, so exclusive, that even the smallest, simplest, most unimportant words take to themselves an emphatic significance.

Anatole France is able to tell us that Monsieur Bergeret made some naïve remark, or the Abbé Jérôme Coignard uttered some unctuous sally, in so large and deliberate and courtly a way that the mere "he said" or "he began" falls upon us like a papal benediction or like the gesture of a benignant monarch.

There is no style in the world so deeply penetrated with the odour and savour of its author's philosophy. And this philosophy, this atmosphere of mind, is so entirely French that every least idiomatic peculiarity in his native tongue seems willing to lend itself, to the last generous drop of the wine of its essential soul, to the tone and manner of his speech. All the refinements of the most consummate civilisation in the world, all its airy cynicism, all its laughing urbanity, all its whimsical friendliness, seem to concentrate themselves and reach their climax on every page of his books.

A delicate odour of incense and mockery, an odour of consecrated wine and a savour of heathen wit, rise up together from every sentence and disarm us with the insidiousness of their pleasant contrast. His style is so beautiful and characteristic that one cannot read the simplest passage of easy narration from his pen without becoming penetrated with his spirit, without feeling saner, wiser, kindlier, and more disenchanted and more humane.

I cannot resist quoting from the prologue to "Le Puits de Sainte Claire," a certain passage which seems to me peculiarly adapted to the illustration of what I have just said. The writer is, or imagines himself to be, in the city of Siena.

"Sur la voie blanche, dans ces nuits transparentes, la seule recontre que je faisais était celle du R. P. Adone Doni, qui alors travaillait comme moi tout le jour dans l'ancienne académie *degli Intronati*. J'avais tout de suite aimé ce cordelier qui, blanchi dans l'étude, gardait l'humeur riante et facile d'un ignorant.

"Il causait volontiers. Je goûtais son parler suave, son beau langage, sa pensée docte et näive, son air de vieux Silène purifié par les eaux baptismales, son instinct de mime accompli, le jeu de ses passions vives et fines, le génie étrange et charmant dont il etait possédé.

"Assidu à la bibliothèque, il fréquentait aussi le marché, s'arrêtant de préférence devant les contadines, qui vendent des pommes d'or, et prêtant l'oreille à leur libres propos.

Il apprenait d'elles, disait-il, la belle langue toscane. . . . Je crus m'apercevoir en effet qu'il inclinait aux opinions singulières. Il avait de la religion et de la science, mais non sans bizarreries. . . . C'est sur le diable qu'il professait des opinions singulières. Il pensait que le diable était mauvais sans l'être absolument et que son imperfection naturelle l'empêcherait toujours d'atteindre à la perfection du mal. Il croyait apercevoir quelques signes de bonté dans les actions obscures de Satan, et, sans trop l'oser dire, il en augurait la rédemption finale de l'archange méditatif, après la consommation des siècles.

. . . Assis sur la margelle, les mains dans les manches de sa robe, il contemplait avec un paisible étonnement les choses de la nuit.

"Et l'ombre qui l'enveloppait laissait deviner encore dans ses yeux clairs et sur sa face camuse l'expressions d'audace craintive et de gràce moqueuse qui y était profondement empreinte. Nous échangions d'abord des souhaits solennels de bonne santé, de paix et de contentement. . . .

"Tandis qu'il parlait, la lumière de la lune coulait sur sa barbe en ruisseau d'argent. Le grillon accompagnait du bruissement de ses élytres la voix du conteur, et parfois, aux sons de cette bouche, d'où sortait le plus doux des langages humains, répondait la plainte flutée du crapaud, qui, de l'autre côté de la route, écoutait, amical et craintif."

The beautiful delicacy of that single touch "sur la voie blanche, dans ces nuits transparentes" is characteristic of a thousand others of a similar kind sprinkled among his books, where gentle and whimsical spirits discourse upon God and the Universe.

He has a most exquisite genius for these little chance-accompaniments of such human scenes. "L'Orme du Mail" is full of them; and so is "Les Opinions de M. Jérôme Coignard."

In "Sur la Pierre Blanche" the impish humour of accidental encounter brings forward nothing less than the death of Stephen the Proto-Martyr, as an irrelevant interruption to the amorous pleasures of one of his least attractive philosophers.

Full of malicious interest as he is in all the outward events of nations and societies, it is always evident that what Anatole France really regards as worthy of tender consideration is the conversation of quaint minds and the "Humeur riante et facile" of wayward and fantastic souls.

His sense of the fundamental futility of the whole scheme of things is so absolute that what most modern writers would regard as the illogical dreams of superannuated eccentrics he is inclined to treat with smiling reverence and infinite sympathy. Where the whole terrestrial business is only a meaningless blur upon the face of nothingness, why should we not linger by the way, under elm trees, or upon broken fragments of old temples, or on sunny benches in cloistered gardens, and listen to the arbitrary fancies of unpractical and incompetent persons whose countenances express an "audace craintive" and a "gràce moqueuse," and who look with mild wonder and peaceful astonishment at "les choses de la nuit"?

After perusing many volumes of Anatole France, one after another, we come to feel as though nothing in the world were important except the reading of unusual books, the conversation of unusual people, and the enjoyment of such philosophical pleasures as may be permitted by the gods and encouraged by the approbation of a friendly and tolerant conscience.

One always rises from the savouring of his excellent genius with a conviction that it is only the conversation of one's friends, varied by such innocent pleasures of the senses as may be in harmony with the custom of one's country, which renders in the last resort the madness of the world endurable.

He alone, of all modern writers, creates that leisurely atmosphere of noble and humorous dignity—familiar enough to lovers of the old masters—according to which every gesture and word of the most simple human being comes to be endowed with a kind of royal distinction. By the very presence in his thought of the essential meaninglessness of the world, he is enabled to throw into stronger relief the "quips and cranks and wanton wiles" of our pathetic humanity.

Human words—the words of the most crackbrained among us—take to themselves a weight and dignity from the presence behind them of this cosmic purposelessness. The less the universe matters, the more humanity matters. The less meaning there is in the macrocosm the more tenderly and humorously must every microcosm be treated.

It thus comes about that Anatole France, the most disillusioned and sceptical of writers, is also the writer whose books throw over the fancies and caprices of humanity the most large and liberal benediction.

To realise how essentially provincial English and American writers are, one has only to consider for a moment the absolute impossibility of such books as "L'Orme du Mail," "Le Mannequin" or "Monsieur Bergeret à Paris" appearing in either of these countries.

This amiable and smiling scepticism, this profound scholarship, this subtle interest in theological problems, this ironical interest in political problems, this detachment of tone, this urbane humanism, make up an "ensemble" which one feels could only possibly appear in the land of Rabelais and Voltaire.

Think of the emergence of a book in London or New York bearing such quotations at the heads of the chapters as those which are to be found in "Le Puits de Sainte Claire"! The mere look of the first page of the volume, with its beautifully printed Greek sentence about τὰ φυσικὰ καὶ τὰ ἠθικὰ καὶ τὰ μαθηματικὰ, lifts one suddenly and with a delicious thrill of pleasure, as if from the touch of a cool, strong, youthful hand, into that serene atmosphere of large speculations and unbounded vistas which is the inheritance of the great humane tradition: the tradition, older than all the dust of modern argument, and making every other mental temper seem, in comparison, vulgar, common, bourgeois and provincial.

The chapter headed "Saint Satyre" is prefaced

by a beautiful hymn from the "Breviarum Romanum"; while the story named "Guido Cavalcanti" begins with a long quotation from "Il Decameron di Messer Giovanni Boccaccio." I take the first instance that comes to my hand; but all his books are the same. And one who reads Anatole France for the sake of an exciting narrative, or for the sake of illuminating psychology, or for the sake of some proselytising theory, will be hugely disappointed. None of these things will he find; nor, indeed, anything else that is tiresomely and absurdly modern.

What he will find will be the old, sweet, laughing, mellow world of rich antique wisdom; a world where the poetry of the ancients blends harmoniously with the mystical learning of the fathers of the church; a world where books are loved better than theories and persons better than books; a world where the humours of the pathetic flesh and blood of the human race are given their true value, as more amusing than any philosophy and as the cause and origin of all the philosophies that have ever been!

Anatole France is incorrigibly pagan. The pleasures of the senses are described in all his books with a calm smiling assurance that ultimately these are the only things that matter!

I suppose that no author that ever lived is so irritating to strong-minded idealists. He does not give these people "the ghost of a chance." He serenely assumes that all ideals are of human, too human, origin, and that no ideals can stand up long against the shocks of life's ironic caprices.

And yet while so maliciously introducing, with laconic Voltairian gibes, the wanton pricking of human sensuality, he never forgets the church. In nothing is he more French; in nothing is he more civilised, than in his perpetual preoccupation with two things—the beauty and frailty of women and the beauty and inconsistency of Christianity.

The clever young men who write books in England and America seem possessed by a precisely opposite purpose; the purpose of showing that Christianity is played out and the purpose of showing that women are no longer frail.

That sort of earnest-minded attempt to establish some kind of mystical substitute for the religion of our fathers, which one is continually meeting in modern books and which has so withering an effect both upon imagination and humour, is never encounted in Anatole France. He is interested in old tradition and he loves to mock at it. He is interested in human sensuality and he loves to mock at it; but apart from traditional piety struggling with natural passion, he finds nothing in the human soul that arrests him very deeply.

Man, to Anatole France, is a heathen animal who has been baptised; and the humour of his whole method depends upon our keeping a firm hold upon both these aspects of our mortal life. In a world where men propagated themselves like plants or trees and where there was no organised religious tradition, the humour of Anatole France would beat its wings in the void in vain. He requires the sting of sensual desire and he requires an elaborate ecclesiastical system whose object is the restraint of sensual desire. With these two chords to play upon he can make sweet music. Take them both away and there could be no Anatole France.

The root of this great writer's genius is *irony*. His whole philosophy is summed up in that word, and all the magic of his unequalled style depends upon it.

Sometimes as we read him, we are stirred by a dim sense of indignation against his perpetual tone of smiling, patronising, disenchanted, Olympian pity. The word "pity" is one of his favourite words, and a certain kind of pity is certainly a profound element in his mocking heart.

But it is the pity of an Olympian god, a pity that cares little for what we call justice, a pity that refuses to take seriously the objects of his commiseration. His clear-sighted intelligence is often pleased to toy very plausibly with a certain species of revolutionary socialism. But, I suppose few socialists derive much satisfaction from that devastating piece of irony, the Isle of the Penguins; where everything moves in circles and all ends as it began.

SUSPENDED JUDGMENTS

The glacial smile of the yawning gulf of eternal futility flickers through all his pages. Everything is amusing. Nothing is important. Let us eat and drink; let us be urbane and tolerant; let us walk on the sunny side of the road; let us smell the roses on the sepulchres of the dead gods; let us pluck the violets from the sepulchres of our dead loves. All is equal—nothing matters. The wisest are they who play with illusions which no longer deceive them and with the pity that no longer hurts them. The wisest are they who answer the brutality of Nature with the irony of Humanity. The wisest are they who read old books, drink old wine, converse with old friends, and let the rest go.

And yet—and yet—

There is a poem of Paul Verlaine dedicated to Anatole France which speaks like one wounded well nigh past enduring by the voices of the scoffers.

Ah, les Voix, mourez donc, mourantes que vous êtes
Sentences, mots en vain, metaphores mal faites,
Toute la rhétorique en fuite des péchés,
Ah, les Voix, mourez donc, mourantes que vous êtes!

   ·   ·   ·   ·   ·   ·   ·   ·   ·

Mourez parmi la voix terrible de l'Amour!

   ·   ·   ·   ·   ·   ·   ·   ·   ·

PAUL VERLAINE

PAUL VERLAINE

TO turn suddenly to the poetry of Paul Verlaine from the mass of modern verse is to experience something like that sensation so admirably described by Thoreau when he came upon a sentence in Latin or in Greek lying like a broken branch of lovely fresh greenery across the pages of some modern book.

Verlaine more than any other European poet is responsible for the huge revolution in poetry which has taken in recent times so many and so surprising shapes and has deviated so far from its originator's method.

There is little resemblance between the most striking modern experiments in what is called "free verse" and the manner in which Verlaine himself broke with the old tradition; but the spirit animating these more recent adventures is the spirit which Verlaine called up from the "vasty deep," and with all their divergence from his original manner these modern rebels have a perfect right to use the authority of his great name, "car son nom," as Coppée says, in his tenderly written preface to his "Choix de Poésies," "éveillera toujours le souvenir d'une poésie absolument nouvelle et qui a pris dans

197

les lettres françaises l'importance d'une décou-
verte."

The pleasure with which one returns to Verlaine from wandering here and there among our
daring contemporaries is really nothing less than
a tribute to the essential nature of all great
poetry; I mean to the soul of music in the thing.
Some of the most powerful and original of modern poets have been led so far away from this
essential soul of their own great art as to treat
the music of their works as quite subordinate to
its intellectual or visual import.

As far as I am able to understand the theories
of the so-called "imagists," the idea is to lay the
chief stress upon the evocation of clearly out-
lined shapes—images clean-cut and sharply defined, and, while personal in their choice, essentially objective in their rendering—and upon
the absence of any traditional "beautiful words"
which might blur this direct unvarnished impact
of the poet's immediate vision.

It might be maintained with some plausibility
that Verlaine's poetry takes its place in the "im-
pressionistic" period, side by side with "impres-
sionistic" work in the plastic arts, and that for
this reason it is quite natural that the more modern poets, whose artistic contemporaries belong
to the "post-impressionistic" school, should devi-
ate from him in many essential ways. Personally I am extremely unwilling to permit Verlaine to be taken possession of by any modern

PAUL VERLAINE

tendency or made the war-cry of any modern camp.

Though by reason of his original genius he has become a potent creative spirit influencing all intelligent people who care about poetry at all, yet, while thus inspiring a whole generation—perhaps, considering the youth of many of our poetic contemporaries, we might say *two* generations—he belongs almost as deeply to certain great eras of the past. In several aspects of his temperament he carries us back to François Villon, and his own passionate heart is forever reverting to the Middle Ages as the true golden age of the spirit he represented.

He thus sweeps aside with a gesture the great seventeenth century so much admired by Nietzsche.

> Non. Il fut gallican, ce siècle, et janséniste!
> C'est vers le Moyen Age énorme et délicat,
> Qu'il faudrait que mon cœur en panne naviguât,
> Loin de nos jours d'esprit charnel et de chair triste.

But whatever may have been the spirit which animated Verlaine, the fact remains that when one takes up once more this "Choix de Poésies," "avec un portrait de l'auteur par Eugene Carrière," and glances, in passing, at that suggestive *cinquante-septième mille* indicating how many others besides ourselves have, in the midst of earthquakes and terrors, assuaged their thirst at this pure fount, one recognises once more that the thing that we miss in this modern welter of poetising is simply *music*—music, the first and last necessity, music, the only authentic seal of the eternal Muses.

Directly any theory of poetry puts the chief stress upon anything except music—whether it be the intellectual content of the verses or their image-creating vision or their colour or their tone—one has a right to grow suspicious.

The more subtly penetrated such music is by the magic of the poet's personality, the richer it is in deep intimations of universal human feeling, the greater will be its appeal. But the music must be there; and since the thing to which it forever appeals is the unchanging human sensibility, there must be certain eternal laws of rhythm which no original experiments can afford to break without losing the immortal touch.

This is all that lovers of poetry need contend for as against these quaint and interesting modern theories. Let them prove their theories! Let them thrill us in the old authentic manner by their "free verse" and we will acknowledge them as true descendants of Catullus and Keats, of Villon and Verlaine!

But they must remember that the art of poetry is the art of heightening words by the magic of music. Colour, suggestion, philosophy, revelation, interpretation, realism, impressionism—all these qualities come and go as the fashion of our taste changes. One thing alone remains, as the essential and undying spirit of all true poetry; that it should have that "concord of sweet sounds"—let us say, rather, that concord of high, delicate, rare sounds—which melts us and enthralls us and liberates us, whatever the subject and whatever the manner or the method! Verse which is cramped and harsh and unmelodious may have its place in human history; it may have its place in human soothsaying and human interest; it has no place or lot in poetry. Individual phrases may have their magic; individual words may have their colour; individual thoughts may have their truth; individual sentences their noble rhetoric;—all this is well and right and full of profound interest. But all this is only the material, the atmosphere, the medium, the instrument. If the final result does not touch us, does not move us, does not rouse us, does not quiet us, as *music* to our ears and our souls—it may be the voice of the prophet; it may be the voice of the charmer; it is not the voice of the immortal god.

Verlaine uses the term *nuance* in his "ars poetica" to express the evasive quality in poetry which appeals to him most and of which he himself is certainly one of the most delicate exponents; but remembering the power over us of certain sublime simplicities, remembering the power over us of certain great plangent lines in Dante and Milton, where there is no "nuance" at all, one hesitates to make this a dogmatic doctrine.

SUSPENDED JUDGMENTS

But in what he says of music he is supremely right, and it is for the sake of his passionate authority on this matter—the authority of one who is certainly no formal traditionalist—that I am led to quote certain lines.

They occur in "Jadis et Naguère" and are placed, appropriately enough, in the centre of the volume of Selections which I have now before me.

De la musique avant toute chose,
Et pour cela préfère l'Impair
Plus vague et plus soluble dans l'air,
Sans rien en lui qui pèse ou qui pose.

Il faut aussi que tu n'ailles point
Choisir tes mots sans quelque méprise :
Rien de plus cher que la chanson grise
Où l'Indécis au Précis se joint.

Car nous voulous la Nuance encor,
Pas la Couleur, rien que la nuance !
Oh ! la nuance seule fiance
Le rêve au rêve et la flûte au cor !

Fuis du plus loin la Pointe assassine,
L'Esprit cruel et le Rire impur,
Qui font pleurer les yeux de l'Azur,
Et tout cet ail de basse cuisine !

Prends l'éloquence et tords-lui sou cou !
Tu feras bien, en train d'énergie
De rendre un peu la Rime assagie
Si l'on n'y veille, elle ira jusqu'où ?

.   .   .   .

PAUL VERLAINE

De la musique encore et toujours!
Que ton vers soit la chose envolée
Qu'on sent qui fuit d'une âme allée
Vers d'autres cieux à d'autres amours.

Que ton vers soit la bonne aventure
Éparse au vent crispé du matin
Qui va fleurant la menthe et le thym . ..
Et tout le reste est littérature.

Yes; that is the sigh which goes up from one's heart, in these days when there is so much verse and so little poetry;—"et tout le reste est littérature"!

Clever imagery, humorous realism, philosophical thoughts, bizarre fancies and strange inventions—it is all vivid, all arresting, all remarkable, but it is only literature! This is a fine original image. That is a fine unexpected thought. Here indeed is a rare magical phrase. Good! We are grateful for these excellent things. But poetry? Ah! that is another matter.

This music of which I speak is a large and subtle thing. It is not only the music of syllables. It is the music of thoughts, of images, of memories, of associations, of spiritual intimations and far-drawn earth-murmurs. It is the music which is hidden in reality, in the heart of reality; it is the music which is the secret cause why things are as they are; the music which is their end and their beginning; it is the old deep Pythagorean mystery; it is the music of the flowing tides, of the drifting leaves, of the breath of the sleepers, of the passionate pulses of the lovers; it is the music of the rhythm of the universe, and its laws are the laws of sun and moon and night and day and birth and death and good and evil.

Such music is itself, in a certain deep and true sense, more instinct with the mystery of existence than any definite image or any definite thought can possibly be. It seems to contain in it the potentiality of all thoughts, and to stream in upon us from some Platonic "beyond-world" where the high secret archetypes of all created forms sleep in their primordial simplicity.

The rhythmic cadences of such music seem, if I dare so far to put such a matter into words, to exist independently of and previously to the actual thoughts and images in which they are finally incarnated.

One has the sense that what the poet first feels is the obscure beauty of this music, rising up wordless and formless from the unfathomable wells of being, and that it is only afterwards, in a mood of quiet recollection, that he fits the thing to its corresponding images and thoughts and words.

The subject is really nothing. This mysterious music may be said to have created the subject; just as the subject, when it is itself called into existence, creates its images and words and

mental atmosphere. Except for the original out-
welling of this hidden stream, pouring up from
unknown depths, there would be no thought, no
image, no words. A beautiful example of this
is that poem entitled "Promenade Sentimentale,"
which is one of the Paysages Tristes in the
"Poèmes Saturniens."

It is a slight and shadowy thing, of no elaborate construction,—simply a rendering of the
impression produced upon the mind by sunset
and water; by willows and water-fowl and water-
lilies. A slight thing enough; but in some mysterious way it seems to blend with all those vague
feelings which are half memories and half
intimations of something beyond memory,
which float round the margins of all human
minds.

We have seen these shadowy willows, that dying sunset; we have heard the wail of those melancholy water-fowl; somewhere—far from here
—in some previous incarnation perhaps, or in the
"dim backward" of pre-natal dreaming. It all
comes back to us as we give ourselves up to the
whispered cadences of this faint sweet music;
while those reiterated syllables about "the great
water-lilies among the rushes" fall upon us like
a dirge, like a requiem, like the wistful voice of
what we have loved—once—long ago—touching
us suddenly with a pang that is well-nigh more
than we can bear.

SUSPENDED JUDGMENTS

Le couchant dardait ses rayons suprêmes
Et le vent berçait les nénuphars blêmes ;
Les grands nénuphars entre les roseaux
Tristement luisaient sur les calmes eaux.
Moi, j'errais tout seul, promenant ma plaie
Au long de l'étang, parmi la saulaie
Où la brume vague évoquait un grand
Fantôme laiteux se désespérant
Et pleurant avec la voix des sarcelles
Qui se rappelaient en battant des ailes
Parmi la saulaie où j'errais tout seul
Promenant ma plaie ; et l'épais linceul
Des ténèbres vint noyer les suprêmes
Rayons du couchant dans ses ondes blêmes
Et des nénuphars parmi les roseaux
Des grands nénuphars sur les calmes eaux.

Verlaine is one of those great original poets the thought of whose wistful evocations coming suddenly upon us when we are troubled and vexed by the howl of life's wolves, becomes an incredible mandragora of healing music.

I can remember drifting once, in one of those misty spring twilights, when even the streets of Paris leave one restless, dissatisfied and feverishly unquiet, into the gardens of the Luxembourg. There is a statue there of Verlaine accentuating all the extravagance of that extraordinary visage—the visage of a satyr-saint, a "ragamuffin angel," a tatterdemalion scholar, an inspired derelict, a scaramouch god,—and I recollect how, in its marble whiteness, the thing leered and peered at me with a look that seemed to

have about it all the fragrance of all the lilac-
blossoms in the world, mixed with all the piety
of all our race's children and the wantonness of
all old heathen dreams. It is like Socrates, that
head; and like a gargoyle on the tower of Notre
Dame.

He ought to have been one of those slaves of
Joseph of Arimathæa, who carried the body of
Our Lord from the cross to the rich man's tomb
—a slave with the physiognomy of the god Pan—
shedding tears, like a broken-hearted child, over
the wounded flesh of the Saviour.

There is an immense gulf—one feels it at once
—between Paul Verlaine and all other modern
French writers. What with them is an intellectual attitude, a deliberate æsthetic cult, is with
him an absolutely spontaneous emotion.

His vibrating nerves respond, in a magnetic
answer and with equal intensity, to the two great
passions of the human race: its passion for beauty
and its passion for God.

His association with the much more hard and
self-possessed and sinister figure of Rimbaud was
a mere incident in his life.

Rimbaud succeeded in breaking up the idyllic
harmony of his half-domestic, half-arcadian
ménage, and dragging him out into the world.
But the influence over him of that formidable inhuman boy was not a deep, organic, predestined
thing touching the roots of his being; it was an
episode; an episode tragically grotesque indeed.

and full of a curious interest, but leaving the main current of his genius untouched and unchanged.

Paul Verlaine's response to the beauty of women is a thing worthy of the most patient analysis. Probably there has never lived any human person who has been more thrilled by the slightest caress. One is conscious of this in every page of his work. There is a vibrant spirituality, a nervous abandonment, about his poetry of passion, which separates it completely from the confessions of the great sensualists.

There was nothing heavy or material about Verlaine's response to erotic appeals. His nervous organisation was so finely strung that, when he loved, he loved with his whole nature, with body, soul and spirit, in a sort of quivering ecstasy of spiritual lust.

One is reminded here and there of Heine; in other places—a little—of William Blake; but even these resemblances are too vague to be pressed at all closely.

His nature was undoubtedly child-like to a degree amounting to positive abnormality. He hardly ever speaks of love without the indication of a relation between himself and the object of his passion which has in it an extraordinary resemblance to the perfectly pure feeling of a child for its mother.

It must have been almost always towards women possessed very strongly of the maternal instinct that he was attracted; and, in his attraction, the irresistible ecstasy of the senses seems always mingled with a craving to be petted, comforted, healed, soothed, consoled, assuaged.

In poem after poem it is the tenderness, the purity, the delicacy of women, which draws and allures him. Their more feline, more raptorial attributes are only alluded to in the verses where he is obviously objective and impersonal. In the excessive *gentleness* of his eroticism Verlaine becomes, among modern poets, strangely original; and one reads him with the added pleasure of enjoying something that has disappeared from the love-poetry of the race for many generations.

"By Gis and by saint Charity," as the mad girl in the play sings, there is too much violence in modern love! One grows weary of all this rending and tearing, of all this pantherish pouncing and serpentine clinging. One feels a reaction against this eternal savagery of earth-lust. It is a relief, like the coming suddenly from a hedge of wild white roses after wandering through tropical jungles, to pass into this tender wistful air full of the freshness of the dew of the morning.

No wonder Verlaine fell frequently into what his conscience told him was sin! His "sinning" has about it something so winning, so innocent, so childish, so entirely free from the predatory mood, that one can easily believe that his conscience was often betrayed into slumber. And yet, when it did awaken at last, the tears of his penitence ran down so pitifully over cheeks still wet with the tears of his passion, that the two great emotions may be almost said to have merged themselves in one another—the ecstasy of remorse in the ecstasy of the sin that caused the remorse.

The way a man "makes love" is always intimately associated with the way he approaches his gods, such as they may be; and one need not be in the least surprised to find that Verlaine's attitude to his Creator has a marked resemblance to his attitude to those too-exquisite created beings whose beauty and sweet maternal tenderness so often betrayed him. He evidently enjoys a delicious childish emotion, almost a babyish emotion, in giving himself up into the hands of his Maker to be soothed and petted, healed and comforted. He calls upon his God to punish him just as a child might call upon his mother to punish him, in the certain knowledge that his tears will soon be kissed away by a tenderness as infinite as it is just. God, Christ, Our Lady, pass through the pages of his poems as through the cypress-terraces of some fantastic mediæval picture. The "douceur" of their sweet pitifulness towards him runs like a quivering magnetic current through all the maddest fancies of his wayward imagination.

PAUL VERLAINE

"De la douceur, de la douceur, de la douceur"!
Even in the least pardonable of light loves he
demands this tenderness—demands it from some
poor "fille de joie" with the same sort of tearful craving with which he demands it from the
Mother of God.

He has a pathetic mania for the consoling
touch of tender, pitiful hands. All through his
poetry we have reference to such hands. Sometimes they are only too human. Sometimes they
are divine. But whether human or divine they
bring with them that magnetic gift of healing
for which, like a hurt and unhappy infant, he is
always longing.

Les chéres mains qui furent miennes
Toutes petites, toutes belles,
Après ces méprises mortelles
Et toutes ces choses païennes,

Après les rades et les grèves,
Et les pays et les provinces,
Royales mieux qu'au temps des princes
Les chéres mains m'ouvrent les rêves.
. . . .

Ment-elle, ma vision chaste,
D'affinité spirituelle,
De complicité maternelle,
D'affection étroite et vaste?
. . . .

That collection of passionate cries to God
which ends with a sort of rhapsody of pleading
prayer, entitled "Sagesse," begins—and one does

not feel that it is in the least inappropriate—
with

Beauté des femmes, leur faiblesse, et ces mains pâles
Qui font souvent le bien et peuvent tout le mal.

It is very curious to note the subtle manner
in which, for all his declarations about the Middle Ages, he is attracted irresistibly to that wonderful artificial fairy-land, associated for us for
all time with the genius of Watteau, wherein
pale roses and fountains and yew-hedges are the
background for the fatal sweetness of Columbine
and the dancing feet of Arlequino.

This Garden-of-Versailles cult, with its cold
moonlight and its faint music has become, with
the sad-gay Pierrot as its tutelary deity, one of
the most appealing "motifs" in modern art.

Almost all of us have worshipped, at some time
or another, at this wistful fairy shrine, and have
laid our single white rose on its marble pavement,
under the dark trees.

Yes; Verlaine may boast of his faithful loyalty
to the "haute théologie et solide morale, guidé
par la folie unique de la Croix" of that "Moyen
Age énorme et délicat" which inspires his spirit.
The fact remains that none—none among all
the most infatuated frequenters of the perverse
fairy-land of Watteau's exquisite dreams—
gives himself up more wantonly to the artifice
within artifice, to the mask below mask, of these
dancers to tambourines amid the "boulingrins

du parc aulique" of mock-classic fantasies. He gives himself up to this Watteau cult all the more easily because he himself has so infantile a heart. He is like a child who enters some elaborate masked ball in his own gala dress. It is natural to him to be perverse and wistful and tragically gay. It is natural to him to foot it in the moonlight along with the Marquis of Carabas.

That Nuit du Walpurgis classique of his, with its "jardin de Lenôtre, correct, ridicule et charmant," is one of the most delicate evocations of this *genre*. One sees these strange figures, " ces spectres agités," as if they were passing from twilight to twilight through the silvery mists of some pale Corot-picture, passing into thin air, into the shadow of a shadow, into the dream of a dream, into nothingness and oblivion; but passing gaily and wantonly—to the music of mandolines, to the blowing of fairy horns!

> N'importe! ils vont toujours, les fébriles fantômes,
> Menant leur ronde vaste et morne, et tressautant
> Comme dans un rayon de soleil des atomes,
>   Et s'évaporent à l'instant
>
> Humide et blême où l'aube éteint l'un après l'autre
> Les cors, en sorte qu'il ne reste absolument
> Plus rien—absolument—qu'un jardin de Lenôtre
>   Correct, ridicule et charmant.

In the same vein, full of a diaphanous gaiety light as the flutter of dragon-fly wings, is that "caprice" in his Fêtes Galantes entitled Fantoches.

> Scaramouche et Pucinella
> Qu'un mauvais dessein rassembla
> Gesticulent, noirs sur la lune.
>
> Cependant l'excellent docteur
> Bolonais cueille avec lenteur
> Des simples parmi l'herbe brune.
>
> Lors sa fille, piquant minois
> Sous la charmille, en tapinois
> Se glisse demi-nue, en quête
>
> De son beau pirate espagnoi
> Dont un langoureux rossignol
> Clame la détresse à tue-tête.

Is that not worthy of an illustration by Aubrey Beardsley? And yet has it not something more naïve, more infantile, than most modern trifles of that sort? Does not it somehow suggest Grimm's Fairy Stories?

There is one mood of Paul Verlaine, quite different from this, which is extremely interesting if only for its introduction into poetry of a certain impish malice which we do not as a rule associate with poetry at all.

Such is the poem called Les Indolents, with its ribald refrain, like the laughter of a light-footed Puck flitting across the moon-lit lawns, of

PAUL VERLAINE

Hi! Hi! Hi! les amants bizarres!

.   .   .   .   .   .

Eurent l'inexpiable tort
D'ajourner une exquise mort.
Hi! Hi! Hi! les amants bizarres!

Such also are those extraordinary verses under the title Colloque Sentimental which trouble one's imagination with so penetrating a chill of shivering disillusionment.

For some reason or other my own mind always associates these terrible lines with a particular corner of a public garden in Halifax, Yorkshire; where I seem to have seen two figures once; seen them with a glacial pang of pain that was like the stab of a dagger of ice frozen from a poisoned well.

Dans le vieux parc solitaire et glacé
Deux formes ont tout à l'heure passé.

Leurs yeux sont morts et leurs lèvres sont molles
Et l'on entend à peine leurs paroles.

Dans le vieux parc solitaire et glacé
Deux spectres ont évoqué le passé.

—Qu'il était bleu, le ciel, et grand l'espoir!
—L'espoir a fui, vaincu, vers le ciel noir.

I have omitted the bitter dialogue—as desolate and hollow in its frozen retorts as the echoes of iron heels in a granite sepulchre—but the whole piece has a petrified forlornness about it

which somehow reminds one of certain verses of
Mr. Thomas Hardy.

One of my own favourite poems of Verlaine
is one whose weird and strange beauty will appeal, I fear, to few readers of these sketches; but
if I could put into words the indescribable power
which it exercises over my own mood I should
be doing something to mitigate its remoteness
from normal feelings. It is a wild mad thing,
this poem—a fantasia upon a melancholy and
terrible truth—but it has the power of launching
one's mind down long and perilous tides of speculation.

It is like a "nocturne" written by a musician
who has wandered through all the cities of Europe with a company of beggar-players, playing
masques of death to the occupants of all the ceme-
teries. He names the poem Grotesques; and it
comes among the verses called Eaux-Fortes,
dedicated to François Coppée.

> C'est que, sur leurs aigres guitares
> Crispant la main des libertés
> Ils nasillent des chants bizarres,
> Nostalgiques et révoltés;
>
> C'est enfin que dans leurs prunelles
> Rit et pleure—fastidieux—
> L'amour des choses éternelles,
> Des vieux morts et des anciens dieux!
> .   .   .   .
> Les juins brûlent et les décembres
> Gélent votre chair jusqu'aux os,

Et la fièvre envahit vos membres
Qui se déchirent aux roseaux.

Tout vous repousse et tout vous navre
Et quand la mort viendra pour vous
Maigre et froide, votre cadavre
Sera dédaigné par les loups!

I cannot resist the feeling that where the inmost essential genius of Verlaine is to be found is neither in his religious poems nor his love-poems; no, nor even in his singular fantasies.

I find it in certain little evasive verses, the fleeting magic of which evaporates, under any attempt to capture or define it, like the perfume from that broken alabaster box from which the woman anointed the feet of the Saviour. Such a poem is that strangely imaginative one, with a lovely silveriness of tone in its moth-like movements, and full of a mystery, soft, soothing and gentle, like the whisper of a child murmuring its happiness in its sleep, which is called Impression Fausse for some delicate reason that I, alas! lack the wit to fathom.

Dame souris trotte
Noire dans le gris du soir
Dame souris trotte
Grise dans le noir.

On sonne la cloche,
Dormez, les bons prisonniers,
On sonne la cloche:
Faut que vous dormiez,

.   .   .   .   .

SUSPENDED JUDGMENTS

Dame souris trotte,
Rose dans les rayons bleus,
Dame souris trotte
Debout, paresseux!

Perhaps of all the poems he ever wrote the one
most full of his peculiar and especial atmosphere
—grey and sad and cool and deep and unlike
anything else in the world—is that entitled Ré-
versibilities; though here again I am out of my
depths as to the full significance of this title.

Entends les pompes qui font
Le cri des chats.
Des sifflets viennent et vont
Comme en pourchas.
Ah, dans ces tristes décors
Les Déjàs sont les Encors!

O les vagues Angélus!
(Qui viennent d'où)
Vois s'allumer les Saluts
Du fond d'un trou.
Ah, dans ces mornes séjours
Les Jamais sont les Toujours!

Quels rêves épouvantés
Vous grands murs blancs!
Que de sanglots répétés,
Fous ou dolents!
Ah, dans ces piteux retraits
Les Toujours sont les Jamais!

Tu meurs doucereusement,
Obscurément,

PAUL VERLAINE

Sans qu'on veille, O cœur aimant,
Sans testament!
Ah, dans ces deuils sans rachats
Les Encors sont les Déjàs!

It is perhaps because his essential kingdom is not bound by the time-limits of any century or age but has its place in that mysterious country beyond the margins of all change, where the dim vague feelings of humanity take to themselves shadowy and immortal forms and whisper and murmur of what except in music can never be uttered, that he appeals to us so much more than other recent poets.

In that twilight-land of delicate mystery, by those pale sea-banks dividing what we feel from what we dream, the silvery willows of indefinable memory bow themselves more sadly, the white poplars of faint hope shiver more tenderly, the far-off voices of past and future mingle with a more thrilling sweetness, than in the garish daylight of any circumscribed time or place.

In the twilight-country over which he rules, this fragile child of the clairvoyant senses, this uncrowned king of beggars and dreams, it may truly and indeed seem that "les jamais sont les toujours."

His poetry is the poetry of water-colours. It is water seen through water. It is white painted upon white. It is sad with the whispers of falling rain. It is grey with the passage of softly-sliding mists. It is cool and fresh with the dews of morning and of evening.

Like a leaf whirling down from one of those tremulous poplar-trees that hang over the Seine between the Pont Neuf and the Quai Voltaire —whirling lightly and softly down, till it touches the flowing water and is borne away—each of these delicate filmy verses of his falls upon our consciousness; draws up from the depths its strange indescribable response; and is lost in the shadows.

One is persuaded by the poetry of Verlaine that the loveliest things are the most evasive things, the things which come most lightly and pass most swiftly. One realises from his poetry that the rarest intimations of life's profound secret are just those that can only be expressed in hints, in gestures, in whispers, in airy touches and fleeting signs.

One comes to understand from it that the soul of poetry is and was and must always be no other thing than *music*—music not merely of the superficial sound of words, but of those deeper significances and those vaguer associations which words carry with them; music of the hidden spirit of words, the spirit which originally called them forth from the void and made them vehicles for the inchoate movements of man's unuttered dreams.

Paul Verlaine—and not without reason—became a legend even while he lived; and now that he is dead he has become more than a legend. A legend and a symbol! Wherever the spirit of art finds itself misunderstood, mistrusted, disavowed, disinherited; driven into the taverns by the stupidity of those who dwell in "homes," and into the arms of the submerged by the coldness and heartlessness of those who walk prosperously upon the surface; the figure of this fantastic child, this satyr-saint with the Socratic forehead, this tearful mummer among the armies of the outcasts, will rise up and write his prophecy upon the wall.

For the kingdom of art is as the kingdom of heaven. The clever ones, the wise ones, the shrewd ones, the ones that make themselves friends with Mammon, and build themselves houses of pleasure for their habitation, shall pass away and be forgotten forever.

The justice of the gods cancels the malice of the righteous, and the devoted gratitude of humanity tears up the the contemptuous libels of the world.

He has come into his own, as all great poets must at last, in defiance of the puritan, in defiance of public opinion, and in spite of all aspersion. He has come into his own; and no one who loves poetry can afford to pass him by.

For while others may be more witty, more learned, more elaborate, none can be more melodious. His poetry is touched with the music that is beyond all argument. He lives by his sincerity. He lives by his imagination.

The things that pertain the deepest to humanity are not its fierce fleshly passions, its feverish ambitions, its proud reasonings, its tumultuous hopes. They are the things that belong to the hours when these obsessing forces fade and ebb and sink away. They are the things that rise up out of the twilight-margins of sleep and death; the things that come to us on softly stepping feet, like child-mothers with their first-born in their arms; the things that have the white mists of dawn about them and the cool breath of evening around them; the things that hint at something beyond passion and beyond reason; the things that sound to us like the sound of bells heard through clear deep water; for the secret of human life is not in its actions or its voices or its clamorous desires, but in the intervals between all these—when all these leave it for a moment at rest—and in the depths of the soul itself the music becomes audible, the music which is the silence of eternity.

REMY DE GOURMONT

REMY DE GOURMONT

THE death of Remy de Gourmont is one of the greatest losses that European literature has suffered since the death of Oscar Wilde. The supreme critic is as rare as the supreme artist, and de Gourmont's critical genius amounted to a miracle of clairvoyance.

He wrote of everything—from the etymological subtleties of the French language down to the chaste reluctances of female moles. He touched everything and he touched nothing that he did not adorn.

In America he is unfortunately far less well known than he deserves, though an admirable translation of "A Night in the Luxembourg," published in Boston, and a charming and illuminating essay by Mr. Robert Parker, have done something to remove this disgrace. As Mr. Parker truly observes, the essence of de Gourmont's genius is to be found in an insatiable curiosity which the absolute closing of any vista of knowledge by the final and authoritative discovery of truth would paralyse and petrify. He does not, as Mr. Parker justly says, seek for truth with any hope or even any particular wish, to find it. Truth found would be truth spoiled. He seeks it from sheer love of the pursuit. In this respect he is precisely of the stuff out of which great essayists are made. He is also placed in that special position from which the illusive phenomena of this challenging world are best caught, best analysed, and best interpreted, as we overtake them in their dreamy passage from mystery to mystery.

The mere fact of his basic assumption that final truth in any direction is undiscoverable—possibly undesirable also—sets him with the wisest and sanest of all the most interesting writers. It sets him "en rapport" with nature, too, in a very close and intimate affiliation. It sets him at one spring at the very parting of the ways where all the mysteries meet. Nature loves to reveal the most delicate side-lights and the most illuminating glimpses to those who take this attitude. Such disinterestedness brings its own reward.

To love truth for the sake of power or gain or pride or success is a contemptible prostitution; to love it for its own sake is a tragic foolishness. What is truth—in itself—that it should be loved? But to love it for the pleasure of pursuing it, that is the temper dear to the immortal gods. For this is indeed their own temper, the very way they themselves—the shrewd undying ones—regard the dream shadows of the great kaleidoscope.

It is a subtle and hard saying this, that truth must be played with lightly to be freely won, but

it has a profound and infinite significance. Illuminating thoughts—thoughts with the bloom
and gloss and dew of life itself upon them—do
not come to the person who with puritanical aus-
terity has grown lean in his wrestling. They
come when we have ceased to care whether they
come or not. They come when from the surface
of the tide and under the indifferent stars we
are content to drift and listen, without distress,
to the humming waters.

As Goethe says, it is of little avail that we go
forth with our screws and our levers. Tugged
at so and mauled, the magic of the universe slips
away from out of our very fingers. It is better to stroll negligently along the highways of
the world careless of everything except "the
pleasure which there is in life itself," and then,
in Goethe's own phrase, "Such thoughts will
come of themselves and cry like happy children—
'Here we are.'"

There is indeed required—and herein may be
found the secret of Remy de Gourmont's evasive
talent—a certain fundamental *irresponsibility*,
if we are to become clairvoyant critics of life.
As soon as we grow responsible, or become conscious of responsibility, something or other comes
between us and the clear object of our curiosity,
blurring its outline and confusing its colours.
Moral scruples, for instance, as to how precisely
this new fragment of knowledge or this new aspect of art is likely to affect the inclinations of

the younger generation; religious scruples as to whether this particular angle of cosmic vision will redound to the glory of God or detract from it or diminish it; political or patriotic scruples as to whether this particular "truth" we have come to overtake will have a beneficial or injurious effect upon the fortunes of our nation; domestic scruples as to whether we are justified in emphasising some aspect of psychological discrimination that may be dangerous to those stately and ideal illusions upon which the more sacred of human institutions rest.

Looked at from this point of view it might seem as if it were almost impossible for a thoroughly responsible or earnest-minded man to become an ideal critic. Such a one keeps his mind so closely and gravely fixed upon his ethical "point d'appui," that when he jumps he misses the object altogether. In a certain sense every form of responsibility is obscurantism. We are concerned with something external to the actual thing under discussion; something to be gained or lost or betrayed or guarded; and between the pure image of what we are looking at and our own free souls, float a thousand distorting mists.

The whole philosophical attitude of Remy de Gourmont is full of interest and significance for those who are watching the deeper movements of European thought. At one, in a limited sense, with Bergson and William James in their protests against final or static "truth," de Gourmont's writings, when taken as a whole, form a most salutary and valuable counterpoise to the popular and vulgar implications of this modern mysticism. That dangerous and pernicious method of estimating the truth of things according to what James calls somewhere their "cash-value" receives blow after blow from his swift and ironic intelligence.

Things are what they are and their hidden causes are what they are, quite apart from whether they produce a pleasant or unpleasant effect upon individual lives. The sordid and utilitarian system of judging the value of thoughts and ideas in proportion to their efficiency in the world of practical exigencies does not appeal to this rational and classical mind.

The pragmatism of William James and the instinct-doctrines of Bergson have both been pounced upon by every kind of apologist for supernatural religion and categorical morality; while the method of appealing to the optimistic prejudices of shallow minds by the use of colloquial and mystical images has of recent years been introducing into European thought what might be called "Metaphysical Americanism."

Against this tendency, a tendency peculiarly and especially Anglo-Saxon, the ingrained *Latinity* of de Gourmont's mind indignantly revolts. His point of view is entirely and absolutely classical, in the old French sense of that suggestive word and in accordance with the great French traditions of Rabelais, Voltaire, Stendhal, Renan, and Anatole France.

The new pseudo-philosophy, so vague, so popular, so optimistic, so steeped in mystical morality, which one associates with the writings of so many modern Americans and which finds a certain degree of support in the work of Maeterlinck and Romain Rolland, leaves the intelligence of Remy de Gourmont entirely untouched. He comes to modern problems with the free, gay, mocking curiosity of a twentieth century Lucian. Completely out of his vein and remote from his method is that grave pedagogic tone which has become so popular a note in recent ethical writing, and which, for all his slang of the marketplace, underlies the psychological optimism of William James.

One has only to read a few pages of Remy de Gourmont to be conscious that one has entered once again the large, spacious, free, irresponsible, *heathen* atmosphere of the great writers of antiquity. The lapse of time since those classic ages, the superficial changes of human manners and speech, seem abolished, seem reduced to something that does not count at all. We have nothing here of that self-conscious modernity of tone, that fussy desire to be original and popular, which spoils the charm of so many vigorous writers of our age. It is as though some pleasant companion of Plato—some wise and gay Athenian from the side of Agathon or Phædrus or Charmides—were risen from his tomb by the blue Ionian seas to discourse to us upon the eternal ironies of nature and human life under the lime trees and chestnuts of the Luxembourg gardens. It is as though some philosophic friend of Catullus or Propertius had returned from an age-long holiday within the olive groves of Sirmio to wander with clear-eyed humorous curiosity along the banks of the Seine or among the book-stalls of the Odéon.

Like a thick miasmic cloud, as we read this great pagan critic, all the fogs and vapours of turgid hyperborean superstition are driven away from the face of the warm sun. Once more what is permanent and interesting in this mad complicated comedy of human life emerges in bold and sharp relief.

Artists, novelists, poets, journalists, occultists, abnormalists, essayists, scientists and even theologians, are treated with that humorous and passionate curiosity, full of a spacious sense of the amplitude of and diversity of life's possibilities, which we associate with the classic tradition.

Only in France is the appearance of a writer of this kind possible at all; because France alone of all the nations, and Paris alone of all the cities, of the modern world, has kept in complete and continuous touch with the "open secret" of the great civilisations.

There is no writer more required in America at this moment than Remy de Gourmont, and for that very reason no writer less likely to be received. Curiously enough, in spite of the huge influx of foreigners into the harbour reigned over by the Statue of Liberty, not even England itself is more enslaved by the dark fogs of puritanical superstition than the United States; for there is no place in the world where the brutal ignorance and complacent self-righteousness of the commercial middle classes rampage and revel and trample upon distinction and refinement more savagely than in America. The blame for this must fall entirely upon the English race and upon the descendants of the Puritans. Perhaps a time will come when all these Jews and Slavs and Italians will assert their *intellectual* as they are beginning to assert their *economic* independence, and then no doubt led by the cities of the West—the ones furthest from Boston—there will be a Renaissance of European intelligence in this great daughter of Europe such as will astonish even Paris itself. But this event, as Sir Thomas More says so sadly of his Utopia, is rather to be hoped for than expected.

One hears so often from the mouths of middle-class apologists for the modern industrial system expressions of fear as to the loss of what they call "initiative" under any conceivable socialistic state. One is inclined to ask "initiative towards what"? Towards growing unscrupulously rich, it must be supposed; certainly not towards intellectual experiments and enterprises; for no possible revolutionary régime could be less sympathetic to these things than the one under which we live at present.

The Puritan rulers of America are very anxious to "educate" foreigners in the free "institutions" of their new home. One can only pray that the persons submitted to this process will find some opportunity of adding to their "education" some cursory acquaintance with their own classics; so that when the hour arrives and we wake to find ourselves under the rule of trade-unions or socialistic bureaucrats, our new authorities will know at least something of the "institution," as Walt Whitman somewhere calls it, of intellectual toleration.

Remy de Gourmont himself is very far from being a socialist. He has imbibed with certain important differences, due to his incorrigible Latin temperament, many of the doctrines of Nietzsche; but Nietzsche himself could hardly be more inimical to any kind of mob-rule than this exponent of "subjective idealism."

Remy de Gourmont does not interest himself greatly in political changes. He does not interest himself in political revolutions. Like Goethe, he considers the intellectual freedom of the artist and philosopher best secured under a government that is stable and lasting; better still under a government that confines itself rigidly to its own sphere and leaves manners and morals to the taste of the individual; best of all under that Utopian absence of any government, whether of the many or of the few, whereof all free spirits dream.

Remy de Gourmont has written one immortal philosophical romance in "A Night in the Luxembourg." He has written some exquisite poetry full of a voluptuous and ironic charm; full of that remoteness from sordid reality which befits a lonely and epicurean spirit, a spirit pursuing its own way on the shadowy side of all human roads where the old men dream their most interesting dreams and the young maidens dance their most unreserved dances.

He has written many graceful and lovely prose poems—one hesitates to call them "short stories"—in which the reader is transported away beyond all modern surroundings into that delicate dream world so dear to lovers of Watteau and Poussin, where the nymphs of Arcadia gather, wondering and wistful, about the feet of wandering saints, and where the symbols of Dionysian orgies blend with the symbols of the redemption of humanity.

He has written admirable and unsurpassed criticism upon almost all the contemporary figures of French literature—criticism which in many cases contains a wisdom and a delicacy of feeling quite beyond the reach of the particular figure that preoccupies him at the moment. He has done all this and done it as no one else in

Europe could have done it. But in the last resort it does not seem as though his reputation
would rest either upon his poetry or his prose
poetry or even perhaps upon his "masks," as he
calls them, of personal appreciation.

It rather seems as though his best work—putting "A Night in the Luxembourg" aside—were
to be found in that long series of psychological
studies which he entitles "Promenades Lit-
téraires," "Promenades Philosophiques" and
"Epilogues." If we add to these the volumes
called "La culture des Idées," "Le chemin de
Velours," and "Le Problème du style" we have
a body of philosophical analysis and speculation
the value of which it would be impossible to overrate in the present condition of European
thought.

What we have offered to us in these illuminating essays is nothing less than an inestimable
mass of interpretative suggestion, dealing with
every kind of topic under the sun and throwing light upon every species of open question and
every degree of human mystery.

When one endeavours to distil from all this
erudite mass of criticism—of "criticism of life"
in the true sense of that phrase—the fundamental and quintessential aspects of thought, one
finds the attempt a much easier one than might be
expected from the variety, and in many cases
from the occasional and transitory nature, of the
subjects discussed. It is this particular tone and

temper of mind diffused at large through a discussion of so immense a variety of topics that in the last resort one feels is the man's real contribution to the art of living upon the earth. And when in pursuing the transformations of his protean intelligence through one critical metamorphosis after another we finally catch him in his native and original form, it is this form, with the features of the real Remy de Gourmont, which will remain in our mind when many of its incidental embodiments have ceased to interest us.

The man in his essential quality is precisely what our generation and our race requires as its antipodal corrective. He is the precise opposite of everything most characteristic of our puritan-souled and commercial-minded Democracy. He is all that we are not—and we are all that he is not.

For an average mind evolved by our system and subjected to our influence—the mind and influence of modern English-speaking America—the writings of Remy de Gourmont would be, if apprehended in any true measure according to their real content and significance, the most extreme intellectual and moral outrage that could be inflicted upon us. Properly understood, or even superficially understood, they would wound and shock and stagger and perplex every one of our most sacred prejudices. They would conflict with the whole method and aim of the education which we have received, an education of which the professed object is to fit us for an active, successful and energetic life in the sphere of industrial or commercial or technical enterprises, and to make of us moral, socially-minded, conventional and normal persons. Our education, I mean our American education—for they still teach the classics in a few schools in England—is, in true pragmatic manner, subordinate to what is called one's "life work"; to the turning, as profitably to ourselves as possible, of some well-oiled wheel in the industrial machine.

Such an education, though it may produce brilliant brokers and inspired financiers, with an efflorescence of preachers and base-ball players, certainly cannot produce "humanists" of the old, wise Epicurean type.

But it is not only our education which is at fault. Our whole spiritual atmosphere is alien and antagonistic to the spiritual atmosphere of Remy de Gourmont. He is serious where we are flippant, and we are serious where he is ironical.

Any young person among us who imbibed the mental and moral attitude of Remy de Gourmont would cause dismay and consternation in the hearts of his friends. He would probably have a library. He might even read Paul Claudel.

I speak lightly enough, but the point at issue is not a light one. It is indeed nothing less than a parting of the ways between two civilisations, or, shall we say, between a civilisation which has not lost touch with Athens and Rome and a commercial barbarism buttressed up with "modern improvements."

Remy de Gourmont's genius is in its essence an aristocratic one. He has the reserve of the aristocrat; the aristocratic contempt for the judgment of the common herd; the aristocrat's haughty indifference to public opinion. Writing easily, urbanely, plausibly upon every aspect of human life, he continues the great literary tradition of the beautifully and appropriately named *"humanism"* of the "Revival of Letters."

As Mr. Parker hints, he is one of those who refuse to bow to the intolerable mandate of the dry and sapless spirit of "specialisation." He refuses to leave art to the artist, science to the scientist, religion to the theologian, or the delicate art of natural casuistry to the professional moralist. In the true humanistic temper he claims the right to deal with all these matters, and to deal with them lightly, freely, unscrupulously, irresponsibly, and with no "arrière pensée" but the simple pleasure of the discussion.

He makes us forget Herbert Spencer and makes us think of Plato. He is the wise sophist of our own age, unspoiled by any Socratic "conceptualism," and ready, like Protagoras, to show us how man is the measure of all things and how the individual is the measure of man. The ar-

dour of his intellectual curiosity burns with a
clear smokeless flame. He brings back to the
touchstone of a sort of distinguished common
sense, free from every species of superstition,
all those great metaphysical and moral problems
which have been too often monopolised by the
acrid and technical pedantry of the schools.

He reminds one of the old-fashioned "gentleman of leisure" of the eighteenth century, writing shrewdly and wisely upon every question relating to human life, from punctuation and gram-
mar to the manner in which the monks of the
Thebaid worshipped God. His attitude is always that of the great amateur, never of the little professional. He writes with suggestive imagination, not with exhaustive authority. He
takes up one subject after another that has been,
so to speak, closed and locked to the ordinary layman, and opens it up again with some original
thrust of wholesome scepticism, and makes it
flexible and porous. He indicates change and
fluctuation and malleableness and the organic ca-
priciousness of life, where the professors have
shut themselves up in logical dilemmas. When
it comes to the matter of his actual approach to
these things it will be found that he plunges his
hand boldly into the flowing stream, in the way
of a true essayist dispensing with all the tedious
logical paraphernalia of a writer of "serious
treatises."

His genius is not only aristocratic in quality;

it is essentially what might be called, in a liberal use of the term, the genius of a sensualist.

Remy de Gourmont's ultimate contribution to the art of criticism is the disentangling, from among the more purely rational vehicles of thought, of what we might regard as the sensual or sensuous elements of human receptivity. No one can read his writings with any degree of intelligence without becoming aware that, in his way of handling life, ideas become sensations and sensations become ideas.

More than any critic that ever lived, Remy de Gourmont has the power of interesting us in his psychological discoveries with that sort of thrilling vibrating interest which is almost like a physical touch.

The thing to note in regard to this evocation of a pleasurable shock of mental excitement is that in his case it does not seem produced so much by the sonority or euphonious fall of the actual words—as in the case of Oscar Wilde— or even by the subtler spiritual harmony of rhythmically arranged thought—as in the case of Walter Pater—as by the use of words to liberate and set free the underlying sensation which gives body to the idea, or, if you will, the underlying idea which gives soul to the sensation.

In reading him we seldom pause, as we do with Wilde or Pater, to caress with the tip of our intellectual tongue the insidious bloom and gloss and magical effluence of the actual phrases he uses. His phrases seem, so to speak, to clear themselves out of the way—to efface themselves and to retire in order that the sensational thought beneath them may leap forward unimpeded.

Words become indeed to this great student of the subtleties of human language mere talismans and entrance keys, by means of which we enter into the purlieus of that psychological borderland existing half way between the moving waters of sensibility and the human shores of mental appreciation. Playing this part in his work it becomes necessary that his words should divest themselves, as far as it is humanly possible for them to do so without losing their intelligible symbolic value, of all merely logical and abstract connotation. It is necessary that his words should be light-footed and airily winged, swift, sharp and sudden, so that they may throw the attention of the reader away from themselves upon the actual psychic and psychological thrill produced by each new and exciting idea. They must be fluid and flexible, these words of his, free from rigid or traditional fetters, and prepared at a moment's notice to take new colour and shape from some unexpected and original thought looming up in the twilight below.

They must be quick to turn green, blue, purple, violet—these words—like the flowing waters of some sunlit sea, in order that the mysterious reflections of the wonderful opalescent fish, swimming to and fro in the dim depths, may reach the surface unimpeded by any shadows.

But the chief point about the style of Remy de Gourmont is that it precisely reflects his main fundamental principle, the principle that ideas should strike us with the pleasurable shock of sensations, and that sensations should be porous to and penetrated by ideas.

"En littérature, comme en tout, il faut que cesse la regne des mots abstraits. Une ouvre d'art n'existe que par l'émotion qu'elle nous donne; il suffira de determiner et de caracteriser la nature de cette émotion; cela ira de la métaphysique à la sensualité, de l'idée pure au plaisir physique."

"La métaphysique à la sensualité; l'idée pure au plaisir physique"; it would be impossible to put more clearly than in those words the purpose and aim of this great writer's work.

Contemptuously aloof from the idols of the market-place, contemptuously indifferent to the tyranny of public opinion, with the fixed principle in his mind—almost his only fixed principle —that the majority is always wrong, Remy de Gourmont goes upon his way; passionately tasting, like a great satin-bodied humming bird, every exquisite flower in the garden of human ideas. The wings of his thoughts, as he hovers, beat so quickly as to be almost invisible; and thus it is that in reading him—great scholar of style as he is—we do not think of his words but only of his thought, or rather only of the sensation which his thought evokes.

When it comes to the actual philosophy of Remy de Gourmont we indeed arrive at something which may well cause our Puritan obscurants to open their mouths with amazement. He is perhaps the only perfectly frank and unmitigated "hedonist" which European literature at this hour offers.

He advocates pleasure as the legitimate and sole end of man's endeavours and aspirations upon this earth. Pleasure imaginatively dealt with indeed, and transformed from a purely physical into a cerebral emotion; but pleasure frankly, candidly, shamelessly accepted at its natural and obvious value.

Here, then, comes at last upon the scene a writer as free from the moralistic aftermath of two thousand years of criminalising of human instincts as he is free from the supernatural dogmas that have given support to this darkening of the sunshine.

Nietzsche, of course, was before him with his formidable philosophic hammer; but Nietzsche himself was by temperament too spiritual, too cold, too aloof from the common instincts of humanity to do more than hew out an opening through the gloomy thickets of the ascetic forest. He was himself too entirely intellectual, too high and icy and austere and imaginative ever to bring the actual feet of the dancers, and the lutes and flutes of the wanton singers into the sunlit path to which he pointed the way.

His cruel praise of the more predatory and rapacious among the emancipated spirits gives, too, a somewhat harsh and sinister aspect to the whole thing. The natural innocence of genuine pagan delight draws back instinctively from the savage excesses of the Nietzschean "blond beast." The poor fauns and dryads of the free ancient world hesitate trembling and frightened on the very threshold of their liberty when this great Zarathustra offers them a choice between frozen Alpine peaks of heroic desolation and blood-stained jungles frequented by Borgian tigers.

In his own heart Nietzsche was much more of a mediæval saint than a predatory "higher man," but the natural human instinct of any sane and sun-loving pagan may well shrink back dismayed from any contact with this savage "will to power," which, while destroying the quiet cloistered gardens of monastic seclusion, hurls us into the path of these new tyrants. The less rigorous "religious orders" of the faith of Christendom would seem to offer to these poor dismayed "revenants" from the ancient world a much quieter and happier habitation than the mountain tops where blows the frozen wind of "Eternal Recurrence," or the smouldering desert sands where stalk the tawny lions of the "higher morality." The "Rule of Benedict" would in this sense be a refuge for the timorous unbaptised, and the

"Weeds of Dominic" a protection for the gentle infidel.

After reading Remy de Gourmont, with his wise, friendly ironic interest in every kind of human emotion, one is inclined to feel that, after all, in the large and tolerant courts of some less zealous traditional "order" there might be more pleasant air to breathe, more peaceful sunshine, more fresh and dewy rose-gardens, than in a world dominated by the Eagle and the Serpent óf the Zarathustrian Overman.

Remy de Gourmont would free us from the rule of dogmatist and moralist, but he would free us from these without plunging us into a yet sterner ascesis. The tone and temper advocated by him is one eminently sane, peaceful, quiet, friendly and gay. He does not free us from a dark responsibility to God to plunge us under the yoke of a darker responsibility to posterity. He would free us from every kind of responsibility. He would reduce our life to a beautiful unrestricted "Abbey of Thelema," over the gates of which the great Pantagruelian motto "Fay ce que vouldray" would be written in letters of gold.

What one is brought to feel in reading Remy de Gourmont is that the liberty of the individual to follow his intellectual and psychological tastes unimpeded by any sort of external authority is much more important for civilisation at large and much more conducive to the interests of posterity than any inflexible rules, whether they be laid upon us by ecclesiastical tradition, by puritanical heretics or by prophetic supermen.

It is really *liberty*—first and last—in the full beautiful meaning of that great human word, that Remy de Gourmont claims for us; though he is perfectly aware that such liberty can never be enjoyed except by those whose genuine intellectual emancipation renders them fit to enjoy it. It is always for the liberty of *man* as an individual, never for *men* as a herd, that he contends; as his favourite phrase, "subjective idealism," constantly insists.

And, above all, it is perfect and untrammelled liberty for the artist that he demands. One of his most suggestive and interesting essays is upon the topic of the influence of the "young girl" upon contemporary literature.

This is indeed carrying the war into the enemy's camp; for if the "young girl" has interfered with the freedom of the artist in France, what has she done in England and America? "What are they doing here?" cried Goethe once, teased and fretted by the presence of this restricting influence. "Why don't they keep them in their convents?"

And it is this very cry, the cry of the impatient artist longing to deal freely and largely with every mortal aspect of human life, that Remy de Gourmont echoes.

It is indeed a serious and difficult problem; and it is one of the problems thrust inevitably

upon us by the spread of education and the con-
sequent cheapening and vulgarising of education
under the influence of democracy.

But it can have only one answer, the great and
memorable answer given to all scrupulous protectors of virtue by John Milton in his "Areopa-
gitica." It is better that this or the other person should come to harm by the bad use of a
good book than that the life-blood of an immortal spirit, embalmed in any beautiful work of art,
should be wasted upon the dust and never reach
the verdict of posterity.

What are they doing here, these difficult young
persons and their still more difficult guardians?

This—this sacred Elysian garden of the great
humanistic tradition of classic wisdom and classic art—must not be invaded by clamorous babes
and agitated elders, must not be profaned either
by the plaudits or the strictures of the unlet-
tered mob. Somewhere in human life, and where
should it be if not in the cloistered seclusion of
noble literature?—there must be an escape from
the importunities of such people and from the
responsibilities of the ignorance they so jealously
guard.

In the days when men wrote for men—and
for women of the calibre of Aspasia or Margaret
of Navarre—this problem did not emerge. It
was not wise perhaps at Athens to abuse Cleon,
though—heaven knows—that was often enough
done; nor in Rome to satirise Cæsar, though that

too was now and again most prosperously
achieved! It was dangerous in the time of Rabelais to throw doubt on the authority of the
church. But this new tyranny, this new oppression of letters, this unfortunate cult of the susceptible "young person," is far more deadly to
the interests of civilisation than any interference
by church or state. There was always to be
found some wise and classic-minded cardinal to
whom one could appeal, some dilettante Maecenas
to whom one might dedicate one's work.

But now the flood-gates are open; the dam
is up; and the great tide of unmitigated philistinism, hounded on by dreadful protectors of
dreadful "young persons," invades the very cita-
del of civilisation itself, and pours its terrible
"pure"scum and its popular sentimental mud over
the altars of the defenceless immortals. No one
asks that these tyrannical young people and their
anxious guardians should read the classics or
should read the works of such far-descended in-
heritors of the classical tradition who, like Remy
de Gourmont, seek to keep the sacred fire alight.
Let them hold their hands off! Let them go back
to their schools and their presbyteries.

Democracy may be a great improvement upon
the past, just as modern religion may be an improvement upon ancient religion. But one thing
democracy must not be allowed to do; it must
not be allowed to substitute the rule of a puritanical middle-class, led by pietistic sentimentalists,

for the despotism of a Cæsar or a Sforza or a Malatesta in the sphere of the intellect. The intellect of the race must be held sacred, must be held intact; and its artists and writers permitted to go their way and follow their "subjective idealism" as they please, without let or hindrance.

What would be the use of persecuting genius into absolute sterility if after years and years of suppression human instincts were left the same, only with no subtle criticism or free creative art to give them beauty, refinement, interpretation and the magic of a noble style?

Remy de Gourmont, like all the profoundest intelligences of our race, like the great Goethe himself, is a spiritual anarchist.

Standing apart from popular idols and popular catch-words he converses with the great withdrawn souls of his own and previous ages, and hands on to posterity the large, free, urbane atmosphere of humanistic wisdom.

On the whole perhaps it would be well to keep his writings out of the New World. They might stir up pessimistic feelings. They might make us dissatisfied with lecture rooms and moving picture shows. They might undermine our interest in politics.

"La métaphysique à la sensualité—l'idée pure au plaisir physique!" Such language has indeed a dangerous sound.

To be obsessed by a passionate and insatiable

curiosity with regard to every sensation known to human senses; to be anxious to give this curiosity complete scope, so that nothing, literally nothing, shall escape it; to be endowed with the power of putting the results of these investigations into clear fascinating words, words that allure us into passing through them and beyond and behind them into the sensation of intellectual discovery which they conceal; this indeed, in our democratic age, is to be a very dubious, a very questionable writer!

For this shameless advocate of pleasure as the legitimate aim of the human race, sex and everything connected with sex comes naturally to be of paramount interest. Sex in every conceivable aspect, and religion in its best aspect—that is to say in its ritualistic one—are the things round which the cerebral passion of this versatile humanist hovers most continually.

In his prose poems and in his poetry these two interests are continually appearing, and, more often than not, they appear together fatally and indissolubly united.

"The Book of Litanies" is the title, for instance, he is pleased to give to one of his most characteristic experiments in verse; the one that contains that amazing poem addressed to the rose, with its melancholy and sinister refrain which troubles the memory like a swift wicked look from a beautiful countenance that ought to be pure and cold in death.

And how lovely and significant are those words "The Pilgrim of Silence," which is the name he seems to select for his own wandering and insatiable soul.

The Pilgrim of Silence! Pilgrim moving, aloof from the clamours of men, from garden to garden of melancholy and sweet mystery; pilgrim passing night by night along moon-lit parterres of impossible roses; pilgrim seeking "wild sea-banks" where strange-leaved glaucous plants whisper their secrets to the sharp salt wind; pilgrim of silence, for whom the gentlest murmur of the troubled senses of feverish humanity has its absorbing interest, every quiver of those burning eyelids its secret intimation, every sigh of that tremulous breast its burden of delicate confession; pilgrim of silence moving aloof from the howls of the mob and the raucous voices of the preachers, moving from garden to garden, from sea-shore to sea-shore; cannot even you—oh pilgrim of the long, long quest—give us the word, the clue, the signal, that shall answer the riddle of our days, and make the twilight of our destiny roll back? Pilgrim of silence, have you only silence to offer us at the last, after all your litanies to all the gods living and dead? Is silence your last word too?

Thus we can imagine Simone, the tender companion of our wanderer, questioning him as they walk together over the dead memories of all the generations.

Ah yes! Simone may question her pilgrim—
her pilgrim of silence—even as, in his own "Nuit
au Luxembourg," the youth to whom our Lord
discoursed so strangely, questioned the Master
as to the ultimate mystery and received so ambiguous a response. ·

And Simone likewise shall receive her answer, as we all—whether we be descendants of
the Puritans, crossing Boston Common, or aliens
of the sweat-shops of New York, crossing Washington Square, or unemployed in Hyde Park, or
nursery-maids in the Jardin des Plantes—shall receive ours, as we walk over the dead leaves of
the centuries.

Simone, aimes-tu le bruit des pas sur les feuilles
mortes?

Quand le pied les écrase, elles pleurent comme
des âmes,
Elle font un bruit d'ailes ou de robes de femme.

Simone, aimes-tu le bruit des pas sur les feuilles
mortes?

Viens; nous serons un jour de pauvres feuilles
mortes.
Viens; déjà la nuit tombe et le vent nous emporte.

Simone, aimes-tu le bruit des pas sur les feuilles
mortes?

REMY DE GOURMONT

"Le bruit des pas sur les feuilles mortes"—such indeed must be, at the last, the wisdom of this great harvester of human passions and perversions.

"Feuilles mortes," and the sound of feet that go by; that go by and return not again!

Remy de Gourmont leaves in us a bitter aftersense that we have not altogether, or perhaps even nearly, sounded the stops of his mystery. "The rest is silence" not only because he is dead, but because it seems as if he mocked at us—he the Protean critic—until his last hour.

His remote epicurean life—the life of a passionate scholar of the Renaissance—baffles and evades our curiosity.

To analyse Remy de Gourmont one would have to be a Remy de Gourmont.

He is full of inconsistencies. Proudly individualistic, an intellectual anarchist free from every scruple, he displays an objective patience almost worthy of Goethe himself in his elaborate investigations into the mysteries of life and the mysteries of the art that expresses life.

Furiously enamoured of thrilling æsthetic sensations he can yet wander, as those who know his "Promenades" can testify, through all manner of intricate and technical details.

Capable in his poetry and prose-poems of giving himself up to every sort of ambiguous and abnormal caprice, he is yet in his calmer hours able to fall back upon a sane, serene and sun-lit wisdom, tolerant towards the superstitions of humanity, and full of the magic of the universe. Never for a single moment in all of his writings are we allowed to forget the essential wonder and mystery of sex. Sex, in all its caprices and eccentricities, in all its psychological masks and ritualistic symbols, interests him ultimately more than anything else. It is this which inspires even his critical work with a sort of physiological thrill, as though the encounter with a new creative intelligence were an encounter between lover and beloved.

Remy de Gourmont would have sex and sex-emotions put frankly into the fore-ground of everything, as far as art and letters are concerned. He would take the timid hyperborean Muse of the modern world and bathe her once more in the sun-lit waters of the Heliconian Spring. He would paganize, Latinize and Mediterraneanize the genius of Europe.

Much of his writing will fall into oblivion. It is too occasional, too topical, too fretted by the necessity of clearing away the half-gods so that the gods may arrive. But certain of his books will live forever; assured of that smiling and amiable immortality, beyond the reach of all vulgar malice, which the high invisible ones give to those who have learnt the sacramental secret that only through the senses do we understand the soul, and only through the soul do we understand the senses.

WILLIAM BLAKE

WILLIAM BLAKE

THE strange and mysterious figure of William Blake seems continually to appear at the end of almost every vista of intellectual and æsthetic interest down which we move in these latter days.

The man's genius must have been of a unique kind; for while writers like Wordsworth and Byron seem now to have stiffened into dignified statues of venerated and achieved pre-eminence, he—the contemporary of William Cowper—exercises now, half way through the second decade of the twentieth century, an influence as fresh, as living, as organic, as palpable, as that of authors who have only just fallen upon silence.

His so-called "Prophetic Books" may be obscure and arbitrary in their fantastic mythology. I shall leave the interpretation of these works to those who are more versed in the occult sciences than I am, or than I should greatly care to be; but a prophet in the most true sense of that distinguished word, Blake certainly was—and to prove it one need not touch these Apocalyptic oracles.

Writing while Cowper was composing evangelical hymns under the influence of the Rev. Dr. Newton, and while Burns was celebrating his

Highland Mary, Blake anticipates many of the profoundest thoughts of Nietzsche, and opens the "charmed magic casements" upon these perilous fairy seas, voyaged over by Verlaine and Hauptmann and Maeterlinck and Mallarmé.

When one considers the fact that he was actually writing poems and engraving pictures before the eighteenth century closed and before Edgar Allan Poe was born, it is nothing short of staggering to realise how, not only in literature but in art, his astounding genius dominates our modern taste.

It might almost seem as if every single one of the poets and painters of our age—all these imagists and post-impressionists and symbolists and the rest—had done nothing during the sensitive years of their life but brood over the work of William Blake. Even in music, even in dancing—certainly in the symbolic dancing of Isadora Duncan—even in the stage decorations of our Little Theatres, one traces the mystical impulse he set in motion, and the austere lineaments, not exactly classical or mediæval, but partaking of the nature of both, of his elemental evocations.

It were, of course, not really possible to suppose that all these people—all the most imaginative and interesting artists of our day—definitely subjected themselves to the influence of William Blake. The more rational way of accounting for the extraordinary resemblance is to conceive that Blake, by some premonitory inspiration of the world-spirit "brooding upon things to come," anticipated in an age more emotionally alien to our own than that of Apuleius or of St. Anselm, the very "body and pressure" of the dreams that were to dominate the earth.

When one considers how between the age of Blake and the one in which we now live, extend no less than three great epochs of intellectual taste, the thing becomes almost as strange as one of his own imaginations.

The age of Sir Walter Scott and Jane Austen, of Wordsworth and Byron, followed immediately upon his. Then we have the age of Thackeray and Tennyson and the great Mid-Victorians. Then finally at the end of the nineteenth century we have the epoch dominated in art by Aubrey Beardsley, and in literature by Swinburne and Oscar Wilde.

Now in our own age—an age that feels as though Wilde himself were growing a little old-fashioned—we find ourselves returning to William Blake and discovering him to be more entirely in harmony with the instincts of our most secret souls than any single genius we could name actually working in our midst. It is as though to find our completest expression, the passionate and mystical soul of our materialistic age were driven back to an author who lived a hundred years ago. This phenomenon is by no means unknown in the history of the pilgrimage of the human spirit; but it has never presented itself in so emphatic a form as in the case of this extraordinary person.

In the early ages of the world, the result without doubt would be some weird deification of the clairvoyant prophet. William Blake would become a myth, a legend, an avatar of the divine Being, a Buddha, a Zoroaster, a wandering Dionysus. As it is, we are forced to confine ourselves to the fascinating pleasure of watching in individual cases, this or that modern soul, "touched to fine issues," meeting for the first time, as it may often happen, this century-buried incarnation of their own most evasive dreams.

I myself, who now jot down these fragmentary notes upon him, had the privilege once of witnessing the illumination—I can call it by no other name—produced upon the mind of the greatest novelist of America and the most incorrigibly realistic, by a chance encounter with the "Songs of Innocence."

One of the most obvious characteristics of our age is its cult of children. Here—in the passion of this cult—we separate ourselves altogether, both from our mediæval ancestors who confined their devotion to the divine child, and from the classical ages, who kept children altogether in the background.

"When I became a man," says the apostle, "I put away childish things," and this "putting away of childish things" has always been a special note of the temper and attitude of orthodox Protestants for whom these other Biblical words, spoken by a greater than St. Paul, about "becoming as little children," must seem a sort of pious rhetoric.

When one considers how this thrice accursed weight of Protestant Puritanism, the most odious and inhuman of all the perverted superstitions that have darkened man's history, a superstition which, though slowly dying, is not yet, owing to its joyless use as a "business asset," altogether dead, has, ever since it was spawned in Scotland and Geneva, made cruel war upon every childish instinct in us and oppressed with unspeakable dreariness the lives of generations of children, it must be regarded as one of the happiest signs of the times that the double renaissance of Catholic Faith and Pagan Freedom now abroad among us, has brought the "Child in the House" into the clear sunlight of an almost religious appreciation.

Let me not, however, be misunderstood. It would be a grievous and ludicrous mistake to associate the child-cult which runs like a thread of filmy star-light through the work of William Blake with the somewhat strained and fantastic attitude of child-worship which inspires such poetry as Francis Thompson's "Love in Dian's Lap," and gives a ridiculous and affected air to so many of our little ones themselves. The child of Blake's imagination is the immortal and undying child to be found in the heart of every man and every woman. It is the child spoken of in some of his most beautiful passages, by Nietzsche himself—the child who will come at the last, when the days of the Camel and the days of the Lion are over, and inaugurate the beginning of the "Great Noon."

> "And there the lion's ruddy eyes
> Shall flow with tears of gold
> And pitying the tender cries
> And walking round the fold,
> Saying, 'Wrath by his weakness
> And by his health sickness
> Are driven away
> From our immortal day.'"

Using boldly and freely, and with far more genuine worship than many orthodox believers, the figure and idea of Christ; it is not exactly the Christ we know in traditional Catholic piety, to whom in association with this image of the man-child, Blake's mind is constantly turning.

With a noble blasphemy—dearer, one may hope, to God, than the slavishness of many evangelical pietists—he treats the Christian legend with the same sort of freedom that the old Greek poets used in dealing with the gods of Nature.

The figure of Christ becomes under his hands, as we feel sometimes it does under the hands of the great painters of the Renaissance, a god among other gods; a power among other powers, but one possessed of a secret drawn from the hidden depths of the universe, which in the end is destined to prevail. So far does Blake stray from the barriers of traditional reverence, that we find him boldly associating this Christ of his —this man-child who is to redeem the race—with a temper the very opposite of an ascetic one.

What makes his philosophy so interesting and original is the fact that he entirely disentangles the phenomena of sexual love from any notion or idea of sin or shame. The man-child whose pitiful heart and whose tenderness toward the weak and unhappy are drawn from the Christ-Story, takes almost the form of a Pagan Eros— the full-grown, soft-limbed Eros of later Greek fancy—when the question of restraint or re-nunciation or ascetic chastity is brought for-ward.

What Blake has really done, be it said with all reverence, and far from profane ears—is to steal the Christ-child out of his cradle in the church of his worshippers and carry him into the cham-bers of the East, the chambers of the Sun, into the "Green fields and happy groves" of primitive Arcadian innocence, where the feet of the dancers are light upon the dew of the morning, and where the children of passion and of pleasure sport and play, as they did in the Golden Age.

In that wonderful picture of his representing the sons of God "shouting together" in the primal joy of creation, one has a vision of the large and

noble harmony he strove after between an emancipated flesh and a free spirit. William Blake,
in his Adamic innocence of "sin," has something
in him that suggests Walt Whitman, but unlike
Whitman he prefers to use the figure of Christ
rather than any vague "ensemble" of nature-
forces to symbolise the triumphant nuptials of
soul and body.

Sometimes in his strange verses one has the
impression that one is reading the fragmentary
and broken utterances of some great ancient poet-
philosopher—some Pythagoras or Empedocles—
through whose gnomic oracles runs the rhythm
of the winds and tides, and for whose ears the
stars in their courses have a far-flung harmony.

He often seems to make use of the Bible and
Biblical usages, very much as the ancient poets
made use of Hesiod or of Homer, treating such
writings with reverence, but subordinating what
is borrowed from them to new and original purpose.

> "Hear the voice of the Bard,
> Who present, past and future sees,
> Whose ears have heard
> The Holy Word
> That walked among the ancient trees.
>
> "Calling the lapséd soul
> And weeping in the evening dew,
> That might control
> The starry pole
> And fallen, fallen light renew!

WILLIAM BLAKE

"O Earth, O Earth, return!
Arise from out the dewy grass!
  Night is worn
  And the Morn
Rises from the slumbrous mass.

"Turn away no more;
Why wilt thou turn away?
  The starry floor
  The watery shore
Is given thee till break of day."

If I were asked to name a writer whose work conveys to one's mind, free of any admixture of rhetoric or of any alloy of cleverness, the very impact and shock of pure inspired genius, I would unhesitatingly name William Blake. One is strangely conscious in reading him of the presence of some great unuttered power—some vast demiurgic secret—struggling like a buried Titan just below the surface of his mind, and never quite finding vocal expression.

Dim shapes—vast inchoate shadows—like dreams of forgotten worlds and shadows of worlds as yet unborn, seem to pass backwards and forwards over the brooding waters of his spirit. There is no poet perhaps who gives such an impression of primordial creative force—force hewing at the roots of the world and weeping and laughing from sheer pleasure at the touch of that dream stuff whereof life is made. Above his head, as he laughs and weeps and sings, the branches of the trees of the forest of night stir

and rustle under the immense spaces, and, floating above them, the planets and the stars flicker
down upon him with friendly mysterious joy.

No poet gives one the impression of greater
strength than William Blake; and this is em-
phasised by the very simplicity and childishness
of his style. Only out of the strength of a lion
could come such honeyed gentleness. And if he
is one of the strongest among poets he is also
one of the happiest.

Genuine happiness—happiness that is at the
same time intellectual and spontaneous—is far
rarer in poetry than one might suppose. Such
happiness has nothing necessarily to do with an
optimistic philosophy or even with faith in God.
It has nothing at all to do with physical well-
being or the mere animal sensations of eating
and drinking and philandering. It is a thing of
more mysterious import and of deeper issues
than these. It may come lightly and go lightly,
but the rhythm of eternity is in the beating of its
wings, and deep calls to deep in the throbbing of
its pulses.

As Blake himself puts it—

> "He who bends to himself a joy
> Does the winged life destroy ;
> But he who kisses the joy as it flies
> Lives in Eternity's sun-rise."

In the welling up, out of the world's depths,
of happiness like this, there is a sense of calm,

of serenity, of immortal repose and full-brimmed ecstasy. It is the "energy without disturbance" which Aristotle indicates as the secret of the life of the eternal Being himself. It is beyond the ordinary pleasures of sex, as it is beyond the ordinary difference between good and evil. It is human and yet inhuman. It is the happiness of da Vinci, of Spinoza, of Goethe. It is the happiness towards which Nietzsche all his life long struggled desperately, and struggled in vain.

One touches the fringe of the very mystery of human symbols—of the uttermost secret of *words* in their power to express the soul of a writer— when one attempts to analyse the child-like simplicity of William Blake's style. How is it that he manages with so small, so limited a vocabulary, to capture the very "music of the spheres"? We all have the same words at our command; we all have the same rhymes; where then lies this strange power that can give the simplest syllables so original, so personal, a shape?

> "What the hammer?   What the chain?
> In what furnace was thy brain?
> What the anvil?   What dread grasp
> Dare its deadly terrors clasp?"

Just because his materials are so simple and so few—and this applies to his plastic art as well as to his poetry—we are brought to pause more sharply and startlingly in his case than that of almost any other, before the primordial mys-

tery of human expression and its malleableness
under the impact of personality. Probably no
poet ever lived who expressed his meaning by the
use of such a limited number of words, or of
words so simple and childish. It is as though
William Blake had actually transformed himself
into some living incarnation of his own Vir-
gilian child-saviour, and were stammering his oracles to mankind through divine baby-lips.

What matter? It is the one and the same Urbs
Beata, Calliopolis, Utopia, New Rome, New At-
lantis, which these child-like syllables announce,
trumpet heralded by the angels of the Revelation,
chanted by the high-souled Mantuan, sung by
David the King, or shouted "over the roofs of the
world" by Walt Whitman.

It is the same mystery, the same hope for the
human race.

> "I will not cease from mental strife
> Nor shall my sword sink from my hand
> Till I have built Jerusalem
> In England's green and pleasant Land!"

One of the most curious and interesting things
in Blake's work is the value he places upon tears.
All his noble mythological figures, gathering in
verse after verse, for the great battle against
brutality and materialism, come "weeping" to the
help of their outraged little ones. Gods and
beasts, lions and lambs, Christ and Lucifer,
fairies and angels, all come "weeping" into the

struggle with the forces of stupidity and tyranny.

He seems to imply that to have lost the power of shedding tears is to have dehumanized oneself and put oneself outside the pale. "A tear is an intellectual thing," and those who still have the power of "weeping" have not quite lost the key to the wisdom of the eternal gods./ It is not only the mysterious and foreordained congruity of rhyme that leads him to associate in poem after poem—until for the vulgar mind, the repetition becomes almost ludicrous—this symbolic "weeping" with the sweet sleep which it guards and which it brings.

The poet of the veiled child at the heart of the world is naturally a poet of the mystery of tears and the mystery of sleep. And William Blake becomes all this without the least tincture of sentimentality. That is where his genius is most characteristic and admirable. He can come chanting his strange gnomic tunes upon tears and upon sleep, upon the loveliness of children, upon life and death, upon the wonder of dews and clouds and rain and the soft petals of flowers which these nourish, without—even for one moment—falling into sentiment or pathos.

All through his strange and turbulent life he was possessed of the power of splendid and terrible anger. His invectives and vituperations bite and flay like steel whips. The "buyers and sellers" in the temple of his Lord are made to

skip and dance. He was afraid of no man living—nor of any man's god.

Working with his own hands, composing his
poems, illustrating them, engraving them, print-
ing them, and binding them in his own work-
shop, he was in a position to make Gargantuan
sport of the "great" and the "little" vulgar.

He went his own way and lived as he pleased;
having something about him of that shrewd,
humorous, imperturbable "insouciance" which
served Walt Whitman so well, and which is so
much wiser, kindlier and more human a shield
for an artist's freedom, than the sarcasms of a
Whistler or the insolence of a Wilde.

Careless and nonchalant, he "travelled the open
road," and gave all obscurantists and oppressors
to ten million cart-loads of horned devils!

It is my privilege to live, on the South Coast,
not so many miles from that village of Felpham
where he once saw in his child-like fantasies, a
fairy's funeral. That funeral must have been
followed after Blake's death by many others; for
there are no fairies in Felpham now. But
Blake's cottage is there still—to be seen by any
who care to see it—and the sands by the sea's
edge are the "yellow sands," flecked with white
foam and bright green sea-weed of Ariel's
song; and on the sea-banks above grow tufts of
Homeric Tamarisk.

It is astonishing to think that while the laconic George Crabbe, "Nature's sternest painter,"

was writing his rough couplets in the metre of Alexander Pope, and while Doctor Johnson was still tapping the posts of his London streets, as he went his way to buy oysters for his cat, William Blake—in mind and imagination a contemporary of Nietzsche and Whitman—should have been asserting the artist's right (why should we not say the individual's right, artist or no artist?) to live as he pleases, according to the morals, manners, tastes, inclination and caprices, of his own absolute humour and fancy.

This was more than one hundred years ago. What would William Blake think of our new world,—would it seem to him to resemble his New Jerusalem of child-like happiness and liberty?—our world where young ladies are fined five dollars if they go into the sea without their stockings? Well! at Felpham they do not tease them with stockings.

What makes the genius of William Blake so salutary a revolutionary influence is the fact that while contending so savagely against puritanical stupidity, he himself preserves to the end, his guilelessness and purity of heart.

There are admirable writers and philosophers, whose work on behalf of the liberation of humanity is rendered less disinterested by the fact that they are fighting for their personal inclinations rather than for the happiness of the world at large. This could never be said of William Blake. A more unselfish devotion to the spiritual interests of the race than that which inspired him from beginning to end could hardly be imagined. But he held it as axiomatic that the spiritual interests of the race can only be genuinely served by means of the intellectual and moral freedom of the individual. And certainly in his own work we have a beautiful and anarchical freedom.

No writer or artist ever succeeded in expressing more completely the texture and colour of his thoughts. Those strange flowing-haired old men who reappear so often in his engravings, like the "splendid and savage old men" of Walt Whitman's fancy, seem to incorporate the very swing and sweep of his elemental earth-wrestling; while those long-limbed youths and maidens, almost suggestive of El Greco in the way their bodies are made, yearn and leap upwards towards the clear air and the cloudless blue sky, in a passion of tumultuous escape, in an ecstasy of resurrection.

It is extraordinary how Blake's peculiar use of very simple rhymes, with the same words repeated over and over again, enhances the power of his poetry—it does more than enhance it—it is the body of its soul. One approaches here the very mystery of style, in the poetic medium, and some of its deepest secrets. Just as that "metaphysic in sensuality" which is the dominant impulse in the genius of Remy de Gourmont expresses itself in constant echoes and reiterated liturgical repetitions—such as his famous "fleur hypocrite, fleur du silence"—until one feels that the "refrain" in poetry has become, in an especial sense, his predominant note, so these constantly recurring rhymes in the work of Blake, coming at the end of very short lines, convey, as nothing else could do, the child-like quality of the spirit transfused through them. They are child-like; and yet they could not have been written by any one but a grown man, and a man of formidable strength and character.

The psychology of the situation is doubtless the same as that which we remark in certain very modern artists—the ones whose work is most of all bewildering to those who, in their utter inability to become as "little children," are as completely shut out from the kingdom of art as they are from the kingdom of heaven.

The curious spell which these simple and in some cases infantile rhymes cast over us, ought to compel the more fanatical adherents of "free verse" to rearrange their ideas. Those who, without any prejudice one way or the other, are only anxious to enjoy to the full every subtle pleasure which the technique of art is able to give, cannot help finding in the unexpected thrill produced by these sweet, soft vibrations of verbal melody—like the sound of a golden bell rung far down under the humming waters—a direct revelation of the tender, strong soul behind them, for whose hidden passion they find a voice.

After all, it is in the final impression produced upon our senses and intellect by a great artist, and not in any particular quality of a particular work of art, that—unless we are pedantic virtuosos—we weigh and judge what we have gained. And what we have gained by William Blake cannot be over-estimated.

His poems seem to associate themselves with a thousand evanescent memories of days when we have been happy beyond the power of calamity or disappointment. They associate themselves with those half-physical, half-spiritual trances—when, suddenly in the outskirts of a great city perhaps, or on the banks of some inland river, we have remembered the long line of breaking surf, and the murmurs and the scents of the sea. They associate themselves with the dreamy indescribable moments when crossing the wet grass of secluded misty meadows, passing the drowsy cattle and the large cool early morning shadows thrown by the trees, we have suddenly come upon cuckoo flowers or marigolds, every petal of which seems burdened with a mystery almost intolerably sweet.

Like the delicate pictures of early Italian art, the poems of Blake indicate and suggest rather than exhaust or satiate. One is never oppressed by too heavy a weight of natural beauty. A single tree against the sky—a single shadow upon the pathway—a single petal fallen on the grass; these are enough to transport us to those fields of light and "chambers of the sun" where the mystic dance of creation still goes on; these are enough to lead us to the hushed dew-drenched lawns where the Lord God walks in the garden "in the cool of the day."

One associates the poetry of William Blake, not with the mountain peaks and gorgeous foliage and rushing torrents of a landscape that clamours to be admired and would fain overpower us with its picturesque appeal, but with the quietest, gentlest, softest, least assuming background to that "going forth" to our work, "and our labour until the evening," which is the normal destiny of man.

The pleasant fields of Felpham with their hawthorne hedges, the little woods of Hertfordshire or Surrey with their patches of bluebells, were all that he needed to set him among the company of the eternal gods.

For this is the prerogative of imagination, that it can reconcile us to life where life is simplest and least adorned; and this is the reluctance and timidity of imagination that it shrinks away into twilight and folds its wings, when the pressure of reality is too heavy, and the materials of beauty too oppressive and tyrannous.

BYRON

BYRON

I T is in a certain sense a lamentable indictment
upon the sheepishness and inertness of the
average crowd that a figure like that of
Byron should have been so exceptional in his own
day and should be so exceptional still. For, god-
like rascal as he was, he was made of quite normal stuff.

There was nothing about him of that rare magical quality which separates such poets as Shelley
or Edgar Allan Poe or Paul Verlaine from the
mass of ordinary people. The Byronic type, as
it is called, has acquired a certain legendary
glamour; but it is nothing, when we come really
to analyse it, but the universal type of vain, im-
petuous, passionate youth, asserting itself with
royal and resplendent insolence in defiance of
the cautious discretion of middle-aged conventions.

Youth is essentially Byronic when it is natural
and fearless and strong; and it is a melancholy
admission of something timid and sluggish in us
all that we should speak "with bated breath and
whispering humbleness" of this brilliant figure.
A little more courage, a little less false mod-

esty, a little more sincerity, and the lambs of our democratic age would all show something of that leonine splendour.

There is nothing in Byron so far above the commonplace that he is out of the reach of average humanity. He is made of the same clay as we all are made of. His vanity is our vanity, his pride our pride, his vices our vices.

We are on the common earth with him; on the natural ground of our normal human infirmities; and if he puts us to shame it is only because he has the physical force and the moral courage to be himself more audaciously and frankly than we dare to be.

His genius is no rare hot-house flower. It is no wild and delicate plant growing in a remote and inhuman soil. It is simply the intensification, to a point of fine poetic fury, of emotions and attitudes and gestures which we all share under the pressure of the spirit of youth.

It is for this reason—for the reason that he expressed so completely in his wayward and imperious manner the natural feelings of normal youthfulness—that he became in his own day so legendary and symbolic a personage, and that he has become in ours a sort of flaming myth. He would never have become all this; he would never have stirred the fancy of the masses of people as he has; if there were not in his temperament something essentially simple, human, and within the comprehension of quite ordinary minds.

It might indeed be maintained that what Oscar Wilde is to the rarer and more perverse minority, Byron is to the solid majority of downright simple philistines.

The average British or American "plain blunt man" regards, and always will regard, such writers as Shelley and Poe and Verlaine and Wilde with a certain uneasy suspicion. These great poets must always seem to him a little weird and morbid and apart from common flesh and blood. He will be tempted to the end to use in reference to them the ambiguous word "degenerate." They strike him as alien and remote. They seem to have no part or lot in the world in which he lives. He suspects them of being ingrained immoralists and free-lovers. Their names convey to his mind something very sinister, something dangerous to the foundations of society.

But the idea of Byron brings with it quite different associations. The sins of Byron seem only a splendid and poetic apotheosis of such a person's own sins. The rebelliousness of Byron seems a rebelliousness not so much deliberate and intellectual as instinctive and impulsive. It seems a normal revolt against normal restrictions.. The ordinary man understands it and condones it, remembering the fires of his own youth.

Besides, Byron was a lord.

Goethe declared to Eckermann that what irritated many people against Byron was the power and pride of his personality—the fact that his personality stood out in so splendid and emphatic a way.

Goethe was right. The brilliance of Byron's personality is a thing which causes curious annoyance to certain types of mind. But these minds are not the normal ones of common intelligence. They are minds possessed of the sort of intellectual temper naturally antagonistic to reckless youth. They are the Carlyles and the Merediths of that spiritual and philosophical vision to which the impassioned normality of Byron with his school-boy ribaldry must always appear ridiculous.

I believe it will be found that those to whom the idea of Byron's brilliant and wayward personality brings exquisite pleasure are, in the first place, quite simple minds, and, in the second place, minds of a disillusioned and un-ethical order who have grown weary of "deep spiritual thinkers," and are ready to enjoy, as a refreshing return to the primitive emotions, this romantic swashbucklerism which proves so annoying to earnest modern thought.

How like a sudden reverberation of the old immortal spirit of romance, the breath of whose saddest melancholy seems sweeter than our happiness, is that clear-toned song of passion's exhaustion which begins

"We'll go no more a-roving
By the light of the moon"

and which contains that magnificent verse,

BYRON

"For the sword outwears the sheath,
And the soul wears out the breast,
And the heart must pause to breathe,
And love itself have rest."

It is extraordinary the effect which poetry of this kind has upon us when we come upon it suddenly, after a long interval, in the crowded pages, say, of some little anthology.

I think the pleasure which it gives us is due to the fact that it is so entirely sane and normal and natural; so solidly and massively within the circle of our average apprehension; so expressive of what the common flesh and blood of our elemental humanity have come to feel as permanent in their passions and reactions. It gives us a thrilling shock of surprise when we come upon it unexpectedly—this kind of thing; the more so because the poetry we have grown accustomed to, in our generation, is so different from this; so mystical and subjective, so remote from the crowd, so dim with the trailing mists of fanciful ambiguity.

It is very unfortunate that one "learned by heart," as a child, so much of Byron's finest poetry.

I cannot imagine a more exciting experience than a sudden discovery at this present hour, with a mind quite new and fresh to its resounding grandeur, of that poem, in the Hebrew Melodies, about Sennacherib.

"And the sheen of their spears was like stars on the sea
When the blue wave rolls nightly on deep Galilee."

Have not those lines the very wonder and terror and largeness of ancient wars?

"And there lay the steed with his nostril all wide,
And thro' it there rolled not the breath of his pride,
And the foam of his gasping lay white on the turf
And cold as the spray of the rock-beating surf!"

Our modern poets dare not touch the sublime
naïveté of poetry like that! Their impressionist,
imagist, futurist theories make them too self-conscious. They say to themselves—"Is that word
a 'cliché' word? Has that phrase been used several times before? Have I been carefully and
precisely *original* in this? Is that image clear-
cut enough? Have I reverted to the 'magic' of
Verlaine and Mallarmé and Mr. Yeats? Do I
suggest the 'cosmic emotion' of Walt Whitman'?"

It is this terror of what they call "cliché
words" which utterly prevents them from writing poetry which goes straight to our heart like
Byron's; poetry which refreshes our jaded epicurean senses with a fine renaissance of youth.

Their art destroys them. Their art enslaves
them. Their art lames and cripples them with
a thousand meticulous scruples.

Think what it would be, in this age, suddenly
to come upon a poet who could write largely and
carelessly, and with a flaming divine fire, about

the huge transactions of life; about love and war
and the great throbbing pulses of the world's historic events! They cannot do it—our poets—
they cannot do it; and the reason of their inability is their over-intellectuality, their heavily burdened artistic conscience. They are sedentary
people, too, most unhealthily sedentary, our moderns who write verse; sedentary young people,
whose environment is the self-conscious Bohemia
of artificial Latin Quarters. They are too clever,
too artistic, too egotistic. They are too afraid
of one another; too conscious of the derisive flap-
ping of the goose-wings of the literary journal!
They are not proud enough in their personal individuality to send the critics to the devil and go
their way with a large contempt. They set themselves to propitiate the critics by the wit of
technical novelty and to propitiate their fellow
craftsmen by avoiding the inspiration of the
past.

They do not write poetry for the pleasure of
writing it. They write poetry in order that they
may be called poets. They aim at originality instead of sweeping boldly ahead and being content
to be themselves as God made them.

I am strongly of opinion that much of the
admiration lavished on these versifiers is not due
to our enjoyment of the poetry which they write
—not, I mean, of the sheer poetic elements in it—
but to our interest in the queer words they dig up
out of the archives of philological bric-à-brac, to

our astonishment at their erotic extravagances, to our satisfaction at being reminded of all the superior shibboleths of artistic slang, the use of which and the understanding of which prove us to be true initiates in the "creative world" and no poor forlorn snakes of outworn tradition.

Our modern poets cannot get our modern artists out of their heads. The insidious talk of these sly artists confuses the simplicity of their natural minds. They are dominated by art; whereas the real sister of the muse of poetry is not "art" at all, but music.

They do not see, these people, that the very carelessness of a great poet like Byron is the inevitable concomitant of his genius; I would go so far as to call his carelessness the mother of his genius and its guardian angel.

I cannot help thinking, too, that if the artistic self-consciousness of our generation spoils its free human pleasure in great poetry, the theories of the academic historians of literature do all they can to make us leave the poetry of the past in its deep grave. It seems to me that of all futile and uninteresting things what is called "the study of literature" is the very worst.

To meddle with such a preposterous matter at all damns a person, in my thinking, as a supreme fool. And yet this is, par excellence, the sort of tediousness in which devotees of culture complacently wallow. As if it mattered where Byron slips in in "the great Renaissance of Wonder";

or where Rossetti drifts by, in the portentous "Pre-Raphaelite Movement"!

It is strange to me how boys and girls, brought up upon this "study of literature," can ever endure to see the look of a line of poetry again! Most of them, it seems, *can* hardly bear that shock; and be it far from me to blame them. I should surmise that the mere names of Wordsworth, Byron, Shelley, etc., would fall upon their ears with a dreariness of memory like the tolling of chapel-bells.

They are queer birds, too, these writers of commentaries upon literature.

At one time in my life I myself absorbed such "critical literature" with a morbid avidity, as if it had been a drug; and a drug it is—a drug dulling one to all fine and fresh sensations—a drug from the effects of which I am only now, at this late hour, beginning slowly to recover. They set one upon a completely wrong track, bringing forward what is unessential and throwing what is essential into the background. Dear heavens! how well I recall those grey discriminations. Wordsworth was the fellow who hit upon the idea of the *anima mundi*. Shelley's "philosophy of life" differed from Wordsworth's in that *his* universal spirit was a thing of pure Love, whereas the other's was a matter of pure Thought.

Pure Love! Pure Thought! Was there ever such petrifying of the evasive flame? "Words! Words! Words!" I suspect that the book the sweet Prince was reading when he met Polonius in the passage was a book of essays on the poets.

The worst of this historical-comical-philosophical way of going to work is that it leaves one with the feeling that poetry is a sort of intellectual game, entirely removed from the jostling pressure of actual life, and that poets when once dead are shoved into their academic pigeon-holes to be labelled like things under glass cases. The person who can rattle off such descriptive labels the quickest is the person of culture. Thus history swallows up poetry; thus the "comparative method" swallows up history; and the whole business is snatched away from the magical flow of real life and turned into the dreariness of a mausoleum. How refreshing, how salutary, to turn from all thoughts as to what Byron's "place in literature" was to such thrilling poetry as

> "She walks in beauty like the night
> Of cloudless climes and starry skies,
> And all that's best of dark and bright
> Meet in her aspect and her eyes—"

or to such sonorous lines full of the reverberating echoes of pent-up passion as those which begin

> "There is none of Beauty's daughters."

One has only to recall the way these simple careless outbursts have burned themselves in upon one's lips, when one's feelings were stirred to the old tune, to realise how great a poet Byron was.

BYRON

"Fare thee well and, if forever,
Still forever fare thee well!"

Can such things ever grow "stale and rung-upon," however much the chilly hand of a pedantic psychology seeks to brush the bloom away from the wings of the bird of paradise? Those poems to the mysterious Thyrza, can any modern eroticism equal them, for large and troubled abandonment; natural as gasping human speech and musical as the murmur of deep waters?

Byron is frankly and outrageously the poet of *sentiment*. This is good. This is what one craves for in vain in modern verse. The infernal seriousness of our grave youngsters and their precious psychological irony make them terrified of any approach to sentiment. They leave such matters with supreme contempt to the poor little devils who write verses for the local newspapers. They are too clever to descend to sentiment. It is their affair to show us the absurdity of sentiment.

And yet the world is full of this thing. It has the rising sap of a thousand springs in its heart. It has the "big rain" of the suppressed tears of a hundred generations in its sobbing music.

It is easy to say that Byron's sentiment was a pose.

The precise opposite of this is the truth. It is our poetic cleverness, our subjective imagery and cosmic irony, which is the pose; not his frank and boyish expression of direct emotion.

We write poetry for the sake of writing poetry. He wrote to give vent to the passions of his heart.

We compose a theme upon "love" and dedicate it to any suitable young woman the colour of whose eyes suits the turn of our metaphors. He loved first and wrote poetry afterwards—as the occasion demanded.

That is why his love-poetry is so full of vibrant sincerity, so rich in blood, so natural, so careless, so sentimental.

That is why there is a sort of conversational ease about his love-poetry, and here and there lapses into what, to an artistic sense, might seem bathos, absurdity, or rhetoric. Lovers are always a little absurd; and the fear of absurdity is not a sign of deep feeling but of the absence of all feeling.

Every one of Byron's most magnificent love-lyrics has its actual circumstantial cause and impulse in the adventures of his life. He does not spin out vague wordy platonic rhapsodies upon love-in-general. He addresses a particular person, just as Burns did—just as Shakespeare did—and his poems are, so to speak, thrilled with the excitement of the great moment's tumultuous pulses, scalded with the heat of its passionate tears.

These moments pass, of course. One need not be derisively cynical over that. Infatuation suc-

ceeds infatuation. Dream succeeds dream.
The loyalty of a life-long love was not his. His
life ended indeed before youth's desperate experiments were over, before the reaction set in.
But the sterner mood had begun.

> "Tread these reviving passions down,
> Unworthy manhood. Unto thee
> Indifferent should the smile or frown
> Of Beauty be."

And the lines end—his last—with that stoical
resignation in the presence of a soldier's fate
which gives to the close of his adventurous enter-
prise on behalf of an oppressed Hellenic world
such a gallant dignity.

> "Then look around and choose thy ground,
> And take thy rest."

If these proud personal touches, of which there
are so many scattered through his work, offend
our artistic modern sense we must remember that
the same tone, the same individual confession of
quite personal emotion, is to be found in Dante
and Milton and Goethe.
The itching mock-modesty of the intellectual
altruist, ashamed to commit himself to the personal note, is not an indication of a great nature.
It is rather a sign of a fussy self-consciousness
under the eyes of impertinent criticism.
What drives the modern philosopher to jeer at
Byron is really a sort of envy of his splendid and

irresponsible personality, that personality whose demonic energy is so radiant with the beautiful glamour of youth.

And what superb strength and high romance there are in certain of his verses when the magnificent anger of the moment has its way with him!

Fill high the bowl with Samian wine!
On Suli's rock and Parga's shore
Exists the remnant of a line
Such as our Doric mothers bore—

No one can help confessing that poetry of this kind, "simple, sensuous and passionate"—to use the great Miltonic definition—possesses, for all its undeniable *rhetoric,* a large and high poetic value.

And at its best, the poetry of Byron is not mere rhetoric. Rhetoric undoubtedly is there. His mind was constantly, like most simple minds when touched to large issues, betrayed by the sweet treachery of rhetoric; but I feel confident that any really subtle critic of the delicate differences between one poetic vein and another, must feel, though he might not be able to express the fineness of the distinction, that there is something here—some breath, some tone, some air, some atmosphere, some royal and golden gesture— which is altogether beyond the reach of all mere eloquence, and sealed with the indescribable seal of poetry.

This real poetic element in Byron—I refer to

something over and above his plangent rhetoric—
arrests us with all the greater shock of sudden
possession, for the very reason that it is so carelessly, so inartistically, so recklessly flung out.

He differs in this, more than in anything else,
from our own poetic contemporaries. Our clever
young poets know their business so appallingly
well. They know all about the theories of
poetry: they know what is to be said for Free
Verse, for Imagism, for Post-Impressionism:
they know how the unrhymed Greek chorus lends
itself to the lyrical exigencies of certain moods:
they know how wonderful the Japanese are, and
how interesting certain Indian cadences may be:
they know the importance of expressing the Ideal
of Democracy, of Femininity, of Evolution, of
Internationalism. There really is nothing in the
whole field of poetic criticism which they do not
know—except the way to persuade the gods to
give us genius, when genius has been refused!

Byron, on the contrary, knows absolutely nothing of any of these things. "When he thinks he
is a child"; when he criticises he is a child; when
he philosophises, theorises, *mysticizes,* he is a
hopeless child. A vast amount of his poetry, for
all its swing and dash and rush, might have been
written by a lamentably inferior hand.

We come across such stuff to-day; not among
the literary circles, but in the poets' corners of
provincial magazines. What is called "Byronic
sentiment," so derided now by the clever young

psychologists who terrorise our literature, has become the refuge of timid old-fashioned people, quite bewildered and staggered by new developments.

I sympathise with such old-fashioned people. The pathetic earnestness of an elderly commercial traveller I once met on the Père Marquette Railway who assured me that Byron was "some poet" remains in my mind as a much more touching tribute to the lordly roué than all the praise of your Arnolds and Swinburnes.

He is indeed "some poet." He is the poet for people who feel the magic of music and the grandeur of imagination, without being able to lay their finger on the more recondite nuances of "creative work," without so much as ever having heard of "imagism."

I have spent whole evenings in passionate readings of "Childe Harold" and the "Poems to Thyrza" with gentle Quaker ladies and demure old maids descended from the Pilgrim Fathers, and I have always left such Apollonian prayer-meetings with a mind purged from the cant of cleverness; washed and refreshed in the authentic springs of the Muses.

So few lords—when you come to think of it—write poetry at all, that it is interesting to note the effect of aristocratic blood upon the style of a writer.

Personally I think its chief effect is to produce a certain magnanimous indifference to the meticulous niceties of the art. We say "drunk as a lord"; well—it is something to see what a person will do, who is descended from Robert Bruce's Douglas, when it is a question of this more heavenly intoxication. Aristocratic blood shows itself in poetry by a kind of unscrupulous contempt for gravity. It refuses to take seriously the art which it practises.

It plays the part of the grand amateur. It is free from bourgeois earnestness. It is this, I suppose, which is so irritating to the professional critic. If you can write poetry, so to speak, with your left hand, in intervals of war and love and adventure, between rescuing girls from sacks destined for the waters of the Bosphorus and swimming the length of the Venetian Grand Canal and recruiting people to fight for Hellenic freedom, you are doing something that ought not to be allowed. If other men of action, if other sportsmen and pleasure-seekers and travellers and wandering free-lances were able to sit down in any cosmopolitan café in Cairo or Stamboul and knock off immortal verses in the style of Byron—verses with no "philosophy" for us to expound, no technique for us to analyse, no "message" for us to interpret, no æsthetic subtleties for us to unravel, no mystical orientation for us to track out, what is there left for a poor sedentary critic to do? Our occupation is gone. We must either enjoy romance for its own sake in a frank, honest, simple manner; confessing that

Byron was "some poet" and letting it go at that; or we must explain to the world, as many of us do, that Byron was a thoroughly bad writer. A third way of dealing with this unconscionable boy, who scoffed at Wordsworth and Southey and insisted that Pope was a great genius, is the way some poor camp-followers of the Moral Ideal have been driven to follow; the way, namely, of making him out to be a great leader in the war of the liberation of humanity, and a great interpreter of the wild magic of nature.

I must confess I cannot see Byron in either of these lights. He scoffs at kings and priests, certainly; he scoffs at Napoleon; he scoffs at the pompous self-righteousness of his own race; he scoffs at religion and sex and morality in that humorous, careless, indifferent "public-school" way which is so salutary and refreshing; but when you ask for any serious devotion to the cause of Liberty, for any definite Utopian outlines of what is to be built up in the world's future, you get little or nothing, except resounding generalities and conventional rhetoric.

Nor are those critics very wise who insist on laying stress upon Byron's contributions to the interpretation of Nature.

He could write "How the big rain comes dancing to the earth!" and his flashing, fitful, sun-smouldering pictures of European rivers and plains and hills and historic cities have their large and generous charm.

But beyond this essentially human and romantic attitude to Nature there is just nothing at all.

"Roll on, thou deep and dark-blue Ocean, roll!"

I confess I caught a keener thrill of pleasure from that all-too-famous line when I suddenly heard it uttered by one of those garrulous ghosts in Mr. Masters's Spoon River cemetery, than I ever did when in childhood they made me learn it.

But, for all that, though it is not an easy thing to put into words, there is a certain grandiose and sonorous beauty, fresh and free and utterly un-affected, about these verses, and many others in "Childe Harold."

As for those long plays of Byron's, and those still longer narrative poems, nothing will induce me to read a line of them again. They have a singularly dusty smell to me; and when I think of them even, I suffer just such a withering sen-sation of ineffable boredom as I used to experi-ence waiting in a certain ante-room in Tunbridge Wells where lived an aged retired general. I as-sociate them with illustrated travels in Palestine.

How Goethe could read "Manfred" with any pleasure passes my comprehension. "Cain" has a certain charm, I admit; but of all forms of all literature the thing which is called Poetic Drama seems to me the most dreary. If poets cannot write for the stage they had better confine them-selves to honest straightforward odes and lyrics.

But it is no use complaining. There is a sort of fate which drives people into this arid path. I sometimes feel as though both Imagination and Humour fled away from the earth when a modern poet takes pen to compose Poetic Drama! The thing is a refuge for those to whom the gods have given a "talent for literature," and have stopped with that gift. The Poetic Drama flourishes in Anglo-Saxon Democracies. It lends itself to the babbling of extreme youth and to the pompous moralising of extreme middle-age.

The odious thing is an essentially modern creation; created, as it is, out of thin vapour, and moulded by melancholy rules of thumb. Drama was Religion to the Greeks, and in the old Elizabethan days great playwrights wrote great poetry.

I suppose if, by some fairy-miracle, *sheep*—the most modern of animals—were suddenly endowed with the privileges of culture, they would browse upon nothing else than Poetic Drama, from All Fools' Day to Candlemas.

But even Manfred cannot be blamed for this withering sterility, this dead-sea of ineptitude. There must be some form of literature found, loose and lax enough to express the Moral Idealism of the second-rate mind; and Poetic Drama lends itself beautifully to this.

Putting aside a few descriptive passages in "Childe Harold" and some score of superb lyrics sprinkled through the whole of the volume, what really is there in Byron at this hour—beyond the irresistible *idea* of his slashing and crimson-blooded figure—to arrest us and hold us, who can read over and over again Christopher Marlowe and John Keats? Very little—singularly little—almost nothing.

Nothing—except "Don Juan"! This indeed is something of a poem. This indeed has the old authentic fire about it and the sweet devilry of reckless youth.

How does one account for the power and authority over certain minds exercised by this surprising production? I do not think it is exactly the wit in it. The wit is often entirely superficial—a mere tricky playing with light resemblances and wordy jingles. I do not feel as though it were the humour in it; for Byron is not really a humorist at all. I think it is something deeper than the mere juxtaposition of burlesque-show jests with Sunday-evening sentimentality. I think it is the downright lashing out, left and right, up and down, of a powerful reckless spirit able "to lash out" for the mere pleasure of doing so. I think it is the pleasure we get from the spectacle of mere splendid energy and devil-may-care animal spirits let loose to run amuck as they please; while genius, like a lovely camp-follower tossed to and fro from hand to hand, throws a redeeming enchantment over the most ribald proceedings.

The people—I speak now of intelligent people—

who love Don Juan, are those who, while timid
and shrinking themselves, love to contemplate emphatic gestures, scandalous advances, Rabelaisian
foolings, clownish tricks; those who love to watch
the mad hurly-burly of life and see the resplendent fire-works go bang; those who love all huge
jests, vituperative cursings, moonlit philander-
ings, scoffing mockeries, honest scurrilities, great
rolling barrels of vulgarity, tuns and vats of ribaldry, and lovely, tender, gondola-songs upon
sleeping waters.

The pleasure which such persons derive from
Byron is the pleasure which the civilised Greeks
derived from Aristophanes, the pleasure of seeing everything which we are wont to treat reverently treated irreverently, the pleasure, most especially, of seeing the pompous great ones of the
world made to dance and skip like drunk puppets.
The literary temperament is so fatally inclined
to fall into a sort of æsthetic gravity, taking its
"philosophy" and its "art" with such portentous
self-respect, that it is extremely pleasant when a
reckless young Alcibiades of a Byron breaks into
the enchanted circle and clears the air with a few
resounding blasts from his profane bassoon.

What happens really in this pantomimic history
of Don Juan, with its huge nonchalance and au-
dacious cynicism, is the invasion of the literary
field by the godless rabble, the rabble who take
no stock of the preserves of art, and go picnicking
and rollicking and scattering their beer-bottles

and their orange-peel in the very glades of the immortals. It is in fact the invasion of Parnassus by a horde of most unmitigated proletarians. But these sweet scamps are led by a real lord, a lord who, like most lords, is ready to out-philistine the philistines and out-blaspheme the blasphemers.

Don Juan would be a hotch-potch of indecency and sentimentality, if it were not for the presence of genius there, of genius which, like a lovely flood of shining sunlight, irradiates the whole thing.

It is nonsense to talk of the "Byronic pose" either with regard to the outrageousness of his cynical wit or with regard to his sentimental Satanism.

Blasphemous wit and Satanic sentiment are the natural reactions of all healthy youthfulness in the presence of the sickening contrasts and diabolic ironies of life.

Such a mood is not by any means a sign of degeneracy. Byron was as far from being a degenerate as he was far from being a saint. It is a sign of sturdy sanity and vigorous strength.

Not to relish the gay brutality of Byron is an indication of something degenerate in ourselves. There is a certain type of person—perhaps the most prurient and disagreeable of all human animals—who is accustomed to indulge in a kind of holy leer of disgust when "brought up sharp" by the Aristophanic lapses of gay and graceless youth. Such a person's mind would be a fruitful study for Herr Freud; but the thought of its simmering cauldron of furtive naughtiness is not a pleasant thing to dwell on, for any but pathological philosophers.

After reading Don Juan one is compelled to recognise that Byron's mind must have been abnormally sane and sound. No one who jests quite at this rate could possibly be a bad man. The bad men—a word to the wise—are those from whose mouth the gay wantonness of the youth of the world is condemned as evil. Such persons ought to be sent for a rest-cure to Cairo or Morocco or Pekin.

The innocence of youth should be protected from a morality which is far more morbid than the maddest Dionysian revel.

It is, to confess it freely, not the satyrishness of Byron at all, but his hard brutality, which, for myself, I find difficult to enjoy.

I seem to require something more mellow, more ironical, more subtle, more humane, in my literature of irreverence. But no doubt this is a racial prejudice. Some obstinate drop of Latin—or, for all I know,—Carthaginian blood in me, makes me reluctant to give myself up to the tough, sane, sturdy brutality of your Anglo-Scot.

I can relish every word of Rabelais and I am not in the least dismayed by Heine's impishness, but I have always found Fielding's and Smollett's grosser scenes difficult mouthfuls to swallow.

They tell me there is a magnanimous generosity
and a large earthy sanity about these humorists.
But to me there is too much horse-play, too much
ruffianism and "bully-ragging." And something
of the same quality offends me in Byron. I lack
the steadiness of nerves to deal with a coarseness
which hits you across the head, much as the old
English clowns hit one another with strings of
sausages.

But because I suffer from this psychological
limitation; because I prefer Sterne to Fielding,
and Lamb to Dickens; I should condemn myself
as an un-catholic fanatic if I presumed to turn
my personal lack of youthful aplomb and gallant
insouciance into a grave artistic principle.

Live and let live! That must be our motto in
literary criticism as it is our motto in other things.
I am not going to let myself call Byron a black-
guard because of something a little hard and insensitive in him which happens to get upon my
own nerves. He was a fine genius. He wrote
noble verses. He has a beautiful face.

Women are, as a rule, less sensitive than men
in these matters of sexual brutality. It may be
that they have learned by bitter experience that
the Byrons of this world are not their worst
enemies. Or perhaps they feel towards them a
certain maternal tenderness; condoning, as mothers will do, with an understanding beyond the
comprehension of any neurotic critic, these rough--
nesses and insensitivenesses in their darlings.

Yes—let us leave the reputation of this great man, as far as his sexual lapses are concerned, to the commonsense and tact of women.

He was the kind of man that women naturally love. Perhaps we who criticise him are not altogether forgetful of that fact when we put our finger upon his aristocratic selfishness and his garish brilliance.

And perhaps the women are right.

It is pleasant at any rate to think so; pleasant to think that one's refined and gentle aunts, living noble lives in cathedral close and country vicarage, still regard this great wayward poet as a dear spoilt child and feel nothing of that instinctive suspicion of him which they feel toward so many "Byrons de nos jours."

When I recall the peculiarly tender look that came into the face of one beautiful old lady—a true "grande dame" of the old-fashioned generation—to whom I mentioned his name, and associate it with the look of weary distaste with which she listened to my discourses upon more modern and more subtle rebels, I am tempted to conclude that what womanly women really admire in a man is a certain energy of action, a certain drastic force, brilliance and hardness, which is the very opposite of the nervous sensitiveness and receptive weakness which is the characteristic of most of us men of letters. I am tempted to go so far as to maintain that a profound atavistic instinct in normal women makes them really contemptuous in their hearts of any purely æsthetic or intellectual type. They prefer poets who are also men of action and men of the world. They prefer poets who "when they think are children." It is not hardness or selfishness or brutality which really alarms them. It is intellect, it is subtlety, it is, above all, *irony*. Byron's unique achievement as a poet is to have flung into poetry the essential brutality and the essential sentiment of the typical male animal, and, in so far as he has done this, all his large carelessness, all his cheap and superficial rhetoric, all his scornful cynicism, cannot hide from us something primitive and appealing about him which harmonises well enough with his beautiful face and his dramatic career.

Perhaps, as a matter of fact, our literary point of view in these later days has been at once over-subtilized and underfed. Perhaps we have grown morbidly fastidious in the matter of delicacies of style, and shrinkingly averse to the slashing energy of hard-hitting, action-loving, self-assertive worldliness.

It may be so; and yet, I am not sure. I can find it in me to dally with the morbid and very modern fancy that, after all, Byron has been a good deal overrated; that, after all, when we forget his personality and think only of his actual work, he cannot be compared for a moment, as an original genius, with such persons—so much less appealing to the world-obsessed feminine mind—as William Blake or Paul Verlaine!

Yes; let the truth be blurted out—even though it be a confession causing suffering to one's pride —and the truth is that I, for one, though I can sit down and read Matthew Arnold and Remy de Gourmont and Paul Verlaine, for hours and hours, and though it is only because I have them all so thoroughly by heart that I don't read the great Odes of Keats any more, shall *never again,* not even for the space of a quarter of an hour, not even as a psychological experiment, turn over the pages of a volume of Byron's Poetical Works!

I think I discern what this reluctance means. It means that primarily and intrinsically what Byron did for the world was to bring into prominence and render beautiful and appealing a certain fierce rebellion against unctuous domesticity and solemn puritanism. His political propagandism of Liberty amounts to nothing now. What amounts to a great deal is that he magnificently and in an engaging, though somewhat brutal manner, broke the rules of a bourgeois social code.

As a meteoric rebel against the degrading servility of what we have come to call the "Nonconformist Conscience" Byron must always have his place in the tragically slow emancipation of the human spirit. The reluctance of an ordinary sensitive modern person, genuinely devoted to poetry, to spend any more time with Byron's verses than what those great familiar lyrics printed in all the anthologies exact, is merely a proof that he is not the poet that Shelley, for instance, is.

It is a melancholy commentary upon the "immortality of genius" and that "perishing only with the English language" of which conventional orators make so much, that the case should be so; but it is more important to be honest in the admission of our real feelings than to flatter the pride of the human race.

The world moves on. Manners, customs, habits, moralities, ideals, all change with changing of the times.

Style alone, the imaginative rendering in monumental words of the most personal secrets of our individuality, gives undying interest to what men write. Sappho and Catullus, Villon and Marlowe, are as vivid and fresh to-day as are Walter de la Mare or Edgar Lee Masters.

If Byron can only thrill us with half-a-dozen little songs his glory-loving ghost ought to be quite content.

To last in any form at all, as the generations pass and the face of the planet alters, is a great and lucky accident. To last so that men not only read you but love you when a century's dust covers your ashes is a high and royal privilege.

To leave a name which, whether men read your work or not, whether men love your memory or not, still conjures up an image of strength and joy and courage and beauty, is a great reward.

To leave a name which must be associated for

all time with the human struggle to free itself from false idealism and false morality is something beyond any reward. It is to have entered into the creative forces of Nature herself. It is to have become a fatality. It is to have merged your human, individual, personal voice with the voices of *the elements which are beyond the elements*. It is to have become an eternally living portion of that unutterable central flame which, though the smoke of its burning may roll back upon us and darken our path, is forever re-creating the world.

Much of Byron's work, while he lived, was of necessity destructive. Such destruction is part of the secret of life. In the world of moral ideals destroyers have their place side by side with creators. The destroyers of human thoughts are the winged ministers of the thoughts of Nature. Out of the graves of ideals something rises which is beyond any ideal. We are tossed to and fro, poets and men of action alike, by powers whose intentions are dark, by unknown forces whose faces no man may ever see. From darkness to darkness we stagger across a twilight-stage.

With no beginning that we can imagine, with no end that we can conceive, the mad procession moves forward. Only sometimes, at moments far, far apart, and in strange places, do we seem to catch the emergence, out of the storm in which we struggle, of something that no poet nor artist nor any other human voice has ever uttered, something that is as far beyond our virtue as it is beyond our evil, something terrible, beautiful, irrational, *mad*—which is the secret of the universe!

EMILY BRONTË

EMILY BRONTË

THE name of Emily Brontë—why does it produce in one's mind so strange and startling a feeling, unlike that produced by any other famous writer?

It is not easy to answer such a question. Certain great souls seem to gather to themselves, as their work accumulates its destined momentum in its voyage down the years, a power of arousing our imagination to issues that seem larger than those which can naturally be explained as proceeding inevitably from their tangible work.

Our imagination is roused and our deepest soul stirred by the mention of such names without any palpable accompaniment of logical analysis, without any well-weighed or rational justification.

Such names touch some response in us which goes deeper than our critical faculties, however desperately they may struggle. Instinct takes the place of reason; and our soul, as if answering the appeal of some translunar chord of subliminal music, vibrates in response to a mood that baffles all analysis.

We all know the work of Emily's sister Charlotte; we know it and can return to it at will, fathoming easily and at leisure the fine qualities of it and its impassioned and romantic effect upon us.

But though we may have read over and over again that one amazing story—"Wuthering Heights"—and that handful of unforgettable poems which are all that Emily Brontë has bequeathed to the world, which of us can say that the full significance of these things has been ransacked and combed out by our conscious reason; which of us can say that we understand to the full all the mysterious stir and ferment, all the far-reaching and magical reactions, which such things have produced within us?

Who can put into words the secret of this extraordinary girl? Who can define, in the suave and plausible language of academic culture, the flitting shadows thrown from deep to deep in the unfathomable genius of her vision?

Perhaps not since Sappho has there been such a person. Certainly she makes the ghosts of de Staël and Georges Sand, of Eliot and Mrs. Browning, look singularly homely and sentimental.

I am inclined to think that the huge mystery of Emily Brontë's power lies in the fact that she expresses in her work—just as the Lesbian did—the very soul of womanhood. It is not an easy thing to achieve, this. Women writers, clever and lively and subtle, abound in our time, as they have abounded in times past; but for some inscrutable reason they lack the demonic energy, the occult spiritual force, the instinctive fire, wherewith to give expression to the ultimate mystery of their own sex.

I am inclined to think that, of all poets, Walt Whitman is the only one who has drawn his reckless and chaotic inspiration straight from the uttermost spiritual depths of the sex-instincts of the male animal; and Emily Brontë has done for her sex what Walt Whitman did for his.

It is a strange and startling commentary upon the real significance of our sexual impulses that, when it comes to the final issue, it is not the beautiful ruffianism of a Byron, full of normal sex-instinct though that may be, or the eloquent sentiment of a Georges Sand, penetrated with passionate sensuality as that is, which really touch the indefinable secret. Emily Brontë, like Walt Whitman, sweeps us, by sheer force of inspired genius, into a realm where the mere *animalism* of sexuality, its voluptuousness, its lust, its lechery, are absolutely merged, lost, forgotten: fused by that burning flame of spiritual passion into something which is beyond all earthly desire.

Emily Brontë—and this is indicative of the difference between woman and man—goes even further than Walt Whitman in the spiritualising of this flame. In Whitman there is, as we all know, a vast mass of work, wherein, true and magical though it is, the earthly and bodily elements of the great passion are given enormous emphasis. It is only at rare moments—as happens with ordinary men in the normal experience of the world—that he is swept away beyond the reach of lust and voluptuousness. But Emily Brontë seems to dwell by natural predilection upon these high summits and in these unsounded depths. The flame of the passion in her burns at such quivering vibrant pressure that the fuel of it—the débris and rubble of our earth-instincts —is entirely absorbed and devoured. In her work the fire of life licks up, with its consuming tongue, every vestige of materiality in the thing upon which it feeds, and the lofty tremulous spires of its radiant burning ascend into the illimitable void.

It is of extraordinary interest, as a mere psychological phenomenon, to note the fact that when the passion of sex is driven forward by the flame of its conquering impulse beyond a certain point it becomes itself transmuted and loses the earthy texture of its original character.

Sex-passion when carried to a certain pitch of intensity loses its sexuality. It becomes pure flame; immaterial, unearthly, and with no sensual dross left in it.

It may even be said, by an enormous paradox, to become sexless. And this is precisely what one feels about the work of Emily Brontë. Sex-passion in her has been driven so far that it has come round "full circle" and has become sexless passion. It has become passion disembodied, passion absolute, passion divested of all human weakness. The "muddy vesture of decay" which "grossly closes in" our diviner principle has been burnt up and absorbed. It has been reduced to nothing; and in its place quivers up to heaven the clear white flame of the secret fountain of life.⟋

But there is more in the matter than that. Emily Brontë's genius, by its abandonment to the passion of which I have been speaking, does not only burn up and destroy all the elements of clay in what, so to speak, is above the earth and on its surface; but it also, burning downwards, destroys and annihilates all dubious and obscure materials which surround the original and primordial human will. Round and about this lonely and inalienable will it makes a scorched and blackened plain of ashes and cinders. Ambiguous feelings are turned to ashes there; and so are doubts, hesitations, timidities, trepidations, cowardices. The aboriginal will of man, of the unconquerable individual, stands alone there in the twilight, under the grey desolate rain of the outer spaces. Four-square it stands, upon adamantine foundations, and nothing in heaven or earth is able to shake it or disquiet it.

It is this isolation, in desolate and forlorn integrity, of the individual human will, which is the deepest element in Emily Brontë's genius. Upon this all depends, and to this all returns. Between the will and the spirit deep and strange nuptials are celebrated; and from the immortality of the spirit a certain breath of life passes over into the mortality of the will, drawing it up into the celestial and invisible region which is beyond chance and change.

From this abysmal fusion of the "creator spiritus" with the human will rises that adamantine courage with which Emily Brontë was able to face the jagged edges of that crushing wheel of destiny which the malign powers of nature drive remorselessly over our poor flesh and blood. The uttermost spirit of the universe became in this manner *her* spirit, and the integral identity of the soul within her breast hardened into an undying resistance to all that would undermine it.

Thus she was able to endure tragedy upon tragedy without flinching. Thus she was able to assert herself against the power of pain as one wrestling invincibly with an exhausted giant.

Calamity after calamity fell upon her house, and the stark desolation of those melancholy Yorkshire hills became a suitable and congruous background for the loneliness of her strange life; but against all the pain which came upon her, against all the aching pangs of remorseless fate, this indomitable girl held grimly to her supreme vision.

No poet, no novelist who has ever lived has been so profoundly affected by the conditions of his life as was this invincible woman. But the conditions of her life—the scenery of sombre terror which surrounded her—only touched and affected the outward colour and rhythm of her unique style. In her deepest soul, in the courage of her tremendous vision, she possessed something that was not bounded by Yorkshire hills, or any other hills; something that was inhuman, eternal and universal, something that was outside the power of both time and space.

By that singular and forlorn scenery—the scenery of the Yorkshire moors round about her home —she was, however, in the more flexible portion of her curious nature inveterately influenced. She does not precisely describe this scenery—not at any rate at any length—either in her poems or in "Wuthering Heights"; but it sank so deeply into her that whatever she wrote was affected by it and bears its desolate and imaginative imprint.

It is impossible to read Emily Brontë anywhere without being transported to those Yorkshire moors. One smells the smell of burning furze, one tastes the resinous breath of pine-trees, one feels beneath one's feet the tough fibrous stalks of the ling and the resistant stems and crumpled leaves of the bracken.

Dark against that pallid greenish light of a dead sunset, which is more than anything else characteristic of those unharvested fells, one can perceive always, as one reads her, the sombre form of some gigantic Scotch-fir stretching out its arms across the sky; while a flight of rooks, like enormous black leaves drifting on the wind, sail away into the sunset at our approach.

One is conscious, as one reads her, of lonely

marsh-pools turning empty faces towards a grey heaven, while drop by drop upon their murky waters the autumn rain falls, sadly, wearily, without aim or purpose.

And most of all is one made aware of the terrible desolation—desolation only rendered more desolate by the presence of humanity—of those half-ruined farm-houses, approached by windy paths or deep-cut lanes, which seem to rise, like huge fungoid things, here and there over that sad land.

It is difficult to conceive they have not sprung —these dwellings of these Earnshaws and Lintons—actually out of the very soil, in slow organic growth leading to slow organic decay. One cannot conceive the human hands which *built* them; any more than one can conceive the human hands which planted those sombre hedges which have now become so completely part of the scenery that one thinks of them as quite as aboriginal to the place as the pine-trees or the gorse-bushes.

Of all shapes of all trees I think the shape of an old and twisted thorn-tree harmonises best with one's impression of the "milieu" of Emily Brontë's single tragic story; a thorn-tree distorted by the wind blowing from one particular quarter, and with its trunk blackened and hollowed; and in the hollow of it a little pool of rain-water and a few dead soaked leaves.

The extraordinary thing is that she can produce these impressions incidentally, and, as it were, unconsciously. They are so blent with her spirit, these things, that they convey themselves to one's mind indirectly and through a medium far more subtle than any eloquent description.

I cannot think of Emily Brontë's work without thinking of a certain tree I once saw against a pallid sky. A long way from Yorkshire it was where I saw this tree, and there were no limestone boulders scattered at its feet; but something in the impression it produced upon me—an impression I shall not lightly forget—weaves itself strangely in with all I feel about her, so that the peculiar look of wintry boughs, sad and silent against a fading west, accompanied by that natural human longing of people who are tired to be safely buried under the friendly earth and "free among the dead," has come to be most indelibly and deeply associated with her tragic figure.

Those who know those Yorkshire moors know the mysterious way in which the quiet country lanes suddenly emerge upon wide and desolate expanses; know how they lead us on, past ruined factories and deserted quarries, up the barren slopes of forlorn hills; know how, as one sees in front of one the long white road vanishing over the hill-top and losing itself in the grey sky, there comes across one's mind a strange, sad, exquisite feeling unlike any other feeling in the world; and we who love Emily Brontë know that this is the feeling, the mood, the atmosphere of the soul, into which her writings throw us.

The power of her great single story, "Wuthering Heights," is in a primary sense the power of romance, and none can care for this book for whom romance means nothing.

What is romance? I think it is the instinctive recognition of a certain poetic glamour which an especial kind of grouping of persons and things —of persons and things seen under a particular light—is able to produce. It does not always accompany the expression of passionate emotion or the narration of thrilling incidents. These may arrest and entertain us when there is no romance, in my sense at any rate of that great word, overshadowing the picture.

I think this quality of romance can only be evoked when the background of the story is heavily laden with old, rich, dim, pathetic, human associations. I think it can only emerge when there is an implication of thickly mingled traditions, full of sombre and terrible and beautiful suggestiveness, stimulating to the imagination like a draught of heavy red wine. I think there must be, in a story of which the flavour has the true romantic magic, something darkly and inexplicably fatal. I think it is necessary that one should hear the rush of the flight of the Valkyries and the wailing upon the wind of the voices of the Eumenides.

Fate—in such a story—must assume a half-human, half-personal shape, and must brood, obscurely and sombrely, over the incidents and the characters.

The characters themselves must be swayed and dominated by Fate; and not only by Fate. They must be penetrated through and through by the scenery which surrounds them and by the traditions, old and dark and superstitious and malign, of some particular spot upon the earth's surface.

The scenery which is the background of a tale which has the true romantic quality must gather itself together and concentrate itself in some kind of symbolic unity; and this symbolic unity —wherein the various elements of grandeur and mystery are merged—must present itself as something almost personal and as a dynamic "motif" in the development of the plot.

There can be no romance without some sort of appeal to that long-inherited and atavistic feeling in ordinary human hearts which is responsive to the spell and influence of old, unhappy, lovely, ancient things; things faded and falling, but with the mellowness of the centuries upon their faces. In other words, nothing can be romantic which is *new*. Romance implies, above everything else, a long association with the human feelings of many generations. It implies an appeal to that background of our minds which is stirred to reciprocity by suggestions dealing with those old, dark, mysterious memories which belong, not so much to us as individuals, as to us as links in a great chain.

There are certain emotions in all of us which go much further and deeper than our mere personal feelings. Such are the emotions roused in us by contact with the mysterious forces of life and death and birth and the movements of the seasons; with the rising and setting of the sun, and the primordial labour of tilling the earth and gathering in the harvest. These things have been so long associated with our human hopes and fears, with the nerves and fibres of our inmost being, that any powerful presentment of them brings to the surface the accumulated feelings of hundreds of centuries.

New problems, new adventures, new social groupings, new philosophical catchwords, may all have their vivid and exciting interest. They cannot carry with them that sad, sweet breath of planetary romance which touches what might be called the "imagination of the race" in individual men and women.

"Wuthering Heights" is a great book, not only because of the intensity of the passions in it, but because these passions are penetrated so profoundly with the long, bitter, tragic, human associations of persons who have lived for generations upon the same spot and have behind them the weight of the burden of the sorrows of the dead.

It is a great book because the romance of it

emerges into undisturbed amplitude of space, and asserts itself in large, grand, primitive forms unfretted by teasing irrelevancies.

The genius of a romantic novelist—indeed, the genius of all writers primarily concerned with the mystery of human character—consists in letting the basic differences between man and man, between man and woman, rise up, unimpeded by frivolous detail, from the fathomless depths of life itself.

The solitude in which Emily Brontë lived, and the austere simplicity of her granite-moulded character, made it possible for her to envisage life in larger, simpler, less blurred outlines than most of us are able to do. Thus her art has something of that mysterious and awe-inspiring simplicity that characterises the work of Michelangelo or William Blake.

No one who has ever read "Wuthering Heights" can forget the place and the time when he read it. As I write its name now, every reader of this page will recall, with a sudden heavy sigh at the passing of youth, the moment when the sweet tragic power of its deadly genius first took him by the throat.

For me the shadow of an old bowed acacia-tree, held together by iron bands, was over the history of Heathcliff; but the forms and shapes of that mad drama gathered to themselves the lineaments of all my wildest dreams.

I can well remember, too, how on a certain long

straight road between Heathfield and Burwash, the eastern district of Sussex, my companion— the last of our English theologians—turned suddenly from his exposition of St. Thomas, and began quoting, as the white dust rose round us at the passing of a flock of sheep, the "vain are the thousand creeds—unutterably vain!" of that grand and absolute defiance, that last challenge of the unconquerable soul, which ends with the sublime cry to the eternal spark of godhead in us all—

"Thou, thou art being and breath;
And what thou art can never be destroyed!"

The art of Emily Brontë—if it can be called art, this spontaneous projection, in a shape rugged and savage, torn with the storms of fate, of her inmost identity—can be appreciated best if we realise with what skill we are plunged into the dark stream of the destiny of these people through the mediatory intervention of a comparative stranger. By this method, and also by the crafty manner in which she makes the old devoted servant of the house of Earnshaw utter a sort of Sophoclean commentary upon the events which take place, we are permitted to feel the magnitude of the thing in true relief and perspective.

By these devices we have borne in upon us, as in no other way could be done, the convincing sense which we require, to give weight and mass to the story, of the real continuity of life in those savage places.

By this method of narration we have the illusion of being suddenly initiated into a stream of events which are not merely imaginary. We have the illusion that these Earnshaws and Lintons are really, actually, palpably, undeniably, living—living somewhere, in their terrible isolation, as they have always lived—and that it is only by some lucky chance of casual discovery that we have been plunged into the mystery of their days.

One cannot help feeling aware, as we follow the story of Heathcliff, how Emily Brontë has torn and rent at her own soul in the creation of this appalling figure. Heathcliff, without father or mother, without even a Christian name, becomes for us a sort of personal embodiment of the suppressed fury of Emily Brontë's own soul. The cautious prudence and hypocritical reserves of the discreet world of timid, kindly, compromising human beings has got upon the nerves of this formidable girl, and, as she goes tearing and rending at all the masks which cover our loves and our hates, she seems to utter wild discordant cries, cries like those of some she-wolf rushing through the herd of normal human sheep.

Heathcliff and Cathy, what a pair they are! What terrifying lovers! They seem to have arisen from some remote unfathomed past of the world's earlier and less civilised passions. And yet, one occasionally catches, as one goes through the world, the Heathcliff look upon the face of a man and the Cathy look upon the face of a woman.

In a writer of less genius than Emily Brontë Heathcliff would never have found his match; would never have found his mate, his equal, his twin-soul.

It needed the imagination of one who had both Heathcliff and Cathy in her to dig them both out of the same granite rock, covered with yellow gorse and purple ling, and to hurl them into one another's arms.

From the moment when they inscribed their initials upon the walls of that melancholy room, to the moment when, with a howl like a madman, Heathcliff drags her from her grave, their affiliation is desperate and absolute.

This is a love which passes far beyond all sensuality, far beyond all voluptuous pleasure. They get little good of their love, these two— little solace and small comfort.

But one cannot conceive their wishing to change their lot with any happier lovers. They are what they are, and they are prepared to endure what fate shall send them.

When Cathy admits to the old servant that she intends to marry Linton because Heathcliff was unworthy of her and would drag her down, "I love Linton," she says—"but *I am* Heathcliff!" And this "*I am* Heathcliff" rings in our ears as the final challenge to a chaotic pluralistic world full of cynical disillusionment, of the desperate spirit of which Emily Brontë was made.

The wild madness of such love—passing the love of men and women—may seem to many readers the mere folly of an insane dream.

Emily Brontë—as she was bound to do—tosses them forth, that inhuman pair, upon the voyaging homeless wind; tosses them forth, free of their desperation, to wander at large, ghosts of their own undying passions, over the face of the rain-swept moors. But to most quiet and sceptical souls such an issue of the drama contradicts the laws of nature. To most patient slaves of destiny the end of the ashes of these fierce flames is to mingle placidly with the dark earth of those misty hills and find their release in nothing more tragic than the giving to the roots of the heather and the bracken a richer soil wherein to grow.

None of us know! None of us can ever know! It is enough that in this extraordinary story the wild strange link which once and again in the history of a generation binds so strangely two persons together, almost as though their association were the result of some æon-old everlasting Recurrence, is once more thrown into tragic relief and given the tender beauty of an austere imagination.

Not every one can feel the spell of Emily Brontë or care for her work. To some she must always remain too ungracious, too savage, too uncompromising. But for those who have come to care for her, she is a wonderful and a lovely figure; a figure whose full significance has not even yet been sounded, a figure with whom we must come more and more to associate that liberation of what we call love from the mere animalism of sexual passion, which we feel sometimes, and in our rarer moments, to be one of the richest triumphs of the spirit over the flesh.

It may be that Emily Brontë is right. It may be that a point can be reached—perhaps is already being reached in the lives of certain individuals—where sexual passion is thus surpassed and transcended by the burning of a flame more intense than any which lust can produce.

It may be that the human race, as time goes on, will follow closer and closer this ferocious and spiritual girl in tearing aside the compromises of our hesitating timidity and plunging into the ice-cold waters of passions so keen and translunar as to have become chaste. It may be so —and, on the other hand, it may be that the old sly earth-gods will hold their indelible sway over us until the "baseless fabric" of this vision leaves "not a rack behind"! In any case, for our present purpose, the reading of Emily Brontë strengthens us in our recognition that the only wisdom of life consists in leaving all the doors of the universe open.

Cursed be they who close any doors! Let that be our literary as it is our philsophical motto.

¶ Little have we gained from books, little from our passionate following in the steps of the great masters, if, after all, we only return once more to the narrow prejudices of our obstinate personal convictions.

From ourselves we cannot escape; but we can, unfortunately, hide ourselves from ourselves. We can hide ourselves "full-fathom-five" under our convictions and our principles. We can hide ourselves under our theories and our philosophies. It is only now and again, when, by some sudden devastating flash, some terrific burst of the thunder of the great gods, the real lineaments of what we are show up clearly for a moment in the dark mirror of our shaken consciousness.

It is well not to let the memory of those moments pass altogether away.

The reading of the great authors will have been a mere epicurean pastime if it has not made us recognise that what is important in our life is something that belongs more closely to us than any opinion we have inherited or any theory we have gained or any principle we have struggled for.

It will have been wasted if it has not made us recognise that in the moments when these outward things fall away, and the true self, beyond the power of these outward things, looks forth defiantly, tenderly, pitifully upon this huge strange world, there are intimations and whispers of something beyond all that the philosophers have ever dreamed, -hidden in the reservoirs of being and ready to touch us with their breath.

Our reading of these noble writings will have been no more than a gracious entertainment if we have not come to see that the enormous differences of their verdicts prove conclusively that no one theory, no one principle, can cover the tremendous field. But such reading will have had but a poor effect if because of this radical opposition in the voices reaching us we give up our interest in the great quest.

For it is upon our retaining our interest that the birthright of our humanity depends.

We shall never find what we seek; that is certain enough. We should be gods, not men, if we found it. But we should be less than men, and beasts—if we gave up the interest of the search, the tremulous vibrating interest, which, like little waves of ether, hovers over the cross-roads where all the great ways part.

Something outside ourselves drives us on to seek it—this evasive solution of a riddle that seems eternal—and when, weary with the effort of refusing this or the other premature solution, weary with the effort of suspending our judgment and standing erect at that parting of the ways, we long in our hearts to drift at leisure down one of the many soothing streams, it is only the knowledge that it is not our intrinsic inmost self that so collapses and yields up the high prerogative of doubt, but some lesser self in us, some tired superficial self, which keeps us back from that betrayal.

The courage with which Emily Brontë faced life, the equanimity with which she faced death, were in her case closely associated with the quiet desolate landscape which surrounded her.

As my American poet says, it is only in the country that we can look upon these fatal necessities and see them as they are. ⟋To be born and to die fall into their place when we are living where the smell of the earth can reach us.

There will always be a difference between those who come from the country and those who come from the town; and if a time ever arrives when the cities of men so cover the earth that there will be room no longer for any country-bred persons in our midst, something will in that hour pass away forever from art and literature, and, I suspect, from philosophy too. ⟋

For you cannot acquire this quality by any pleasant trips through picturesque scenery. It is either in you or it is not in you. You either have the slow, tenacious, humorous, patient, imaginative instincts of the country-born; or you have the smart, quick, clever, witty, fanciful, lively, receptive, caustic turn of mind of those bred in the great cities.

We all come to the town, "some in rags and some in jags and some in velvet gowns"; but the country-born always recognises the country-born, and there is a natural affinity between them.

I suspect that those who have behind them no local, provincial traditions will find it difficult to understand Emily Brontë.

She did not deal in elaborate description; but the earth-mould smells sweet, and the roots of the reeds of the pond-rushes show wavering and dim in the dark water, and "through the hawthorn blows the cold wind," and the white moon drifts over the sombre furze-covered hills; and all these things have passed into her style and have formed her style, and all these things are behind the tenacity with which she endures life, and behind the immense mysterious hope with which, while regarding all human creeds as "unutterably vain," she falls back so fiercely upon that "amor intellectualis Dei" which is the burning fire in her own soul.

—"Thou, thou art being and breath;
And what thou art can never be destroyed!"

JOSEPH CONRAD

JOSEPH CONRAD

THE inherent genius of a writer is usually a deeper and more ingrained thing than the obvious qualities for which the world commends him, and this is true in a very profound sense in Conrad's case.

We have only touched the fringe of the matter when we say that he has possessed himself of the secret of the sea more completely than any who write in English except Shakespeare and Swinburne.

We have only touched the fringe of the matter when we say he has sounded the ambiguous stops of that mysterious instrument, the heart of the white man exiled from his kind in the darkness of tropical solitudes.

These things are of immense interest, but the essence of Conrad's genius lies behind and beyond them; lies, in fact, if I am not mistaken, in a region where he has hardly a single rival.

This region is nothing more nor less than that strange margin of our minds, where memories gather which are deeper than memories, and where emotions float by and waver and hover and alight, like wild marsh-birds upon desolate sea-banks.

Conrad's genius, like the genius of all great writers who appeal to what is common and universal in us, to what unites the clever and the simple, the experienced and the inexperienced, is revealed in something much less accidental and arbitrary than the selection of any striking background, however significant, of ocean-mystery or jungle solitude.

The margin of the mind! Margin, mid-way between the known and the unknown! Do not the obscure images, called up by the feelings such words suggest, indicate far more intimately than any description of tropical rivers or Malay seas, the sort of spiritual atmosphere in which he darkly gives us many strange clues?

I seem to see this shadowy borderland, lying on the extreme "bank and shoal" of our human consciousness, as a place like that across which Childe Roland moved when he came to the "dark tower."

I seem to visualise it as a sort of dim marshland, full of waving reeds and deep black pools. I seem to see it as a place where patches of dead grass whistle in a melancholy wind, and where half-buried trunks of rain-soaked trees lift distorted and menacing arms.

Others may image it in a different way, perhaps with happier symbols; but the region I have in my mind, crossed by the obscure shapes of dimly beckoning memories, is common to us all.

You can, if you like, call this region of faint

rumours and misty intimations the proper sphere
and true hunting-ground of the new psychology.
As a matter of fact, psychologists rarely approach
it with any clairvoyant intelligence. And the
reason of that is, it is much further removed from
the material reactions of the nerves and the
senses than the favourite soil of these people's
explorations.

So thin and shadowy indeed is the link between
the vague feelings which flit to and fro in this
region and any actual sensual impression, that it
almost seems as though this subconscious borderland were in contact with some animistic inner
world—not exactly a supernatural world, but a
world removed several stages back from the material one wherein our nerves and our senses
function; a world wherein we might be permitted
to fancy the platonic archetypes dwelling,
archetypes of all material forms; or, if you will,
the inherent "souls" of such forms, living their
own strange inner life upon a plane of existence
beyond our rational apprehension.

It is certain that there are many moments in
the most naïve people's experience when, as they
walk in solitude along some common highway, the
shape of a certain tree or the look of a certain
hovel, or the indescribable melancholy of a certain
road-side pool, or the way the light happens to fall
upon a heap of dead leaves, or the particular manner in which some knotted and twisted root pro-
trudes itself from the bank, awakes quite sud-

denly, in this margin of the mind of which I speak, the strangest and subtlest feelings.

It is as though something in the material thing before us—some inexplicable "soul" of the inanimate—rushed forth to meet our soul, as if it had been *waiting* for us for long, long years.

I am moving, in this matter of the essential secret of Conrad, through a vague and obscure twilight. It is not easy to express these things; but what I have in my thoughts is certainly no mere fancy of mystical idealism, but a quite definite and actual experience, or series of experiences, in the "great valley" of the mind.

When Almayer, for instance, stares hopelessly and blankly at a floating log in his gloomy river; when the honest fellow in "Chance" who is relating the story watches the mud of the road outside the hotel where Captain Anthony and Flora de Barral are making their desperate arrangements; you get the sort of subconscious "expectancy" which is part of this strange phenomenon, and that curious sudden thrill, "I have been here before! I have seen and heard all this before!" which gives to so many scenes in Conrad that undertone of unfathomable mystery which is so true an aspect of life.

So often are we conscious of it as we read him! We are conscious of it—to give another instance —when Heyst and Lena are talking together in the loneliness of their island of escape, before the unseen enemies descend on them.

The same insight in him and the same extra-ordinary power of making words malleable to his purpose in dealing with these hidden things may be remarked in all those scenes in his books where men and women are drawn together by love.

Conrad takes no interest in social problems. His interest is only stirred by what is permanent and undying in the relations between men and women. These extraordinary scenes, where Gould and his wife, where Antonia Avellanos and her friend, where Willem and Aissa, where Nina and her Malay chief, where Flora and Anthony, Heyst and Lena, and many other lovers, meet and peer into the secret depths of one another's beings, are all scenes possessing that universal human element which no change or reform or revolution or improvement can touch or alter.

Without any theory about their "emancipation," Conrad has achieved for women, in these stories of his, an extraordinary triumph. Well does he name his latest book "Victory." The victory of women over force, over cunning, over stupidity, over brutality, is one of the main threads running through all his work.

And what women they are! I do not recall any that resemble them in all literature.

Less passionate than the women of Dostoievsky, less sentimental than the women of Balzac, less sensual than the women of de Maupassant, Conrad's women have a quality entirely their own, a quality which holds us spell-bound. It is much easier to feel this quality than to describe it. Something of the same element—and it is a thing the positivity of which we have to search out among many crafty negations—may be discerned in some of the women of Shakespeare and, in a lesser degree, in one or two of the young girls in the stories of Turgenief.

I think the secret of it is to be looked for in the amazing poise and self-possession of these women; a self-possession which is indicated in their moments of withdrawn and reserved silence.

They seem at these times to sink down into the very depths of their femininity, into the depths of some strange sex-secret of which they are themselves only dreamily conscious.

They seem to withdraw themselves from their own love, from their own drama, from their own personality, and to lie back upon life, upon the universal mystery of life and womanhood. This they do without, it might seem, knowing what they are doing.

They all, in these strange world-deep silences of theirs, carry upon their intent and sybilline faces something of that mysterious charm—expectant, consecrated, and holy—which the early painters have caught the shadow of in their pictures of the Annunciation.

There is something about them which makes us vaguely dream of the far-distant youth of the world; something that recalls the symbolic and poetic figures of Biblical and Mythological legend.

They tease and baffle us with the mystery of their emotions, with the magical and evasive depths of the feminine secret in them. They make us think of Rebecca at the well and Ruth in the corn-field; of Andromache on the walls of Troy and of Calypso, Brunhilda, Gwenevere, Iphigeneia, Medea, Salome, Lilith.

And all this is achieved by the most subtle and yet by the most simple means. It is brought about partly by an art of description which is unique among English novelists, an art of description which by a few fastidious and delicate touches can make the bodily appearance indicative of the hidden soul; and partly by the cunning insertion of long, treacherous, pregnant silences which reveal in some occult indirect manner the very integral quality of the soul thus betrayed.

The more voluble women of other novelists seem, even while they are expressing their most violent emotions, rather to blur and confuse the mysterious depths of their sex-life than to reveal it. Conrad's women, in a few broken words, in a stammered sentence, in a significant silence, have the power of revealing something more than the tragic emotion of one person. They have the power of revealing what might be called the sub-liminal sex-consciousness of the race itself. They have the power of merging the individuality of the particular speaker into something deeper and larger and wider, into something univer-sal.

Reserve is the grand device by means of which this subconscious element is made evident, is hinted at and glimpsed so magically. When everything is expressed, nothing is expressed. A look, a gesture, a sigh, a whisper, in Conrad, is more significant of the ocean-deep mysteries of the soul than pages of eloquent psychology.

The deepest psychology—that is what one comes at last to feel—can only be expressed indirectly and by means of movements, pictures, symbols, signs. It can be revealed in words; but the words revealing it must ostensibly be concerned with something else.

For it is with the deepest things in human life as with the deepest things in nature; their way must be prepared for them, the mind must be alert to receive them, but they must not be snatched at in any direct attack. They will come; suddenly, sharply, crushingly, or softly as feathers on the wind; but they will only come if we turn away our faces. They will only come if we treat them with the reverence with which the ancients treated the mysterious fates, calling them "The Eumenides"; or the ultimate secret of the universe, calling it Demogorgon; with the reverence which wears the mask of superstition.

The reason why Conrad holds us all—old and young, subtle and simple—with so irresistible a spell, is because he has a clairvoyant intuition for the things which make up the hidden substratum of all our human days—the things which cause us those moments of sharp sweet happiness which come and go on sudden mysterious wings.

His style is a rare achievement; and it is so because he treats the language he uses with such scrupulous and austere reverence.

The mere fact that English was a foreign tongue to him seems to have intensified this quality; as though the hardness and steepness of its challenge forced the latent scholarship in him to stiffen its fibres to encounter it.

When he writes of ships he does not tease us with the pedantry of technical terms. He undertakes the much more human and the much more difficult task of conveying to us the thousand and one vague and delicate associations which bind the souls of seafarers to the vessels that carry them.

His fine imaginative mind—loving with a large receptive wisdom all the quaint idiosyncrasy of lonely and reserved people—naturally turns with a certain scornful contempt from modern steamships. That bastard romance, full of vulgar acclamation over mechanical achievements, which makes so much of the mere size and speed of a trans-Atlantic liner, is waved aside contemptuously by Conrad.

Like all great imaginative spirits, he realizes that for any inanimate object to wear the rich magic of the deep poetic things, it is necessary for it to have existed in the world long enough to have become intimately associated with the hopes and fears, the fancies and terrors, of many generations.

It is simply and solely their newness to human experience which makes it impossible for any of these modern inventions, however striking and sensational, to affcct our imagination with the sense of intrinsic beauty in the way a sailing-ship does.

And it is not only—as one soon comes to feel in reading Conrad—that these old-fashioned ships, with their legendary associations carrying one back over the centuries, are beautiful in themselves. They diffuse the beauty of their identity through every detail of the lives of those who are connected with them. They bring the mystery and terror of the sea into every harbour where they anchor and into every port.

No great modern landing-stage for huge liners, from which the feverish crowds of fashionable tourists or bewildered immigrants disembark, can compare in poetic and imaginative suggestiveness, with any ramshackle dock, east or west, where brigs and schooners and trawlers put in; and real sailors—sailors who *sail* their ships—enter the little smoky taverns or drift homeward down the narrow streets.

The shallow, popular, journalistic writers whose vulgar superficial minds are impressed by the mere portentousness of machinery, are only making once more the old familiar blunder of mistaking size for dignity, and brutal energy for noble strength.

Conrad has done well in his treatment of ships and sailors to reduce these startling modern inventions to their proper place of emotional insignificance compared with the true seafaring tradition. What one thinks of when any allusion is made to a ship in Conrad's works is always a sailing-ship, a merchant ship, a ship about which from the very beginning there is something human, mellow, rich, traditional, idiosyncratic, characteristic, full of imaginative wistfulness and with an integral soul.

One always feels that a ship in Conrad has a *figure-head;* and is it possible to imagine a White Star liner, or a North German Lloyd steamer, with such an honourable and beautiful adornment? Liners are things entirely without souls. One only knows them apart by their paint, their tonnage, or the name of the particular set of financiers who monopolise them.

"Floating hotels" is the proud and inspiring term with which the awed journalistic mind contemplates these wonders.

Well! In Conrad's books we are not teased with "floating hotels." If a certain type of machine-loving person derives satisfaction from thinking how wonderfully these monsters have conquered the sea, let it be remembered that the sea has its *poetic* revenge upon them by abso-

347

lutely concealing from those who travel in this way the real magic of its secret.

No one knows the sea—that, at any rate, Conrad makes quite clear—who has not voyaged over its waves in a sailing vessel.

Of the books which Mr. Conrad has so far written—one hopes that for many years each new Spring will bring a new work from his pen—my own favourites are "Chance" and "Lord Jim," and, after those two, "Victory."

I think the figure of Flora de Barral in "Chance" is one of the most arresting figures in all fiction. I cannot get that girl out of my mind. Her pale flesh, her peculiarly dark-tinted blue eyes, her white cheeks and scarlet mouth; above all, her broken pride, her deep humiliation, her shadowy and abysmal reserve—haunt me like a figure seen and loved in some previous incarnation.

I like to fancy that in the case of Flora, as in the case of Antonia and Nina and Lena and Aissa, Conrad has been enabled to convey, by means of an art far subtler than appears on the surface, a strange revival, in the case of every person who reads the book, of the intangible memories of the sweetness and mystery of such a person's first love.

I believe half the secret of this wonderful art of his, by which we are thus reminded of our first love, is the absolute elimination of the *sensual* from these evasive portraits. And not only of the sensual; of the sentimental as well. In the average popular books about love we have nowadays a sickening revel of sentimentality. Then again, as opposed to this vulgar sentimentality, with its false idealisation of women, we have the realistic sensuality of the younger cleverer writers playing upon every kind of neurotic obsession. I think the greatness of Conrad is to be found in the fact that he refuses to sacrifice the mysterious truth of passion either to sentiment or to sensuality. He keeps this great clear well of natural human feeling free from both these turbid and morbid streams.

A very curious psychological blunder made by many of our younger writers is the attributing to women of the particular kind of sex emotion which belongs essentially to men, an emotion penetrated by lust and darkened by feverish restlessness. From this blunder Conrad is most strangely free. His women love like women, not like vicious boys with the faces of women. They love like women and they hate like women; and they are most especially and most entirely womanlike in the extreme difficulty they evidently always experience in the defining with any clearness—even to themselves—of their own emotions.

It is just this mysterious inability to define their own emotions which renders women at once so annoying and so attractive; and the mere presence of something in them which refuses defini-

tion is a proof that they are beyond both sentiment and sensuality. For sentiment and sensuality lend themselves very willingly to the most
exact and logical analysis. Sensualists love nothing better than the epicurean pleasure of dissect-
ing their own emotions as soon as they are once assured of a discreet and sympathetic listener. The
same is doubly true of sentimentalists. The
women of Conrad—like the women of Shakespeare—while they may be garrulous enough and
witty enough on other matters, grow tongue-tied
and dumb when their great emotions call for overt
expression.

It seems to me quite a natural thing that the
writer who, of all others, has caught the mystery
of ships should be the writer who, of all moderns,
has caught the mystery of women. Women are
very like ships: ships sailing over waters of whose
depths they themselves know nothing; ships upon
whose masts strange wild birds—thoughts wandering from island to island of remote enchantment—settle for a moment and then fly off forever; ships that can ride the maddest and most
tragical storms in safety; ships that some hidden
rock, unmarked on any earthly chart, may sink
to the bottom without warning and without
mercy!

Conrad reveals to us the significant fact that
what the deepest love of women suffers from—
the kind of storm which shakes it and troubles it
—is not sensuality of any sort but a species

of blind and fatal fury, hardly conscious of any definite cause, but directed desperately and passionately against the very object of this love itself. Conrad seems to indicate, if I read him correctly, that this mad, wild, desperate fury with which women hurl themselves against what they love best in a blind desire to hurt it, is nothing less than a savage protest against that deep and inviolable gulf which isolates every human being from every other human being.

'Such a gulf men—in a measure—pass, or dream they pass, on the swift torrent of animal desire; but women are more clairvoyant in these things, and their love being more diffused, and, in a sense, more spiritual, is not so easily satisfied by mere physical possession.

They want to possess more. They want to possess body, soul and spirit. They want to share every thought of their beloved, every instinct, every wish, every ambition, every vision, every remotest dream.

That they are forbidden this complete reciprocity by a profound law of nature excites their savage fury, and they blindly wreak their anger upon the innocent cause of their bewildered unhappiness.

It is their maternal instinct which thus desires to take complete and absolute possession of the object of their love. The maternal instinct is always—as Conrad makes quite clear—at the bottom of the love-passion in the most normal types

351

of women; and the maternal instinct is driven on by a mad relentless force to seek to destroy every vestige of separate independence, bodily, mental or spiritual, in the person it pursues./

Conrad shows with extraordinary subtlety how this basic craving in women, resulting in this irrational and, apparently, inexplicable anger, is invariably driven to cover its tracks by every kind of cunning subterfuge.

This loving anger of women will blaze up into flame at a thousand quite trivial causes. It may take the form of jealousy; but it is in reality much deeper than jealousy. It may take the form of protest against man's stupidity, man's greed, man's vanity, man's lust, man's thick-skinned selfishness; but it is in reality a protest against the law of nature which makes it impossible for a woman to share this stupidity, this vanity, this lust, this greed, and which holds her so cruelly confined to a selfishness which is her own and quite different from the selfishness of man.

One would only have to carry the psychological imagination of Conrad a very little further to recognise the fact that while man is inherently and completely satisfied with the difference between man and woman; satisfied with it and deriving his most thrilling pleasure from it; woman is always feverishly and frantically endeavouring to overcome and overreach this difference, endeavouring, in fact, to feel her way into every nerve and fibre of man's sensibility, so that he shall have nothing left that is a secret from her. That he should have any such secrets—that such secrets should be an inalienable and inevitable part of his essential difference from herself—excites in her unmitigated fury; and this is the hidden cause of those mysterious outbursts of apparently quite irrational anger which have fallen upon all lovers of women since the beginning of the world.

Man wishes woman to remain different from himself. It interests him that she should be different. He loves her for being different. His sensuality and his sentiment feed upon this difference and delight to accentuate it. Women seem in some subtle way to resent the division of the race into two sexes and to be always endeavouring to get rid of this division by possessing themselves of every thought and feeling and mood and gesture of the man they love. And when confronted by the impassable gulf, which love itself is incapable of bridging, a blind mad anger, like the anger of a creative deity balked of his purpose, possesses them body and soul.

Mr. Wilson Follet in his superb brochure upon Conrad, written in a manner so profoundly influenced by Henry James that as one reads it one feels that Henry James himself, writing upon Conrad, could not possibly have done better, lays great stress upon Conrad's complicated and elaborate manner of building up his stories.

Mr. Follet points out, for instance, how in "Chance" we have one layer of personal receptivity after another; each one, as in a sort of rich palimpsest of overlaid impressions, making the material under our hands thicker, fuller, more significant, more symbolic, more underscored and overscored with interesting personal values.

This is perfectly true, and it is a fine arresting method and worthy of all attention.

But for myself I am not in the least ashamed to say that I prefer the art of Conrad at those moments when the narrative becomes quite direct and when there is no waylaying medium, however interesting, between our magnetised minds and the clear straightforward story.

I like his manner best, and I do not scruple to admit it, when his Almayers and Ninas, his Anthonys and Floras, his Heysts and Lenas, are brought face to face in clear uncomplicated visualisation. I think he is always at his best when two passionate and troubled natures—not necessarily those of a man and woman; sometimes those of a man and man, like Lingard and Willem—are brought together in direct and tragic conflict. At such moments as these we get that true authentic thrill of immemorial romance—romance as old as the first stories ever told or sung—of the encounter of protagonist and antagonist; and from the hidden depths of life rise up, clear and terrible and strong, the austere voices of the adamantine fates.

But though he is at his greatest in these direct uncomplicated passionate scenes, I am quite at one with Mr. Wilson Follet in treasuring up as of incalculable value in the final effect of his art all those elaborate by-issues and thickly woven implications which give to the main threads of his dramas so rich, so suggestive, so mellow a background.

Except for a few insignificant passages when that sly old mariner Marlowe, of whom Conrad seems perhaps unduly fond, lights his pipe and passes the beer and utters breezy and bracing sentiments, I can enjoy with unmitigated delight all the convolutions and overlappings of his inverted method of narration—of those rambling "advances," as Mr. Follet calls them, to already consummated "conclusions." In the few occasional passages where Marlowe assumes a moralising tone and becomes bracing and strenuous I fancy I detect the influence of certain muscular, healthy-minded, worthy men, among our modern writers, who I daresay appeal to the Slavonic soul of this great Pole as something quite wonderfully and pathetically English.

With these exceptions I am unwavering in my adherence to his curious and intricate method. I love the way he pours his main narrative, like so much fruity port-wine, first through the sieve of one quaint person's mind and then of another; each one adding some new flavour, some new vein of body or bouquet or taste, to the original stream, until it becomes thick with all the juices of all the living fermentations in the world.

SUSPENDED JUDGMENTS

I think the pleasure I derive from Conrad is largely due to the fact that while he liberates us with a magnificent jerk from the tiresome monotonous sedentary life of ordinary civilised people, he does so without assuming that banal and bullying air of the adventurous swashbuckler, which is so exhausting; without letting his intellectual interests be swamped by these physiological violences and by these wanderings into savage regions.

Most of our English writers, so it appears to me, who leave the quiet haunts of unadventurous people and set off for remote continents, leave behind them, when they embark, all the fineness and subtlety of their intelligence, and become drastic and crude and journalistic and vulgar. They pile up local colour till your brain reels, and they assume a sort of man-of-the-wide-world "knowingness" which is extremely unpleasant.

Conrad may follow his tropical rivers into the dim dark heart of his Malay jungles, but he never forgets to carry with him his sensitiveness, his metaphysical subtlety, his delicate and elaborate art.

What gives one such extraordinary pleasure in his books is the fact that while he is writing of frontier-explorers and backwoods-peddlers, of ivory-traffickers and marooned seafarers, he never forgets that he is a philosopher and a psychologist.

This is the kind of writer one has been secretly

craving for, for years and years; a writer who can liberate us from the outworn restrictions of civilised life, a writer who can initiate us into all the magical mysteries of dark continents and secret southern islands, without teasing us with the harsh sterilities of a brain devoid of all finer feelings.

This is the sort of writer one hardly dared to hope could ever appear; a writer capable of describing sheer physical beauty and savage elemental strength while remaining a subtle European philosopher. I suppose it would be impossible for a writer of English blood to attain such a distinction—to be as crafty as a Henry James, moving on velvety feline paws through the drawing-rooms of London and the gardens of Paris; and yet to be leading us through the shadows of primordial forests, cheek by jowl with monstrous idolatries and heathen passions.

But what renders the work of Conrad so extraordinarily rich in human value is not only that he can remain a philosopher in the deserted outposts of South-Pacific Islands, but that he can remain a tender and mellow lover of the innumerable little things, little stray memories and associations, which bind every wanderer from Europe, however far he may voyage, to the familiar places he has left behind in the land of his birth.

Here he is a true Slav, a true continental European. Here he is rather Russian—or French, shall I say—than an adopted child of Britain; for the colonising instinct of the British race renders its sentimental devotion to the country of its engendering less burdened with the passionate intimate sorrows of the exile than the nostalgia of the other races.

Conrad has indeed to a very high degree that tender imaginative feeling for the little casual associations of a person's birthplace in town or country, which seems to be a peculiar inheritance of the Slavonic and Latin races, and which for all their sentimental play with the word "home" is not really natural to the tougher-minded Englishman or Scotchman.

One is conscious, all the while one reads of these luckless wanderers in forlorn places, of the very smell of the lanes and the very look of the fields and the actual sounds and stir of the quaint narrow streets and the warm interiors of little friendly taverns by wharfside and by harbourmouth, of the far-off European homes where these people were born.

No modern English writer, except the great, the unequalled Mr. Hardy, has the power which Conrad has, of conveying to the mind that close indescribable intimacy between humanity's passions and the little inanimate things which have surrounded us from childhood.

Conrad can convey this "home-feeling," this warm secure turning of the human animal to the lair which it has made for itself, even into the heart of the tempestuous ocean. He can give

us that curious half-psychic and half-physical
thrill of being in mellow harmony with our material surroundings, even in the little cabin of
some weather-battered captain of a storm-tossed
merchant-ship; and not a sailor, in his books, and
not a single ship in which his sailors voyage, but
has a sort of dim background of long rests from
toil in ancient harbour back-waters where the
cobblestones on the wharf-edge are thick with
weeds and moss, and where the November rain
beats mistily and greyly, as in Russia and in
England, upon the tiled roofs and the lamplit
streets.

It is nothing less than just this human imagination in him, brooding so carefully over the
intimate and sacred relations between our frail
mortality and its material surroundings, that
makes it possible for him to treat with such delicate reverence the ways and customs, the usages
and legendary pieties, of the various half-savage
tribes among whom his exiled Europeans wander.

I am not ashamed to admit that I find the emphasis laid in Conrad's books upon sheer physical
violence a little hurtful to my pleasure in reading
him. What is the cause of this mania for violence? It surely detracts from the charm of his
writing, and it is difficult to see, from any psychological point of view, where the artistic necessity
of it lies. I do not feel that the thing is an erotic
perversion. There is a downright brutality in

it which militates against any subtly voluptuous explanation. Can it be that he is simply and solely appealing here to what he is led to believe is the taste of his Anglo-Saxon readers? No—that, surely, were unworthy of him. That surely must be considered unthinkable! Is it that, being himself of an abnormally nervous and sensitive temperament, he forces himself by a kind of intellectual asceticism to rush upon the pricks of a physiological brutality as the sort of penance a conscientious writer has to pay; has to pay to the merciless cruelty of truth?

No; that does not seem to me quite to cover the case. It is an obscure matter, and I think, in our search for the true solution, we may easily stumble upon very interesting and deeply hidden aspects, not only of Conrad's temperament, but of the temperament of a great many artists and scholars. In all artistic work there is so much that goes on in the darkness, so much secret exploitation of the hidden forces of one's nature, that it is extremely difficult to put one's finger upon the real cause of any particular flaming outbreak.

I have observed this sudden and tempestuous "obsession of violence" in the moods of certain highly-strung and exquisitely wrought-upon women; and it is possible that the heavy, dull, thick, self-complacent brutality of Nature and average human nature is itself so hurting and rending a thing to the poignant susceptibilities of

a noble spirit, that, out of a kind of desperate revenge upon it, it goes to the extreme limit itself
and, so to speak, out-Tamberlaines Tamberlaine
in bloody massacre.

What, however, really arrests and holds us in
Conrad is not the melodramatic violence of these
tempestuous scenes, but the remote psychological
impulses at work behind them.

Where, in my opinion, he is supremely great,
apart from his world-deep revelations of direct
human feeling, is in his imaginative fusion of
some particular spiritual or material motif
through the whole fabric of a story.

Thus the desolate "hope against hope" of poor
Almayer becomes a thing of almost bodily presence in that book; a thing built up, fragment by
fragment, piece by piece, out of the very forlornness of his surroundings, out of the débris and
litter of his half-ruined dwelling, out of the rot-
ting branches of the dim misty forest, out of the
stakes and piles of his broken-down wharf, out
of the livid mud of his melancholy river.

Thus the sombre and tragic philosophy of
Heyst's father—that fatalism which is beyond
hope and beyond pity—overshadows, like a
ghastly image of doom seated upon a remote
throne in the chill twilight of some far Ultima
Thule, all the events, so curious, so ironic, so
devastating, which happen to his lethargic and
phlegmatic son. It is this imaginative element in
his work which, in the final issue, really and truly

counts. For it is a matter of small significance whether the scene of a writer's choice be the uplands of Wessex or the jungles of the tropics, as long as that ironic and passionate consciousness of the astounding drama—of men and women being the baffled and broken things they are—rises into unmitigated relief and holds us spell-bound. And beyond and above this overshadowing in his stories of man's fate by some particular burden of symbolic implication, Conrad flings the passionate flame of his imagination into the words of every single sentence.

That is why his style is a thing of such curious attraction. That is why it has such sudden surprises for us, such sharp revelations, such rare undertones. That is why after reading Conrad it is difficult to return to the younger English writers of the realistic school.

One enjoys, in savouring the style of Conrad, a delicious ravishing thrill in the mere look of the words, as we see them so carefully, so scrupulously laid side by side, each with its own burden of intellectual perfume, like precious vases full of incense on the steps of a marble altar. To write as delicately, as laboriously, as exquisitely as this, upon the stark, rough, raw materials of murder and suicide and madness and avarice and terror and desperation; to write as elaborately and richly as this, when dealing with the wild secrets of drunken sailors and the mad revenges of half-bestial savages, is great mastery. And it is more than mastery. It is a spiritual triumph. It is a proof that the soul of man, confronting the worst terrors that can come upon it, is still capable of turning all things into grist for its mill.

For Conrad, while he finds nothing except meaningless and purposeless chance in the ways of Nature, is inspired by a splendid tenacity of courage in resisting any desperate betrayal of human joy.

Like that amazing character in "Lord Jim," who collects butterflies and keeps his affections simple and sweet in the presence of tragedy upon tragedy, he seems to indicate to us, in these stark and woeful stories, that since there is no help in heaven or earth for the persecuted child of man, it is the more necessary that in defiance of the elements, in defiance of chance, yea! in defiance of fate itself, man should sink into his own soul and find in the strength of his own isolated and exiled spirit a courage equal to all that can be laid upon it. Even this would be but a barren comfort if what we found when we sank down thus into ourselves were courage, and courage only. What one comes to feel from the reading of Conrad is that there is nothing in the world which has enduring value—nothing in the world which gives the mad convoluted hurly-burly any kind of dignity or beauty—except only love. And love like this, which is the forlorn hope of the race, is as far from lust as it is far from sentiment or indolent pity. It is the "high old Roman virtue." It is the spirit of comradeship defiant still, under the tottering pillars of a shaken earth.

"Man must abide his going hence, even as his coming hither.. Ripeness is all."

.   .   .   .

"Upon such sacrifices, my Cordelia,
The gods themselves throw incense."

HENRY JAMES

HENRY JAMES

THE greatness of a writer can be estimated by the gap which would yawn in our interpretation of life if we conceived for a moment the expurgation of his whole body of work from our minds.

And what a hole there would be, what a jagged, bleeding, horrible hole, if the books of Henry James—and it is a continuous satisfaction to a lover of literature to think how many of them there are—were flung upon oblivion.

How often as the days of our life drift by, growing constantly more crowded and difficult, do we find ourselves exclaiming, "Only Henry James could describe this! What a situation for Henry James!"

The man has come to get himself associated more—oh, far more—than any other writer of our day, with the actual stir and pressure of environment in which we habitually move. I say "we." By this I mean the great mass of educated people in Europe, England and America. Of the "Masses," as they are called; of the persons by whose labours our middle-class and upper-class life, with its comparative leisure and comfort, is made possible, Henry James has little to say.

SUSPENDED JUDGMENTS

He never or very rarely deals, as Balzac and
de Maupassant and Hardy do, with the farmers
and farm labourers on the land. He never or
very rarely deals with the slums of our great
cities, as did Dickens and Victor Hugo. He confines himself more rigorously than any other novelist of equal power to the ways and manners and
entanglements of people who are "in society," or
who could be in society if they wanted to, or are
on the verge and edge of society.

When the "lower classes"—I use the convenient term; doubtless in the eyes of celestial
hierarchies the situation is reversed—enter at all
into the circle of Mr. James' consciousness, they
enter, either as interesting anarchists, like young
Hyacinth, or as servants. Servants—especially
butlers and valets—play a considerable part, and
so do poor relations and impecunious dependents.

For these latter of both sexes the great urbane
author has a peculiar and tender consideration.
It is not in the least that he is snobbish. Of that
personal uneasiness in the presence of worldly
greatness so unpleasantly prominent in Thackeray there is absolutely nothing. It is only that,
conscientious artist as he is, he is unwilling to
risk any sort of æsthetic "faux pas" by adventur-
ing outside his natural sphere, the sphere to
which he was born. Of gentlefolk who are poor
and of artists and writers who are poor there
are innumerable types strewn throughout his
works.

It were quite unfair to say that he only writes of the idle rich. What he actually does is—as I have said—to write of our upper middle class life, with its aristocrats at the top and its luckless governesses and tutors and journalists at the bottom; as we, who are in it, know it and feel it and suffer from it, every day of our existence.

And, curiously enough, this is a very rare achievement. Of course there is a horde of second-rate writers, cheap hucksters of glittering sentimental wares for the half-educated, who write voluminously of the life of which I am speaking. There are others, more cultivated but endowed with less vivacity, who crowd their pages with grave personages from what are called "liberal professions." But the more imaginative writers of our day are not to be looked for in the drawing-rooms of their wives and daughters.

Mr. Hardy confines himself to the meadows of Blackmoor and the highways and hedges of Dorset Uplands. Mr. Conrad sails down tropical rivers and among the islands of Southern seas. The American Mr. Dreiser ploughs his earth-upheaving path through the workshops of Chicago and the warehouses of Manhattan.

It is Henry James and Henry James alone, who unravels for us the tangled skein of our actual normal-abnormal life, as the destinies twist

and knot it in the civilised chambers of our natural sojourning.

The curious thing is that even among our
younger and most modern writers, no one, except John Galsworthy, really deals with the sort
of life that I have in mind when I speak of the
European "upper classes"; and one knows how
Mr. Galsworthy's noble and chivalrous interest
in social questions militates against the intellectual detachment of his curiosity.

The cleverer authors among our younger
school almost invariably restrict their scope to
what one feels are autobiographical histories of
their own wanderings through the pseudo-latin
quarters of London and Paris. They flood their
pages with struggling artists, emancipated seam-
stresses, demi-mondaine actresses, social re-
formers, and all the rag-tag and bob-tail of sub-
urban semi-culture; whereas in some mysterious
way—probably by reason of their not possessing
imaginations strong enough to sweep them out
of the circle of their own experiences—the more
normal tide of ordinary "upper-class" civilisation passes them untouched.

It is imagination which is lacking, imagination which, as in the case of Balzac and Dostoievsky, can carry a writer beyond the sphere of
his own personal adventures, into the great tides
and currents of the human comedy, and into the
larger air of the permanent life-forces. It is
the universal element which one misses in these

clever and interesting books, that universal element which in the work of Henry James is never
absent, however slight and frivolous his immediate subject or however commonplace and conventional his characters.

Is it, after all, not they,—these younger philosophical realists—but he, the great urbane humanist, who restricts his scope, narrowing it
down to oft-repeated types and familiar scenes,
which, as the world swings forward, seem to
present themselves over and over again as an
integral and classic embodiment of the permanent forces of life? It might seem so sometimes; especially when one considers how little
new or startling "action" there is in Henry
James, how few romantic or outstanding figures
there are to arrest us with the shock of sensational surprise. Or is it, when we get to the
bottom of the difference—this difference which
separates Henry James from the bulk of our
younger novelists—not a matter of subject at
all, but purely a matter of method and mental atmosphere?

May it not, perhaps, turn out that all those
younger men are preoccupied with some purely
personal philosophy of life, some definite scheme
of things—like the pattern idea in "Human Bond-
age"—to which they are anxious to sacrifice their
experiences and subordinate their imaginations?
Are they not all, as a matter of fact, interested
more deeply in hitting home some original phi-

losophical nail, than in letting the vast human tragedy strike them out of a clear sky? But it matters little which way it is. The fact that concerns us now is to note that Henry James has still no rival, nor anything approaching a rival, in his universal treatment of European Society. None, even among our most cynical and disil- lusioned younger writers, are able to get as completely rid as he of any "a priori" system or able to envisage, as he did, in passionate colourless curiosity, the panorama of human characters drawn out along the common road of ordinary civilised life.

Putting Flaubert aside, Henry James is the only one of the great modern novelists to be absolutely free from any philosophical system. Tolstoy, Dostoievsky, Balzac, Hardy, de Maupassant, D'Annunzio—they all have their metaphysical or anti-metaphysical bias, their gesture of faith or denial.

Even Flaubert himself makes a kind of philosophic attitude out of his loathing for the common-place. Henry James alone confronts the universe with only one passion, with only one purpose, with only one obsession—the passion and the purpose of satisfying his insatiable curiosity upon the procession of human motives and the stream of human psychological reactions, which pass him by in their eternal flux.

This cold, calm, detached intellectual curiosity, free from any moral alloy, renders him an extraordinary and unique figure; a figure that would be almost inhuman, if it were not that the fury of his research is softened and mitigated by a deep and tender pity for every sort and condition of frail human creature subjected to his unwearied scrutiny.

This is one of the basic contradictions of Mr. James' fascinating personality, that he is able to retain the clear and Olympian detachment of his purely æsthetic curiosity and yet to betray a tenderness—why should one not say, in the best meaning of that excellent word, a goodness of heart?—in his relations with his characters, and with us, his unknown readers, who so easily might be his characters.

It is one of the profoundest secrets of art itself, this contradiction, and it reveals the fact that however carefully a great spirit may divest itself of philosophy and system there is a residuum of personal character left behind—of personal predilection and taste—which all the artistic objectivity in the world cannot overcome.

I am myself inclined to think that it is this very tenderness and friendliness in Henry James, this natural amiability of disposition which all his detachment and curiosity cannot kill, that makes him so much more attractive a figure than the sombre Flaubert whose passion for literary objectivism is touched by no such charm.

It is a matter of great interest to watch the little tricks and devices of a genius of this kind preparing the ground, as one might put it, for the peculiar harvest of impressions.

What Henry James aims at is a clear field for the psychological emotions of people who have, so to speak, time and leisure to indulge themselves in all the secondary reactions and subtle ramifications of their peculiar feelings.

The crude and intrusive details of any business or profession, the energy-absorbing toil of manual or otherwise exhausting labour, prevent, quite naturally, any constant preoccupation with one's emotional experiences. A Maxim Gorky or a Thomas Hardy will turn the technical labours of his emotionally-stricken people into tragic accomplices of the human drama, making field or factory, as it may happen, dumb but significant participators in the fatal issue. But in their case, and in the case of so many other powerful modern writers, the emotions required are simple and direct, such as harmonise well with the work of men's hands and the old eternal struggle with the elements.

It may be said, and with a great deal of plausibility, that this natural and simple toil adds a dignity and a grandeur to human emotions which must necessarily vanish with the vanishing of its heavy burdens. It may be said that the mere existence of an upper class more or less liberated from such labours and permitted the leisure to make so much of its passing sensations, is itself a grievous indictment of our present system.

This also is a contention full of convincing force. Oscar Wilde himself—the most sophisticated of hedonists—declares in his "Soul of Man" that the inequality of the present system, when one considers æsthetic values alone, is as injurious to the rich as it is pernicious to the poor. Almost every one of the great modern writers, not excluding even the courtly Turgenief, utters bitter and eloquent protests against the injustice of this difference.

Nietzsche alone maintains the necessity of a slave caste in order that the masters of civilisation may live largely, freely, nobly, as did the ancient aristocracies of the classic ages, without contact with the burden and tediousness of labour. And in this—in his habitual and arbitrary neglect of the toiling masses—Henry James is more in harmony with the Nietzschean doctrine than any other great novelist of our age. He is indeed, the only one—except perhaps Paul Bourget, and Bourget cannot in any sense be regarded as his intellectual equal—who relentlessly and unscrupulously rules out of his work every aspect of "the spirit of the revolution."

There is something almost terrifying and inhuman about this imperturbable stolidity of indifference to the sufferings and aspirations of the many too many. One could imagine any intellectual proletarian rising up from his perusal of these voluminous books with a howl of indignation against their urbane and incorrigible author.

I do not blush to confess that I have myself sometimes shared this righteous astonishment. Is it possible that the aloofness of this tender-hearted man from the burden of his age, is due to his American antecedents?

Rich people in America are far less responsible in their attitude towards the working classes, and far less troubled by pricks of conscience than in older countries, where some remote traces of the feudal system still do something towards bridging the gulf between class and class.

One must remember too that, after all, Henry James is a great *déraciné*, a passionate pilgrim from the new world making amorous advances toward the old. It is always difficult, in a country which is not one's own, to feel the sting of conscience with regard to social injustices as sharply as one feels it at home. Travelling in Egypt or Morocco, one seems to take it carelessly for granted that there should be scenes of miserable poverty sprinkled around the picturesque objects of our æsthetic tour.

Well! England and France and Italy are to Henry James like Egypt and Morocco; and as long as he finds us picturesquely and charmingly ourselves; set that is, in our proper setting, and with the picturesque background of local colour behind us—he naturally does not feel it incumbent upon him to worry himself very greatly over our social inequalities.

But there is probably more in it than that.

These things—the presence or the absence of the revolutionary conscience—are matters, when one gets to the bottom of it, of individual temperament, and James, the kindest and most charitable of men in his personal life, was simply untouched by that particular spark of "saeva indignatio."

It was not out of stupidity or any lack of sensitiveness that he let it alone. Perhaps—who can tell?—he, like Nietzsche's Zarathustra, overcame "the temptation of pity," and deliberately turned aside from the "ugliest man's" cries.

One feels in one's more ardent moments, when the wish to smite this accursed economic system some shattering blow becomes red-hot, a little chilled, it must be confessed, when one recalls that immense brow, heavy with brooding intellect, and those dreamy, full-orbed Shakespearian eyes. Was the man, one is tempted to wonder then, too great, too lonely, too wise, to believe in any beautiful desperate change in the tragic "pathos of distance" between man and man? Was indeed the whole mortal business of human life a sort of grand tour of "Egypt and Morocco" to him; a mere long-drawn-out search after æsthetic sensations and a patient satisfying of Olympian curiosity?

No novelist that has ever lived "shows his hand" so little, in the sense of coming before the foot-lights and making gestures to the crowd; but in a deeper implication, none shows it more constantly.

To have a style so marked and sealed, so stamped and dyed for one's own in the integral way James has it, a style so personal and unique that its peculiar flavour rises from every single sentence on the page, is indeed, in a deep sense, to betray one's hidden soul to the world.

This, at any rate, is the only kind of betrayal that we—the general public—are permitted to surprise him in; unless one counts as a personal revelation the grave portentous solemnity of his technical prefaces. Like that amiable girl in Wilhelm Meister who, when asked whether she had ever loved, replied "Never—or always!" Henry James may be said to have never "coined his soul" or always to have coined it.

This style of his—so dyed and ingrained with personality—becomes in his later books, a stumbling-block to many readers; to the readers who want their "story" and have no wish to be teased and distracted "en route." Certainly his style thickens and gathers in fuller intensity as well as diffuses itself in wider atmospheric attenuation as his later manner grows upon him. The thing becomes at once richer and more evasive. But this implies no violent or sudden change, such as might excite suspicion of any arbitrary "tour-de-force." The characteristic elements are there from the beginning. They are only emphasized and drawn out to their logical issues by the process of his development.

From the very start he possesses a style which

HENRY JAMES

has its own flavour. It is only that the perfume of it diffuses itself more insidiously, in proportion as its petals, so to speak, warmed by the sun of maturer experience and subtler imagination, open to the air.

The result of this natural and organic development is precisely what one would have anticipated. Lovers of simple story-telling prefer the earlier work with its Daisy Miller, Roderick Hudson, and The Portrait of a Lady.

Virtuosos of rare psychological achievements and of strange æsthetic experiments prefer his very latest writings, including such a difficult and complicated book as "The Golden Bowl" or the short stories in "The Finer Grain."

On the other hand, those among us who are concerned with sheer beauty of form apart both from exciting subjects and psychological curiosities, hold by the intermediate period—the period extending, let us say, from the beginning of the last five years of the Nineteenth to the end of the first five years of the Twentieth century.

As a matter of fact, "The Golden Bowl," one of his most elaborate and exhaustive masterpieces, was published in November, 1904; and "The Sacred Fount," perhaps the most difficult as it is certainly one of the most characteristic of all his stories, appeared very much earlier. But taking his works as a whole, that epoch—from 1895 to 1905—may be regarded as his apogee, as his "Great Noon."

"The Awkward Age," for instance, the book of all others for which initiated admirers have an insistent devotion, appeared in 1899, while the collection of stories entitled "The Better Sort," which includes that masterpiece of tender-hearted malice "The Beldonald Holbein," came out in 1903.

As I have hinted, the whole question of selecting the period of a great artist's manner which contains his most significant work is largely a matter of taste; and the thing—as we have seen—is complicated by all sorts of over-lappings, reversions, anticipations; but if I were myself pressed to suggest a brief list of books, which might be found to contain the quintessential qualities both of Henry James' attitude and his method, I should certainly include "The Tragic Muse," "The Spoils of Poynton," "What Maisie Knew," "The Ambassadors," "The Private Life" and "The Soft Side," whatever else it were difficult to omit.

Putting everything he wrote together, and letting these many-coloured opals and amethysts of intellectual imagination slide through our passionate fingers, I would perhaps select "The Great Good Place" as the best of all his short stories, and "The Tragic Muse" as the best of all his longer ones.

One sometimes, at unfortunately rare intervals, comes across a person who has really "collected" Henry James from the very beginning.

Such persons are greatly to be envied. I think perhaps, they are the only bibliophiles for whom I have a tenderness; for they prove themselves so much more than bibliophiles; they prove themselves wise and prudent anticipators of the verdict of posterity.

It is impossible to enjoy the reprinted editions, in their tiresome monotony of luxurious bindings, as delicately as one enjoyed these first flowers of the author's genius, dewy with his authentic blessing. I am myself proud to recall the fact that, before the ninteenth century closed, I had secured a whole shelf of these sibylline volumes; buying most of them—I can recall the occasion— in one huge derelict pile from a certain friendly book-shop in Brighton; and leaving the precious parcel, promise of more than royal delights, in some little waiting-room on the sun-bathed Georgian front, while I walked the beach like a Grand Vizier who has received a present from the Sultan.

The only people who are to be more envied than those who have collected Henry James from the beginning—and these alas! are most of them grey-headed now—are the people who, possessed of the true interior unction, have by some accident of obstructing circumstance been debarred from this voluptuous pleasure until late in their experience. What ecstasies such persons have in store for them, what "linked sweetness long-drawn out" of sybaritish enjoyment!

But I was speaking of those secret and interesting preparations that every great artist makes before he gets to work; those clearings of his selected field of operations from the alien and irrelevant growths.

What Henry James requires before he can set his psychological machinery in motion is uninterrupted leisure for the persons of his emotional dramas. Leisure first, and after leisure a certain pleasant congruity of background.

Henry James is indeed the author "par excellence" of a leisured upper class who have time to think and feel, and to dwell at large upon their thoughts and feelings, undisturbed by the spade, the plough, the sword, the counter, the wheels of factories or the roar of traffic. It is amusing to watch the thousand and one devices by which he disentangles his people from the intrusive irrelevancy of work. They are either rich themselves—and it cannot be concealed that money, though not over-emphasised, is never quite eliminated from the field of action—or they are dependent upon rich relatives and friends.

It is for this reason perhaps that there are so few professional people in his books. The absence of lawyers is quite striking; so is the absence of doctors,—though a charming example of the latter profession does certainly appear in "The Wings of a Dove" as the medical attendant upon the dying girl in Venice. I cannot at this moment recall a single clergyman or priest. Is this because these spiritual guides of our race are too poor or too over-worked to serve his purpose, or do we perhaps,—in this regrettable "lacuna"—stumble upon one of the little smiling prejudices of our great conformist? He must have met some black coats, we are compelled to suppose, in the drawing-rooms of his country houses. Did he perhaps, like so many of his discreet and cautious young men, "conform" without "committing himself," in these high places?

If I were asked what types of character—among men I mean—emerge as most characteristic of his interest and as best lending themselves to his method, I should put my finger upon those pathetic middle-aged persons, like Mr. Verver in "The Golden Bowl," or Mr. Longdon in "The Awkward Age," who, full of riches and sad experience, have retired completely from active life, only to exercise from the depths of their sumptuous houses and secluded gardens, a sort of fairy influence upon the fortunes of their younger friends.

In the second place, I would indicate, as characteristic of this author, those wealthy and amiable young men who, as a general rule from America, but sometimes from the country-houses of England, wander at large and with genial "artistic" sympathies through the picturesque cities of Europe, carrying their susceptible hearts and sound moral principles into "pension" and "studio" where they are permitted to encounter those other favourite "subjects" of this cosmopolitan author, the wandering poverty-stricken gentlewoman with her engaging daughters, or the ambiguous adventuress with her shadowy past.

The only persons who seem allowed to work at their trade in Henry James, are the writers and artists. These labour continually and with most interesting results. Indeed no great novelist, not even Balzac himself, has written so well about authors and painters. Paul Bourget attempts it, but there is a certain pedantic air of a craftsman writing about craftsmen, a connoisseur writing about connoisseurs, in his treatment of such things, which detracts from the human interest. Paul Bourget lacks, too, that fine malice, that sly arch humour, which saves Henry James from ever making his artists "professional" or his writers prolix.

But if he describes fellow-labourers thus sympathetically, it must not be forgotten that by far the most fascinating "artistic" person in all his books, is that astonishing Gabriel Nash in "The Tragic Muse." And the rôle of Gabriel Nash is to do nothing at all. To do nothing; but to be perpetually and insidiously enticing others, out of the sphere of all practical duties, responsibilities and undertakings, to renounce everything for art. Anything more charming or characteristic than Gabriel Nash's final departure from the scene, it would be impossible to find. He does not depart. He "goes up"—and "out." He

melts into thin air.   He dissolves like an iridescent vapour.   He is—and then again, he is not.

I sometimes seem to see the portentous Henry
James himself, with his soft plump hands, heavy
forehead and drooping-lidded eyes, flitting to and
fro through the drawing-rooms of our fantastic
civilisation,   like   some   huge   feathery-winged
moth-owl, murmuring, just as Gabriel Nash used
to do, wistful and whimsical protests against all
this tiresome "business of life" which distracts
people from psychology and beauty and amiable
conversation!

Alas! he too has now "passed away"; vanishing as lightly and swiftly as this other, leaving
behind him as the one drastic and spectacular action in a life of pure æsthetic creation, his definite
renunciation of the world of his engendering and
his formal reception into the more leisured atmosphere of the traditions of his adoption.

That he—of all men the most peaceful—should
have taken such a step in the mid-torrent of the
war, is a clinching proof of the value which he
placed upon the sacred shrines of his passionate
pilgrimage.

When we come to take up the actual threads
of his peculiar style, and to examine them one
by one, we cannot fail to note certain marked
characteristics, which separate him entirely from
other writers of our age.

One of the most interesting of these is his way
of handling those innumerable colloquialisms and

light "short-cuts" of speech, which—especially in their use by super-refined people—have a grace and charm quite their own. The literary value of the colloquialisms of upper-class people has never, except here and there in the plays of Oscar Wilde, been exploited as delightfully and effectively as in Henry James.

Just as Charles Lamb will make use of Milton or Sir Thomas Browne or the "Anatomy of Melancholy"; and endow his thefts with an originality all his own, making them seem different in the transposition, and in some mysterious way richer, so Henry James will take the airy levities of his aristocratic youths and the little provocative ejaculations of his well-bred maidens, and out of these weave a filmy, evasive, delicate essence, light as a gossamer-seed and bitter as coloquintida, which, mingled with his own graver and mellower tones, becomes an absolutely new medium in the history of human style.

The interesting thing to observe about all this is that the argot that he makes use of is not the slang of his own America, far less is it the more fantastic colloquialism of the English Public Schools. It is really a sort of sublimated and apotheosized "argot," an "argot" of a kind of platonic archetypal drawing-room; such a drawing-room as has never existed perhaps, but to which all drawing-rooms or salons, if you will, of elegant conversation, perpetually approximate. It is indeed the light and airy speech, eminently natural and spontaneous, but at the same time profoundly sophisticated, of a sort of Utopian aristocracy, that will, in some such delicious hesitations, innuendoes and stammerings, express their "superficiality out of profundity," in the gay, subtle, epicurean days which are to come.

It is only offensive to tiresome realistic people, void of humour as they are void of imagination, this sweet psychological persiflage. To such persons it may even seem a little ridiculous that *everybody*—from retired American Millionaires down to the quaintest of Hertfordshire old maids —should utter their sentiments in this same manner. But such objectors are too pig-headed and stupid to understand the rudimentary conventions of art, or those felicitous "illusions," which, as Charles Lamb reminds us in speaking of some sophisticated old English actors, are a kind of pleasant challenge from the intelligent comedian to his intelligent audience.

One very delicate and dainty device of Henry James is his trick of placing "inverted commas" round even the most harmless of colloquialisms. This has a curiously distinguished and refined effect. It seems constantly to say to his readers —"one knows very well, *we* know very well, how ridiculous and vulgar all this is; but there are certain things that cannot be otherwise expressed!" It creates a sort of scholarly "rapport"—this use of commas—between the gentility of the author and the assumed gentility of the reader, taking the latter into a kind of amiable partnership in ironic superiority.

I say "gentility"—but that is not exactly the word; for there is not the remotest trace of snobbishness in Henry James. It is rather that he indicates to a small inner circle of intellectually detached persons, his recognition of their fastidiousness and their prejudices, and his sly humorous consciousness of the gulf between their classical mode of speech and the casual lapses of ordinary human conversation.

In spite of all his detachment no novelist diffuses his personal temperament so completely through his work as Henry James does. In this sense—in the sense of temperamental style—he is far more personal than Balzac and incomparably more so than Turgenief.

One does not, in reading these great authors, savour the actual style on every page, in every sentence. We have large blank spaces, so to speak, of straightforward colourless narrative. But there are no "blank spaces" in Henry James. Every sentence is penetrated and heavy with the fragrance of his peculiar grace. One might almost say—so strong is this subjective element in the great objective æsthete—that James writes novels like an essayist, like some epicurean Walter Pater, suddenly grown interested in common humanity, and finding in the psychology of ordinary people a provocation and a stimulus as insidious and suggestive as in the lines and colours of mediæval art. This *essayist attitude* accounts largely for those superior "inverted commas" which throw such a clear space of ironic detachment round his characters and his scenes.

On the other hand, what a man he is for concealing his *opinions!* Who can lay his finger on a single formal announcement of moral or philosophical partizanship in Henry James? Who can catch him for a moment declaring himself a conservative, a liberal, a Christian, a pagan, a pantheist, a pluralist, a socialist, a reactionary, a single taxer, a realist, a symbolist, an empiricist, a believer in ideals, a materialist, an advocate of New Thought, an esoteric Buddhist, an Hegelian, a Pragmatist, a Free Lover?

It would be possible to go over this formidable list of angles of human vision, and find evidence somewhere in his books sufficient to make him out an adherent of every one of them. Consider his use of the supernatural for instance. Hardly any modern writer makes so constant, so artistic a use of the machinery of the invisible world; and yet who would have the temerity to say that Henry James believed even so much as in ghosts?

I know nothing of Mr. James' formal religious views, or to what pious communion, if any, that brooding forehead and disillusioned eyes were wont to drift on days of devotion. But I cannot resist a secret fancy that it was to some old-fashioned and not too ritualistic Anglican church that he sometimes may have been met proceeding, in silk hat and well-polished shoes, at the close of a long Autumn afternoon, across the fallen leaves of Hyde Park!

There is an unction, a dreamy thrill about some of those descriptions of town and country churches in conventional England which would suggest that he had no secularistic aversion to these modest usages. Perhaps, like Charles Darwin, he would have answered impertinent questions about his faith by pointing to just such patient unexcluding shrines of drowsy controversy-hating piety.

I cannot see him listening to modernistic rhetorie. I cannot see him prostrated before ritualistic revivals. But I can see him sitting placid and still, like a great well-groomed visitor in "Egypt and Morocco," listening pensively to some old-fashioned clergyman, whose goodness of heart redeems the innocence of his brain; while the mellow sunshine falls through the high windows upon the fair hair of Nanda or Aggie, or Mamie or Nina or Maud, thinking quiet thoughts in front of him.

It is strange how difficult it is to forget the personal appearance of this great man when one reads his works. What a head he had; what weight of massive brooding bulk! When one thinks of the head of Henry James and the head of Oscar Wilde—both of them with something that suggests the classical ages in their flesh-heavy contours—one is inclined to agree with

HENRY JAMES

Shakespeare's Cæsar in his suspicion of "lean men."

Think of the harassed and rat-like physiognomy of nearly all the younger writers of our day! Do their countenances suggest, as these of James and Wilde, that their pens will "drop fatness"? Can one not discern the envious eye, the serpent's tongue, the scowl of the aggressive dissenter, the leer of the street urchin?

How excellent it is, in this modern world, to come upon the "equinimitas" of the great ages! After all, in the confused noises of our human arena, it is something to encounter an author who preserves restraint and dignity and urbanity. It is something more to encounter one who has, in the very depths of his soul, the ancient virtue of magnanimity.

This American visitor to Europe brings back to us those "good manners of the soul" which we were in danger of forgetting; and the more we read the writings of Henry James, the more fully we become aware that there is only one origin of this spiritual charm, this aristocratic grace; and that is a sensitive and noble heart.

The movement of literature at the present time is all towards action and adventure. This is right and proper in its place, and a good antidote to the tedious moralising of the past generation.

The influence of Nietzsche upon the spiritual plane, and that of the war upon the emotional plane, have thrown us violently out of the sphere of æsthetic receptivity into the sphere of heroic and laconic wrestling.

Short stories, short poems, short speeches, short questions, short answers, short pity and short shrift, are the order of the day. Far and far have we been tossed from the dreamy purlieus of his "great good place," with its long sunny hours under misty trees, and its interminable conversations upon smooth-cut lawns! The sweet psychology of terrace-walks is scattered, and the noise of the chariots and the horsemen breaks the magical stillness where lovers philosophised and philosophers loved.

But let none of the strenuous gentlemen, whose abrupt ways seem encouraged by this earthquake, congratulate themselves that refinement and beauty and distinction and toleration have left the world forever, for them to "bustle in." It is not for long. The sun does not stop shining or the dew cease falling or the fountains of rain dry up because of the cruelty of men. It is not for long. The "humanism" of Henry James, with its "still small voice," is bound to return. The stars in their courses fight for it. It is the pleasure of the consciousness of life itself; of the life that, whether with Washington Square, or Kensington Park, or the rosy campaniles of the Giudecca, or the minarets of Sacré-Cœur, or the roofs of Montmartre, or the herbaceous borders and shadowy terraces of English gardens, as its background, must flow and flow and flow, with its tender equivocations and its suppliance of wistful mystery, as long as men and women have any leisure to love or any intelligence to analyse their love!

He is an aristocrat, and he writes—better than any—of the aristocracy; and yet, in the long result, is it of his well-bred levities and of his pleasantly-housed, lightly-living people, that one comes to think? Is it not rather of those tragic and faded figures, figures of sensitive men and sensitive women for whom the world has no place, and of whom few—even among artists—speak or care to speak, with sympathy and understanding?

He has, just here, and in his own way, something of that sheer human pity for desolate and derelict spirits which breaks forth so savagely sometimes, and with so unexpected a passion, from amid the brutalities and sensualities of Guy de Maupassant.

No one who has ever lived has written more tenderly or beautifully of what Charles Lamb would call "superannuated people." Old bachelors, living in a sort of romantic exile, among mementoes of a remote past; old maids, living in an attenuated dream of "what might have been," and playing heart-breaking tricks with their forlorn fancies; no one has dealt more generously, more imaginatively with such as these. He is a little cruel to them sometimes, but with a fine caressing cruelty which is a far greater tribute than indifference; and is there not, after all, a certain element of cruelty in every species of tender love? Though more than any one capable of discerning rare and complicated issues, where to the vulgar mind all would seem grey and dull and profitless, Henry James has, and it is absurd not to admit it, a "penchant" for the abnormal and the bizarre. This element appears more often in the short stories than the longer ones, but it is never very far away.

I sometimes think that many of the gentle and pure-souled people who read this amiable writer go on their way through his pages without discerning this quiver, this ripple, this vibration, of "miching mallecho." On softly-stepping feline feet, the great sleek panther of psychological curiosity glides into very perverse, very dubious paths. The exquisite tenuity and flexibility of his style, light as the flutter of a feather through the air, enable him to wander freely and at large where almost every other writer would trip and stumble in the mud. It is one of the most interesting phenomena in literature, this sly, quiet, half ironic dalliance with equivocal matters.

Henry James can say things that no one else could say, and approach subjects that no one else could approach, simply by reason of the grave whimsical playfulness of his manner and the extraordinary malleableness of his evasive style. It is because his style can be as simple and clear as sunlight, and yet as airy and impalpable as the invisible wind, that he manages to achieve these results.   He uses little words, little harmless innocent words, but by the connotation he gives them, and the way in which he softly flings them out, one by one, like dandelion seeds upon swiftly-sliding water, one is being continually startled into sharp arrested attention, as if—in the silence that follows their utterance—somebody, as the phrase goes, "stepped over one's grave."

How dearly one grows to love all his dainty tricks of speech! That constant repetition of the word "wonderful"—of the word "beautiful" —how beautifully and wonderfully he works it up into a sort of tender chorus of little caressing cries over the astounding tapestry woven by the invisible fates! The charming way his people "drop" their little equivocal innocent-wicked retorts; "drop" them and "fling them out," and "sweetly hazard" them and "wonderfully wail" them, produces the same effect of balanced expectancy and suspended judgment ·that one derives from those ambiguous "so it might seems" of the wavering Platonic Dialogue.

The final impression left upon the mind after one closes one of these fascinating volumes is, it must be confessed, a little sad. So much ambiguity in human life—so much unnecessary suffering—so many mad, blind, wilful misunderstandings! A little sad—and yet, on the other hand, we remain fortified and sustained with a certain interior detachment.

SUSPENDED JUDGMENTS

After all, it is soon over—the whole motley farce—and, while it lasts, nothing in it matters so very greatly, or at any rate matters enough to disturb our amusement, our good-temper, our toleration. Nothing matters so very greatly. And yet everything—each of us, as we try to make our difficult meanings clear, the meanings of our hidden souls, and each of these meanings themselves as we stammer them forth to one another—matters so "wonderfully," so "beautifully"!

The tangled thread of our days may be knotted and twisted; but, after all, if we have the magnanimity to let off lightly those "who trespass against us" we have not learnt our æsthetic lesson of regarding the whole business of life as a complicated Henry James story, altogether in vain.

We have come to regard the world as a more or less amusing Spectacle, without forgetting to be decently considerate of the other shadows in the gilt-framed mirror!

Perhaps, in our final estimate of him, what emerges most definitely as Henry James' *doctrine* is the height and depth and breadth of the gulf which separates those who have taste and sensitiveness from those who have none. That is the "motif" of the "Spoils of Poynton," and I do not know any one of all his books more instinct with his peculiar spiritual essence.

Below every other controversy and struggle in

the world is the controversy between those who
possess this secret of "The Finer Grain" and
those who have it not. There can be no recon-
ciliation, no truce, no "rapport" between these.
At best there can be only mitigated hostility on
the one side, and ironical submission on the other.
The world is made after this fashion and after
no other, and the best policy is to follow our great
artists and turn the contrast between the two into
a cause of æsthetic entertainment.

Duality rules the universe. If it were not for
the fools there would be no wisdom. If it were
not for those who could never understand him,
there could be no Henry James.

One comes at any rate to see, from the exquisite success upon us of this author's method,
how futile it is, in this world whereof the beginning and the end are dreams, to bind an artist
down to tedious and photographic reality.

People do not and perhaps never will—even in
archetypal Platonic drawing-rooms—converse
with one another quite so goldenly; or tell the
amber-coloured beads of their secret psychology
with quite so felicitous an unction. What matter? It is the prerogative of fine and great art
to create, by its shaping and formative imagination, new and impossible worlds for our enjoyment.

And the world created by Henry James is like
some classic Arcadia of psychological beauty—
some universal Garden of Versailles unprofaned

by the noises of the crowd—where among the terraces and fountains delicate Watteau-like figures move and whisper and make love in a soft artificial fairy moonlight dimmed and tinted with the shadows of passions and misty with the rain of tender regrets; human figures without name or place. For who remembers the names of these sweet phantoms or the titles of their "great good places" in this hospitable fairy-land of the harassed sensitive ones of the earth; where courtesy is the only law of existence and good taste the only moral code?

OSCAR WILDE

OSCAR WILDE

THE words he once used about himself—
"I am a symbolic figure"—remain to
this day the most significant thing that
can be said of Oscar Wilde.

It is given to very few men of talent, this peculiar privilege—this privilege of being greater
in what might be called the *shadow of their personality* than in any actual literary or artistic
achievement—and Wilde possesses it in a degree second to none.

"My genius is in my life," he said on another
occasion, and the words are literally and most
fatally true.

In the confused controversies of the present
age it is difficult to disentangle the main issues;
but it seems certain that side by side with political and economic divisions, there is a gulf
growing wider and wider every day between the
adherents of what might be called the Hellenic
Renaissance and the inert, suspicious, unintel-
ligent mob; that mob the mud of whose heavy
traditions is capable of breeding, at one and the
same time, the most crafty hypocrisy and the
most stupid brutality.

It would be hardly a true statement to say
that the Renaissance referred to—this modern

Renaissance, not less formidable than the historic revolt which bears that name—is an insurrection of free spirits against Christianity. It is much rather a reversion to a humane and classic reasonableness as opposed to mob-stupidity and middle-class philistinism—things which only the blundering of centuries of popular misapprehension could associate with the sublime and the imaginative figure of Christ.

It is altogether a mistake to assume that in "De Profundis" Wilde retracted his classic protest and bowed his head once more in the house of Rimmon.

What he did was to salute, in the name of the æsthetic freedom he represented, those enduring elements of human loveliness and beauty in that figure which three hundred years of hypocritical puritanism have proved unable to tarnish. What creates the peculiar savagery of hatred which his name has still the power to conjure up among the enemies of civilisation has little to do with the ambiguous causes of his final downfall. These, of course, gave him up, bound hand and foot, into their hands. But these, though the overt excuse of their rancour, are far from being its real motive-force. To reach that we must look to the nature of the formidable weapon which it was his habit, in season and out of season, to use against this mob-rule—I mean his sense of humour.

The stupid middle-class obscurantism, so alien

to all humane reasonableness, which, in our Anglo-Saxon communities, masquerades under the cloak of a passionate and imaginative religion, is more sensitive to ridicule than to any other form of attack, and Wilde attacked it mercilessly with a ridicule that cut to the bone.

They are not by any means of equal value, these epigrams of his, with which he defended intelligence against stupidity and classical light against Gothic darkness.

They are not as humorous as Voltaire's. They are not as philosophical as Goethe's. Compared with the aphorisms of these masters they are light and frivolous. But for this very reason perhaps, they serve the great cause—the cause of humane and enlightened civilisation—better in our age of vulgar mob-rule than more recondite "logoi."

They pierce the hide of the thickest and dullest; they startle and bewilder the brains of the most crass and the most insensitive. And it is just because they do this that Wilde is so cordially feared and hated. It was, one cannot help feeling, the presence in him of a shrewd vein of sheer boyish bravado, mingled—one might go even as far as that—with a dash of incorrigible worldliness in his own temper, that made his hits so effective and wounding.

It is interesting, with this in mind, to compare Wilde's witticisms with those of Matthew Arnold or Bernard Shaw. The reason that Wilde's lash cuts deeper than either of these other champions of rational humanism, is that he goes, with more classical clearness, straight to the root of the matter.

The author of "Thyrsis" was not himself free from a certain melancholy hankering after "categorical imperatives," and beneath the cap and bells of his theological fooling, Shaw is, of course, as gravely moralistic as any puritan could wish.

Neither of these—neither the ironical schoolmaster nor the farcical clown of our Renaissance of intelligence—could exchange ideas with Pericles, say, or Cæsar, without betraying a puritanical fussiness that would grievously bewilder the lucid minds of those great men.

The philosophy of Wilde's æsthetic revolt against our degraded mob-ridden conscience was borrowed from Walter Pater, but whereas that shy and subtle spirit moved darkly and mysteriously aside from all contact with the vulgar herd, Wilde, full of gay and wanton pride in his sacred mission, lost no opportunity of flaunting his classic orthodoxy in the face of the heretical mob.

Since the death of Wilde, the brunt of the battle for the spiritual liberties of the race has been borne by the sterner and more formidable figure of Nietzsche; but the vein of high and terrible imagination in this great poet of the Superman sets him much closer to the company of the saints and mystics than to that of the instinctive children of the pagan ideal.

Oscar Wilde's name has become a sort of rallying cry to all those writers and artists who suffer, in one degree or another, from the persecution of the mob—of the mob goaded on to blind brutality by the crafty incentives of those conspirators of reaction whose interest lies in keeping the people enslaved. This has come about, in a large measure, as much by the renown of his defects as by reason of his fine quality.

The majority of men of talent lack the spirit and the gall to defy the enemy on equal terms. But Wilde while possessing nobler faculties had an undeniable vein in him of sheer youthful insolence. To the impertinence of society he could oppose the impertinence of the artist, and to the effrontery of the world he could offer the effrontery of genius.

The power of personality, transcending any actual literary achievement, is what remains in the mind when one has done reading him, and this very faculty—of communicating to us, who never saw him or heard him speak, the vivid impact of his overbearing presence—is itself evidence of a rare kind of genius. It is even a little ironical that he, above all men the punctilious and precious literary craftsman, should ultimately dominate us not so much by the magic of his art as by the spell of his wilful and wanton individuality, and the situation is heightened still further by the extraordinary variety of his works and their amazing perfection in their different spheres.

One might easily conceive an artist capable of producing so clean-cut and crystalline a comedy as "The Importance of Being Earnest," and so finished and flawless a tragedy as "Salome," disappearing quite out of sight, in the manner so commended by Flaubert, behind the shining objectivity of his flawless creations. But so far from disappearing, Oscar Wilde manages to emphasise himself and his imposing presence only the more startlingly and flagrantly, the more the gem-like images he projects harden and glitter.

Astoundingly versatile as he was—capable of producing in "Reading Gaol" the best tragic ballad since "The Ancient Mariner," and in "Intentions" one of the best critical expositions of the open secret of art ever written at all—he never permits us for a second to lose touch with the wayward and resplendent figure, so full, for all its bravado, of a certain disarming childishness, of his own defiant personality.

And the fact remains that, perfect in their various kinds though these works of his are, they would never appeal to us as they do, and Oscar Wilde would never be to us what he is, if it were not for the predominance of this personal touch.

I sometimes catch myself wondering what my own feeling would be as to the value of these things—of the "Soul of Man," for instance, or "Intentions," or the Comedies, or the Poems—if the unthinkable thing could be done, and the emergence of this irresistible figure from behind it all could be drastically eliminated. I find myself conscious, at these times, of a faint disturbing doubt; as though after all, in spite of their jewel-like perfection, these wonderful and varied achievements were not quite the real thing, were not altogether in the "supreme manner." There seems to me—at the moments when this doubt arises—something too self-consciously (how shall I put it?) *artistic* about these performances, something strained and forced and far-fetched, which separates them from the large inevitable utterances of classic genius.

I am ready to confess that I am not sure that this feeling is a matter of personal predilection or whether it has the larger and graver weight behind it of the traditional instincts of humanity, instincts out of which spring our only permanent judgments. What I feel at any rate is this: that there is an absence in Wilde's writings of that large cool spaciousness, produced by the magical influence of earth and sky and sea, of which one is always conscious in the greater masters.

"No gentleman," he is said to have remarked once, "ever looks out of the window"; and it is precisely this "never looking out of the window" that produces his most serious limitations.

In one respect I must acknowledge myself grateful to Wilde, even for this very avoidance of what might be called the "magical" element in things. His clear-cut palpable images, carved, as one so often feels, in ebony or ivory or gold, offer an admirable relief, like the laying of one's hand upon pieces of Hellenic statuary, after wandering among the vague mists and "beachéd margents."

Certainly if all that one saw when one "looked out of the window" were Irish fairies with dim hair drifting down pallid rivers, there would be some reason for drawing the curtains close and toying in the lamp-light with cameo-carved profiles of Antinous and Cleopatra!

But nature has more to give us than the elfish fantasies, charming as these may be, of Celtic legend—more to give us than those "brown fauns" and "hoofed Centaurs" and milk-white peacocks, which Wilde loves to paint with his Tiepolo-like brush. The dew of the morning does not fall less lightly because real autumns bring it, nor does the "wide aerial landscape" of our human wayfaring show less fair, or its ancient antagonist the "salt estranging sea" less terrible, because these require no legendary art to endow them with mystery.

Plausible and full of significance as these honeyed arguments in "Intentions" are—and fruitful as they are in affording us weapons wherewith to defend ourselves from the mob—

it is still well, it is still necessary, to place against them the great Da Vinci saying, "Nature is the Mistress of the higher intelligences."

Wilde must be held responsible—along with others of his epoch—for the encouragement of that deplorable modern heresy which finds in bric-a-brac and what are called "objets d'art" a disproportionate monopoly of the beauty and wonder of the world. One turns a little wearily at last from the silver mirrors and purple masks. One turns to the great winds that issue forth out of the caverns of the night. One turns to the sun and to the rain, which fall upon the common grass.

However! It is not a wise procedure to demand from a writer virtues and qualities completely out of his rôle. In our particular race there is far more danger of the beauty and significance of art—together with all its subtler and less normal symbols—perishing under crude and sentimental Nature-worship, than of their being granted too large a place in our crowded house of thought.

After all, the art which Wilde assures us adds so richly to Nature, "is an art which Nature makes." They are not lovers of what is rarest and finest in our human civilisation who would suppress everything which deviates from the common track.

Who has given these people—these middle-class minds with their dull intelligences—the right to decide what is natural or unnatural in the presence of the vast tumultuous forces, wonderful and terrible, of the life-stream which surrounds us?

The mad smouldering lust which gives a sort of under-song of surging passion to the sophisticated sensuality of "Salome" is as much an evocation of Nature as the sad sweet wisdom of that sentence in "De Profundis"—"Behind joy and laughter there may be a temperament, coarse, hard and callous. But behind sorrow there is always sorrow."

What, beneath all his bravado and his paradoxes, Wilde really sought, was the enjoyment of passionate and absorbing emotion, and no one who hungers and thirsts after this—be he "as sensual as the brutish sting itself"—can fail in the end to touch, if only fleetingly with his lips, the waters of that river of passion which, by a miracle of faith if not by a supreme creation of art, Humanity has caused to issue forth from the wounded flesh of the ideal.

It is in his "Soul of Man"—perhaps the wisest and most eloquent revolutionary tract ever written—that Wilde frees himself most completely from the superficial eccentricities of his æsthetic pose, and indicates his recognition of a beauty in life, far transcending Tyrian dyes and carved cameos and frankincense and satin-wood and moon-stones and "Silks from Samarcand."

It is impossible to read this noble defence of

the natural distinction and high dignity of our human days when freed from the slavery of what is called "working for a living," without feeling that the boyish bravado of his insolent wit is based upon a deep and universal emotion. What we note here is an affiliation in revolt between the artist and the masses. And this affiliation indicates that the hideousness of our industrial system is far more offensive than any ancient despotism or slave-owning tyranny to the natural passion for light and air and leisure and freedom in the heart of man.

That Oscar Wilde, the most extreme of individualists, the most unscrupulous of self-asserters, the pampered darling of every kind of sophisticated luxury, should thus lift up his voice on behalf of the wage-earners, is an indication that a state of society which seems proper and inevitable to dull and narrow minds is, when confronted, not with any mere abstract theory of Justice or Political rights, but with the natural human craving for life and beauty, found to be an outrage and an insult.

Oscar Wilde by pointing his derisive finger at what the gross intelligence of our commercial mob calls the "honourableness of work" has done more to clear our minds of cant than many revolutionary speeches.

An age which breeds a world of uninteresting people whose only purpose in life is working for their living is condemned on the face of it. And it is just here that the association between your artist and your "labouring man" becomes physiologically evident. The labourer shows quite clearly that he regards his labour as a degradation, a burden, an interruption to life, a necessary evil.

The rôle of the capitalist-hired preacher is to condemn him for this and to regret the departure from the scene of that imaginary and extremely ridiculous figure, the worker who "took pleasure in his work." If there ever have been such people, they ought, as Wilde says, to be thoroughly ashamed of themselves. Any person who enjoys being turned into a machine for the best part of his days and regards it with pride, is no better than a blackleg or a scab—not a "scab" in regard to a little company of strikers, but a "scab" in regard to the human race; for he is one who denies that life in itself, life with all its emotional, intellectual and imaginative possibilities, can be endured without the gross, coarsening, dulling "anæsthetic" of money-making toil.

This is the word that the social revolution wanted—the word so much more to the point than discourses upon justice and equality and charity. And it is precisely here that the wage-earners of our present system are in harmony with the "intellectuals."

The "wage-earners," or those among them who have in them something more than the souls of scabs, despise and loathe their enforced labour. The artist also despises the second-rate tasks set him by the stupidity and bad taste of his middle-class masters.

The only persons in the community who are really happy in their life's work, as they fantastically call it, are those commercial *ruffians* whose brutal, self-righteous, puritanical countenances one is swamped by—as if by a flood of suffocating mediocrity—in the streets of all our modern cities.

Oscar Wilde is perfectly right. We are living in an age when the world for the first time in its history is literally under the rule of the stupidest, dullest, least intelligent and least admirable of all the classes in the community. Wilde's "Soul of Man" is the condemnation—let us hope the effective condemnation—of this epoch in the journey of the race.

The odium which France—always the protector of civilisation—has stamped upon the word "bourgeois" is no mere passing levity of an irresponsible Latin Quarter. It is the judgment of classic taste—the taste of the great artists and poets of all ages—upon the worst type of person, the type most pernicious to true human happiness, that has ever yet appeared upon the planet. And it is this type, the commercial type, the type that loves the money-making toil it is engaged upon, which rules over us now with an absolute authority, and creates our religion, our morality, our pleasures, our pastimes, our literature and our art.

Oscar Wilde must be forgiven everything in his gay impertinence which may jar upon our more sensitive moments, when one considers what he has done in dragging this great issue into the light and making it clear. He shows that what we have against us is not so much a system of society or a set of laws, as a definite and contemptible type of human character.

Democracy may well appear the most hopeless and lamentable failure in the government of men that history has ever known—but this is only due to the fact that the working classes have until now meekly and mildly received from the commercial classes their notions as to what democracy means.

No one could suppose for a moment that such a thing as the puritanical censorship of art and letters which now hangs, like a leaden weight, round the neck of every writer of original power, would be thrust upon us by the victims of sweatshops and factories. It is thrust upon us, like everything else which is degrading and uncivilised in our present system, by the obstinate stupidity and silly sentiment of the self-righteous middle class, the opponents of everything that is joyous and interesting and subtle and imaginative. It is devoutly to be hoped that, when the revolution arrives, the human persons who force their way to the top and guide the volcanic eruption will be such persons as are absolutely free from every kind of middle-class scruple.

There are among us to-day vigorous and indignant minds who find in the ugliness and moral squalor of our situation, the unhappy influence of Christ and his saints. They are wrong. The history of Oscar Wilde's writings shows that they are wrong.

It is the self-satisfied moralist who stands in the way, not the mystic or the visionary. They spoil everything they touch, these people. They turn religion into a set of sentimental inhibitions that would make Marcus Aurelius blush. They turn faith into pietism, sanctity into morality, and righteousness into a reeking prurience.

After all, it is not on the strength of his opinions, wise and sound as these may be, that Wilde's reputation rests. It rests on the beauty, in its own way never equalled, of the style in which he wrote. His style, as he himself points out, is one which seems to compel its readers to utter its syllables aloud. Of that deeper and more recondite charm which lies, in a sense, outside the sphere of vocal articulation, of that rhythm of the very movements of thought itself which lovers of Walter Pater catch, or dream they catch, in those elaborate delicately modulated sentences, Wilde has little or nothing.

What he achieves is a certain crystalline lucidity, clear and pure as the ring of glass upon glass, and with a mellifluous after-tone or echo of vibration, which dies away upon the ear in a lingering fall—melancholy and voluptuous, or light and tender as the hour and the moment lead.

He is at his best, or at any rate his style shows itself at its best, not in the utterances of those golden epigrams, the gold of which, as days pass, comes in certain cases to look lamentably like gilt, but in his use of those far-descended legendary images gathered up into poetry and art again and again till they have acquired the very tone of time itself, and a lovely magic, sudden, swift and arresting, like the odour of "myrrh, aloes, and cassia."

The style of Wilde is one of the simplest in existence, but its simplicity is the very apex and consummation of the artificial. He uses Biblical language with that self-conscious preciosity —like the movements of a person walking on tiptoe in the presence of the dead—which is so different from the sturdy directness of Bunyan or the restrained rhetoric of the Church of England prayers. There come moments when this premeditated innocence of tone—this lisping in liturgical monosyllables—irritates and annoys one. At such times the delicate unction of his naïveté strikes one, in despite of its gravity, as something a little comic; as though some very sophisticated and experienced person suddenly joined in a children's game and began singing in a plaintive tenderly pitched voice—

"This is the way we wash our hands, wash our hands,
    wash our hands—
This is the way we wash our hands,
    On a cold and frosty morning!"

But it were absurd to press this point too far. Sophisticated though the simplicity of Wilde is, it does actually spring with all its ritualistic tip-toeing straight out of his natural character. He was born artificial, and he was born with more childishness than the great majority of children. I like to picture him as a great Uranian baby, full of querulousness and peevishness, and eating greedily, with a sort of guileless wonder that anyone should scold him for it, every species of forbidden fruit that grows in the garden of life! How infantile really, when one thinks of it, and how humorously solemn the man's inordinate gravity over the touch of soft fabrics and the odour of rare perfumes! One seems to see him, a languid-limbed "revenant," with heavy-lidded drowsy eyes and voluptuous lips, emerging all swathed and wrapped in costly cerements out of the tomb of some Babylonian king.

After all, it remains a tremendous triumph of personality, the manner in which this portly modern Antinous has taken captive our imagination. His influence is everywhere, like an odour, like an atmosphere, like a diffused flame. We cannot escape from him.

In those ridiculous wit-contests with Whistler, from which he always emerged defeated, how much more generous and careless and noble he appears than the wasp-like artist who could rap out so smartly the appropriate retort! He seems like a great lazy king, at such times, caught off his guard by some skipping and clever knave of his spoilt retinue. Perhaps even now no small a portion of the amused and astonished wonder he excites is due to the fact that he really had, what so few of us have, a veritable passion for precious stuffs and woven fabrics and ivory and cedar wood and beads of amber and orchid-petals and pearl-tinted shells and lapis-lazuli and attar of roses.

It is open to doubt whether even among artists, there are many who share Wilde's Hellenic ecstasy in these things. This at any rate was no pose. He posed as a man of the world. He posed as an immoralist. He posed as a paradoxist. He posed in a thousand perverse directions. But when it comes to the colour and texture and odour and shape of beautiful and rare things—there, in his voluptuous delight in these, he was undeniably sincere.

He was of course no learned virtuoso. But what does that matter? The real artist is seldom a patient collector or an encyclopedic authority. That is the rôle of Museum people and of compilers of hand-books. Many thoroughly uninteresting minds know more about Assyrian pottery and Chinese pictures than Oscar Wilde knew about wild flowers.

Knowledge, as he teaches us himself, and it is one of the profoundest of his doctrines, is nothing. Knowledge is external and incidental. The important thing is that one's senses should be passionately alive and one's imagination fearlessly far-reaching.

We can embrace all the treasures of the Herods and all the riches of the Cæsars as we lay our fingers upon a little silver coin, if the divine flame is within us, and, if not, we may excavate a thousand buried cities and return learned and lean and empty. Well, people must make their own choice and go their own way. The world is wide, and Nature has at least this in common with Heaven, that it has many mansions.

The feverish passion for fair things which obsessed Oscar Wilde and carried him so far is not for all the sons of men; nor even, in every hour of their lives, for those who most ardently answer to it. That feverishness burns itself out; that smouldering fire turns to cold ashes. Life flows on, though Salome, daughter of Herodias, lies crushed under the piled-up shields, and though in all the prisons of the world "the damned grotesques make arabesques, like the wind upon the sand."

Life flows on, and the quips and merry jests of Oscar Wilde, his artful artlessness, his insolence, his self-pity, his loyalty and fickleness, his sensuality and tenderness, only fill after all a small space in the heart's chamber of those who read him and stare at his plays and let him go.

But there are a few for whom the tragic wantonness of that strange countenance, with the heavy eyelids and pouting mouth, means something not easily forgotten, not easily put by.

To have seen Oscar Wilde and talked with him gives to such persons a strange significance, an almost religious value. One looks long at them, as if to catch some far-off reflection from the wit of the dead man. They do not seem to us quite like the rest. They have seen Oscar Wilde, and "They know what they have seen." For when all has been said against him that can be said it remains that Oscar Wilde, for good and for evil, in innocence and in excess, in orthodoxy and in rebellion, is a "symbolic figure."

It is indeed easy enough, when one is under the spell of the golden gaiety of his wit, to forget the essential and irresistible truth of so many of his utterances.

That profound association between the "Sorrow that endureth forever" and the "Pleasure that abideth for a moment," which he symbolises under the parable of the Image of Bronze, has its place throughout all his work.

It is a mistake to regard De Profundis as a recantation. It is a fulfilment, a completion, a rounding off. Like a black and a scarlet thread running through the whole tapestry of his tragic story are the two parallel "motifs," the passion of the beauty which leads to destruction and the passion of the beauty which leads to life.

It matters little whether he was or was not received into the Church before he died. In the larger sense he was always within those unexcluding walls, those spacious courts of the Ecclesia of humanity. There was no trace in him, for all his caprices, of that puritanism of denial which breaks the altars and shatters the idols at the bidding of scientific iconoclasm.

What the anonymous instinct of humanity has rendered beautiful by building into it the golden monuments of forlorn hopes and washing it with the salt tears of desperate chances remained beautiful to him. From the narcissus-flowers growing on the marble ledges of Parnassus, where Apollo still weeps for the death of Hyacinth and Pan still mourns the vanishing of Syrinx, to the passion-flowers growing on the slopes of Calvary, he, this lover of eidola and images, worships the white feet of the bearers of dead beauty, and finds in the tears of all the lovers of all the lost a revivifying rain that even in the midst of the dust of our degeneracy makes bloom once more, full of freshness and promise, the mystical red rose of the world's desire.

The wit of his "Golden lads and girls" in those superb comedies may soon fall a little faint and thin upon our ears. To the next generation it may seem as faded and old-fashioned as the wit of Congreve or Sheridan. Fashions of humour change more quickly than the fashions of manner or of dress. The only thing that gives immortality to human writing is the "eternal bronze" of a noble and imaginative style. Out of such divine material, with all his petulances and perversities, Oscar Wilde's style was hammered and beaten. For there is only one quarry of this most precious metal, and the same hand that shapes from it the "Sorrow that endureth forever" must shape from it the "Pleasure that abideth for a moment," and the identity of these two with that immortal bronze is the symbol of the mystery of our life.

The senses that are quickened by the knowledge of this mystery are not far from the ultimate secret. As with the thing sculptured, so with the sculptor.

Oscar Wilde is a symbolic figure.

SUSPENDED JUDGMENT

SUSPENDED JUDGMENT

THE conclusion of any book which has tried to throw into momentary relief the great shadowy figures who have led and misled humanity must necessarily be no more than a new suspension of judgment; of judgment drawing its interest from the colour of the mind of the individual making it, of judgment guarded from the impertinence of judicial decision by its confessed implication of radical subjectivity.

The conclusion of any critical essay must in large measure be lame and halting; must indeed be a whispered warning to the reader to take what has gone before, however ardently expressed, with that wise pinch of true Attic salt which mitigates even a relative finality in these high things.

One comes to feel more and more, as one reads many books, that judicial decisions are laughable and useless in this rare atmosphere, and that the mere utterance of such platitudinous decrees sets the pronouncer of them outside the inner and exclusive pale.

One comes to feel more and more that all that any of us has a right to do is to set down as patiently and tenderly as he may the particular response, here or there, from this side or the other, as it chances to happen, that is aroused in his own soul by those historic works of art, which, whatever principle of selection it is that places them in our hands, have fallen somehow across our path.

It might seem that a direct, natural and spontaneous response, of the kind I have in my mind, to these famous works, were easy enough of attainment. Nothing, on the contrary, is more difficult to secure or more seldom secured.

One might almost hazard the paradox that the real art of criticism only begins when we shake ourselves free of all books and win access to that locked and sealed and uncut volume which is the book of our own feelings.

The art of self-culture—one learns just that when youth's outward-looking curiosity and passion begin to ebb—is the art of freeing oneself from the influence of books so that one may enjoy what one is destined to enjoy without pedantry or scruple. And yet, by the profound law of the system of things, when one has thus freed oneself from the tyranny of literary catchwords and the dead weight of cultivated public opinion, one comes back to the world of books with an added zest. It is then, and only then, that one reads with real unscrupulousness, thinking solely of the pleasure, and nothing of the rectitude or propriety or adequacy of what we take up.

And it is then that the great figures of the master-writers appear in their true light; the light —that is to say—in which we, and not another, have visualised them, felt them, and reacted from them.

It is wonderful what thrilling pleasures there are in store for us in literature when once we have cut ourselves adrift from all this superfluity of cultured opinion, and have given ourselves complete leave to love what we like and hate what we like and be indifferent to what we like, as the world swings round!

I think the secret of making an exquisite use of literature so that it shall colour and penetrate our days is only a small part of what the wisest epicureans among us are concerned with attaining. I think it is one of the most precious benefits conferred on us by every new writer that he flings us back more deeply than ever upon ourselves. We draw out of him his vision, his peculiar atmosphere, his especial quality of mental and emotional tone. We savour this and assimilate it and store it up, as something which we have made our own and which is there to fall back upon when we want it. But beyond our enjoyment of this new increment to our treasury of feeling, we are driven inwards once more in a kind of intellectual rivalry with the very thing we have just acquired, and in precise proportion as it has seemed to us exciting and original we are roused in the depths of our mind to substitute something else for it; and this something else is nothing less than the evocation of our own originality, called up out of the hidden caverns of our

being to claim its own creative place in the communion between our soul and the world,

I can only speak for myself; but my own
preference among writers will always be for
those whose genius consists rather in creating a
certain mental atmosphere than in hammering
out isolated works of art, rounded and complete.

For a flawless work of art is a thing for a
moment, while that more penetrating projection
of an original personality which one calls a
mental or æsthetic atmosphere, is a thing that
floats and flows and drifts and wavers, far beyond
the boundaries of any limited creation. Such an
atmosphere, such a vague intellectual music, in
the air about us, is the thing that really challenges
the responsive spirit in ourselves; challenges it
and rouses it to take the part which it has a right
to take, the part which it alone *can* take, in re-
creating the world for us in accordance with our
natural fatality.

It is only by the process of gradual disillusionment that we come at last to recognise what we
ourselves—undistracted now by any external
authority—need and require from the genius of
the past. For my own part, looking over the
great names included in the foregoing essays, I
am at this moment drawn instinctively only to
two among them all—to William Blake and to
Paul Verlaine; and this is an indication to me that
what my own soul requires is not philosophy or
psychology or wit or sublimity, but a certain

delicate transmutation of the little casual things that cross my way, and a certain faint, low, sweet music, rumouring from indistinguishable horizons, and bringing me vague rare thoughts, cool and quiet and deep and magical, such as have no concern with the clamour and brutality of the crowd.

The greater number of the writers who have dominated us, in the pages that go before, belong to the Latin race, and I cannot but feel that it is to this race that civilisation must come more and more to return in its search for the grandeur and pathos, the humanity and irony of that attitude of mind which serves our spirits best as we struggle on through the confusions and bewilderments of our way.

There is a tendency observable here and there — though the genuinely great minds who give their adherence to it are few and far between— to speak as though the race-element in literature were a thing better away, a thing whose place might be taken by a sort of attenuated idealistic amalgam of all the race-elements in the world, or by something which has no race-element in it at all—something inter-national, inter-racial, humanitarian and cosmopolitan.

People to whom this thin thing appeals often speak quite lightly of blending the traditions of East and West, of Saxon and Celt, of Latin and Teuton, of Scandinavian and Slav.

They do not see that you might as well speak

of blending the temperaments of two opposite types of human personality. They do not see that the whole interest of life depends upon these contrasts. You cannot blend traditions in this academic way, any more than you can blend two human souls that are diametrically different, or two soils or climates which are mutually excluding. This ideal of a cosmopolitan literature that shall include all the local traditions and racial instincts is the sort of thing that appeals to the type of mind which remains essentially dull to the high qualities of a noble style.

No; it is not cosmopolitan literature that we want. It was not of cosmopolitan literature that Goethe was thinking when he used that term "I am a good European," which Nietzsche found so suggestive; it was of classical literature, of literature which, whatever its racial quality, has not lost touch with the civilised traditions of Athens and Rome.

In art, as in everything else, we must "worship our dead"; and the attempt to substitute a vague idealised cosmopolitanism for the living passionate localised traditions that spring like trees and flowers out of a particular soil, out of a soil made dear to us by the ashes of our fathers and consecrated by a thousand pious usages, is an attempt that can result in no great magical works.

Walt Whitman, for all his celebrations of the huge "ensemble" of the world, remains and must always remain profoundly and entirely American.

When Romain Rolland, the author of "Jean Christophe,"—the book of all books most penetrated by the spirit of race distinctions—appalled by the atrocity of the war, calls upon us to substitute the Ideal of Humanity for the ideas of the various tribes of men, he is really (in re-action from the dreadful scenes around him) renouncing those flashes of prophetic insight which gave him such living visions of the diverse souls of the great races. Romain Rolland may speak rhetorically of the "Ideal of Humanity" to be realised in art and letters. The thing is a word, a name, a phrase, an illusion. What we actually have are individuals—individual artists, individual races —each with its own beautiful and tragical fatality.

And what is true of races is true of persons both in life and in criticism. All that is really interesting in us springs in the first place from the traditions of the race to which we belong, springs from the soil that gave us birth and from our sacred dead and the usages and customs and habits which bind us to the past; and in the second place from what is uniquely and peculiarly personal to ourselves, belonging to our intrinsic and integral character and refusing to be swamped by any vague cult of "humanity in general."

To talk of literature becoming universal and planetary, becoming a logical synthesis of the traditions of races and the visions of individuals, is to talk of something that in its inherent nature is contrary to the fundamental spirit of art. It implies a confusion between the spheres of art and philosophy. The function of philosophy is to synthesise and unite. The function of art is to differentiate and distinguish. Philosophy and ethics are perfectly justified in concerning themselves with a "regenerated humanity" in which race-instincts and race-traditions are blotted out. Let them produce such a humanity if they can! But while there are any artists left in the world, or any lovers of art, it will always be to the old inalienable traditions that they will turn; to the old local customs, local pieties, local habits, local altars, and local gods.

To talk vaguely of cosmopolitan art uniting the nations, is to talk foolishly, and it is to talk irreverently. The people who deal in such theories are endeavouring to betray the dead of their own race and the noble pieties and desperate courage of those who made them what they are. It is a sacrilege, this speculation, and a sacrifice of beauty upon the altar of a logical morality.

What one comes more and more to feel is that everything which belongs to poetry and art belongs to the individual, to the individual nation and the individual person. The great modern democracies, with their cult of the average man and their suspicion of the exceptional man, are naturally only too ready to hail as ideal and wonderful any doctrine about literature which flatters their pride.

One of the most plausible forms of rhetorical cant is the cant about the soul of average humanity expressing itself in art, in an art which has sloughed off like an outworn skin all ancient race-instincts and all individual egoism.

There has never been such art in the history of the world as this average man's art, free from tradition and free from personal colour.

There will never be such art, unless it be the great, idealistic, humanitarian, cosmopolitan art of the Moving Picture Show.

But the idea sounds well in popular oratory, and it has a most soothing ointment for the souls of such artists as have neither reverence nor imagination.

It is quite possible that for the general comfort of the race at large—even if not for its happiness—it would be a good thing if philosophers and moralists between them could get rid of the imagination of races as well as the imagination of individuals.

The common crowd are naturally suspicious of imagination of any kind, as they are suspicious of genius of any kind; and this new doctrine of a literature largely and purely "human," wherein the general soul of humanity may find its expression, free from the colour of race-feeling and free from the waywardness of individual men of genius, is just the sort of thing to flatter the unthinking mob.

Why not have art and literature harnessed once and for all to the great rolling chariot of popular public opinion? Why not abolish all individualism at one stroke as a thing dangerous to the public welfare—a thing uncomfortable, undesirable, upsetting?

The same desperate, irrational, immoral imagination which inspires races with a strange madness, inspires individuals too with a strange madness.

Art and Literature are, after all, and there is little use denying it, the last refuge and sanctuary, in a world ruled by machinery and sentiment, of the free, wild, reckless, irresponsible, anarchical imagination of such as refuse to sacrifice their own dreams for the dreams—not less illusive—of the general herd.

We have to face the fact—bitter and melancholy though it may be—that in our great bourgeois-dominated democracies the majority of people would like to trample out the flame of genius altogether; trample it out as something inimical to their peace.

Dante, Shakespeare, Goethe, Balzac, were all completely aware of this instinctive hatred with which the mob of men regard what is exceptional and rare. The Hamlet-spirit of the author of Coriolanus must chuckle bitterly in that grave in Stratford-on-Avon when he learns that the new ideal is the ideal of cosmopolitan literature expressing the soul of the average man.

The clash is bound to come sooner or later between public opinion, concerned to preserve the comfort of its illusions, and the art of the individual artist playing, in noble irresponsibility, with all illusions.

It was his consciousness of this—of the natural antagonism of the mob and its leaders to all great literature—that made Goethe draw back so coldly and proudly from the popular tendencies of his time, and seek refuge among the great individualistic spirits of the classic civilisations. And what Goethe—the good European—did in his hour, the more classical among European writers of our own day do still.

The great style—the style which is like gold and bronze in an age of clay and rubble—remains as the only sure refuge we have from the howling vulgarities of our generation. If books were taken from us—the high, calm, beautiful, ironical books of classic tradition—how, in this age, could the more sensitive among us endure to live at all?

With brutality and insanity and ruffianism, with complacency and stupidity and sentimentalism, jostling us and hustling us on all sides, how could we live, if it were not for the great, calm, scornful anarchists of the soul, whose high inviolable imaginations perpetually refresh and re-create the world?

And we who find this refuge, we who have to win our liberty every day anew by bathing in these classic streams, we too will do well to remember that the most precious things in life are the things that the world can neither give nor take away.

We too—encouraged by these great individualists—have a right to fall back upon whatever individuality may have been left to us; and, resting upon that, sinking into the soul of that, to defy all that public opinion and the voice of the majority may be able to do.

And we shall be wise also if we recognise, before it is too late, that what is most intrinsic and inalienable in ourselves is just that very portion of us which has nothing to do with our work in life, nothing to do with our duty to the community.

We shall be wise if we recognise, before it is too late, that the thing most sacred in us is that strange margin of unoccupied receptivity, upon which settle, in their flight over land and sea, the beautiful wild birds of unsolicited dreams.

We shall be wise if, before we die, we learn a little of the art of suspending our judgment—the art of "waiting upon the spirit."

For it is only when we have suspended our judgment; it is only when we have suspended our convictions, our principles, our ideals, our moralities, that "the still small voice" of the music of the universe, sad and sweet and terrible and tender, drifts in upon us, over the face of the waters of the soul.

The essence of us, the hidden reality of us, is too rare and delicate a thing to bear the crude weight of these sturdy opinions, these vigorous convictions, these social ardours, without growing dulled and hardened.

We all have to bear the burden of humanity; and the artists among us may be thankful that the predatory curse resting upon the rich is very seldom ours: but the burden of humanity must not be allowed to press all joy, all originality, all waywardness, all interest, all imagination out of our lives.

It is not for long, at best or worst, that we know what it is to be conscious of being living children of the human race upon this strange planet.

The days pass quickly, and the seasons and the years. From the graves of the darlings of our souls there comes a voice and a cry. A voice bidding us sink into our own true selves before we too are numbered with the dead; a cry bidding us sacrifice everything before we sacrifice the prerogative of our inmost identity, the right to feel and think and dream as persons born into a high inheritance, the inheritance of the mind that has the right to question all things and to hold fast what pleases it in defiance of opinion and logic and probability and argument.

For it is only when we suspend our judgments

and leave arguing and criticising, that the quiet gods of the moonlit shores of the world murmur their secrets in our ears.

They come without our seeking for them, these rare intimations; without our seeking for them, and, sometimes, without our desiring them; but when they come they come as revelations of something deeper in us than any mere soul of humanity. They come from a region that is as far beyond humanity as it is beyond nature. They come from the fairy-land of that mysterious country wherein dwell the dreams and the fancies of those lonely ones among the sons of men who have been possessed by imagination. They come from the unknown land where those inhabit who are, as the Psalmist says, "free among the dead." They come from the land which we left when we were born, and to which we return when we die. And whether this is a land of nothingness and oblivion none knoweth; for none hath returned to tell us. Meanwhile we can imagine what we will; and we can suspend our last judgment until we ourselves are judged.

REMINISCENT OF DOSTOIEVSKY

WOOD AND STONE
A ROMANCE
By JOHN COWPER POWYS

12mo, 722 pages, $1.50 net

This is an epoch marking novel by an author " who is dramatic as is no other now writing."—*Oakland Enquirer.*

In this startling and original romance, the author turns aside from the track of his contemporaries and reverts to models drawn from races which have bolder and less conventional views of literature than the Anglo-Saxon race. Following the lead of the Great Russian Dostoievsky, he proceeds boldly to lay bare the secret passions, the unacknowledged motives and impulses, which lurk below the placid-seeming surface of ordinary human nature.

It has been reviewed favorably by all of America's principal newspapers, as the following extracts from press notices will indicate:

Boston Transcript: " His mastery of language, his knowledge of human impulses, his interpretation of the forces of nature and of the power of inanimate objects over human beings, all pronounce him a writer of no mean rank. . . . He can express philosophy in terms of narrative without prostituting his art; he can suggest an answer without drawing a moral; with a clearer vision he could stand among the masters in literary achievement."

Chicago Tribune: " Psychologically speaking, it is one of the most remarkable pieces of fiction ever written. . . . I do not hesitate to say that a new novelist of power has appeared upon the scene."

Evening Sun, New York: " Mr. powys, master essayist, comes forward with a first novel which is brilliant in style, absorbing in plot, deep and thoughtful in its purpose."

Philadelphia Press: " It undoubtedly will set a new mark in literature of the contemporary period. . . . Mr. Powys' style is the style of Thomas Hardy."

Philadelphia Record: " Every page is a joy, every chapter a fresh proof of Powys' genius."

N. Y. Evening Post: " The best novel one reviewer has read in a good while."

New York Times: " Mr. Powys is evidently a keen observer of life and responsive to all its phases."

N. Y. Tribune: " A good story well told."

N. Y. Herald: " Here is a novel worth reading."

The Nation: " A book of distinctive flavor."

Review of Reviews: " An exceptional novel . . . a brilliant intellectual piece of work."

Philadelphia North American: " A notable achievement in fictitious literature."

Springfield Republican: " This is a book which will have more than the ephemeral existence of the average novel."

New Haven Courier Journal: " One of the most notable and important novels that has appeared in the last twelve months."

Hartford Courant: " The book is very interesting, provokingly interesting."

Democrat and Chronicle, Rochester: " Among the few works of fiction that stand out in the very forefront of this season's production."

G. ARNOLD SHAW
Publisher to the University Lecturers Association

GRAND CENTRAL TERMINAL   **NEW YORK**

CPSIA information can be obtained
at www.ICGtesting.com
Printed in the USA
BVHW090917201118

533624BV00019B/462/P